D1246997

STANDARD ENCYCLOPEDIA OF

Opalescent Glass

SIXTH EDITION

*IDENTIFICATION
&
VALUES*

MIKE CARWILE

COLLECTOR BOOKS
A Division of Schroeder Publishing

Front Cover: Trident pitcher, amber opalescent, $400.00.

Back Cover: Brideshead pitcher, amber opalescent, $425.00, and tumblers, $75.00 ea.

Cover design: *Beth Summers*
Book design: *Terri Hunter*

COLLECTOR BOOKS

P.O. Box 3009
Paducah, Kentucky 42002-3009

www.collectorbooks.com

Searching for a Publisher?

We are always looking for people knowledgeable within their fields. If you feel that there is a real need for a book on your collectible subject and have a large comprehensive collection, contact Collector Books.

Proudly printed and bound in the United States of America

Contents

Part I:
Opalescent Glass,
1880 – 1930
Page 13

Part II:
Whimsey Pieces
Page 166

Part III:
Opalescent Glass,
1930 – 1970
Page 178

Dedication

To Steve and Radka Sandeman, John and Mary Petrasich, Dave and Vickie Peterson, Seigmar Geiselberger, Ruth Harvey, and Kelvin Russell for the many nice photos as well as additional information provided in updating this new edition.

Acknowledgments

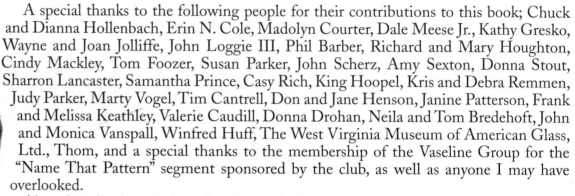

A special thanks to the following people for their contributions to this book; Chuck and Dianna Hollenbach, Erin N. Cole, Madolyn Courter, Dale Meese Jr., Kathy Gresko, Wayne and Joan Jolliffe, John Loggie III, Phil Barber, Richard and Mary Houghton, Cindy Mackley, Tom Foozer, Susan Parker, John Scherz, Amy Sexton, Donna Stout, Sharron Lancaster, Samantha Prince, Casy Rich, King Hoopel, Kris and Debra Remmen, Judy Parker, Marty Vogel, Tim Cantrell, Don and Jane Henson, Janine Patterson, Frank and Melissa Keathley, Valerie Caudill, Donna Drohan, Neila and Tom Bredehoft, John and Monica Vanspall, Winfred Huff, The West Virginia Museum of American Glass, Ltd., Thom, and a special thanks to the membership of the Vaseline Group for the "Name That Pattern" segment sponsored by the club, as well as anyone I may have overlooked.

Also a big thanks to jetbroadband.com for keeping me in touch with the world.

Special Note to Readers

Four years have gone by since the last edition of this book and you will notice some changes in this new edition, which I hope will meet with your approval. In 2006, my co-author Bill Edwards decided to go into a well-deserved state of retirement, and I wish him the best. I hope I can fill his shoes to my reader's satisfaction. Please don't hesitate to contact me should you have any comments, suggestions, corrections, or additions to this book. They will all be considered and certainly appreciated.

Although there are many new patterns and a good number of replacement photos in this new edition, you will also notice that some patterns have been dropped from the front section, the whimsey section, and the after-1930s section as well.

Some patterns were discovered to be newer production items that just didn't fit, even into the after-1930s section (for which I've set a cut-off date of 1970, when Fenton began to use their logo on pieces). Some of the whimsies have also been dropped due to the fact that they were really not true whimsies, but rather production pieces. This decision was primarily made to provide needed room for the continued growth of this publication.

I hope you will enjoy this edition and I do look forward to hearing of new and exciting finds from the many collectors of this beautiful glass.

Introduction

From its inception in the 1880s, opalescent glass has enjoyed a widely receptive audience, both in England, where it was introduced, and here in America, where a young but growing market was ready for any touch of brightness and beauty for the hearth and home.

Early American makers, such as Hobbs, Brockunier and Company (1863 – 1888), Buckeye Glass (1878 – 1896), LaBelle Glass (1872 – 1888), American Glass (1889 – 1891), Nickel Plate Glass (1888 – 1893), and of course, the Northwood Glass Company in its various locations (1888 until its demise in 1924), were the primary producers, especially in early blown opalescent glass production. They were not by themselves, of course. Other companies, such as Model Flint (1893 – 1899), Fostoria Shade & Lamp Co. (1890 – 1894), Consolidated Lamp & Glass (1894 – 1897), Elson Glass (1882 – 1893), West Virginia Glass (1893 – 1896), National Glass (1899 – 1903), Beaumont Glass (1895 – 1906), Dugan Glass (1904 – 1913, which then became Diamond Glass, 1914 – 1931), Coudersport Glass (1900 – 1904), and finally the Jefferson Glass Company (1900 – 1933), added their talents in all sorts of opalescent items in both blown and pressed glass.

The major production covered 40 years (1880 – 1920); however, beginning shortly after the turn of the century, the Fenton Glass Company of Williamstown, West Virginia, joined the ranks of opalescent manufacturers, and has continued production off and on until the present time. Its production from 1907 to 1940 is an important part of the opalescent field and has been covered to some extent in this book. The Fenton factory, along with Dugan Glass and Jefferson Glass, produced quality opalescent glass items long after the rest of the companies had ceased operations, primarily pressed items in patterns they had used for other types of glassware.

In 1899 A. H. Heisey & Company began a very limited production of some opalescent glass in white and blue by adding a milky formula to the glass while it was still in the mould. Patterns known are #1255 Pineapple and Fan in white and vaseline (1898), #2 Plaid Chrysanthemum in vaseline (1904), #1220 Punty Band in white and blue (1904 – 1910), #1280 Winged Scroll in white (1910), #357 Prison Stripe in white (1905), #300 Peerless in blue, and a Pluto candlestick in experimental gold opalescent. Most of these were made in very small amounts for very short periods of time, and by 1915 they were no longer in production.

To understand just what opalescent glass is has always been easy; to explain the process of making this glass is quite another matter. If the novice will think of two layers of glass, one colored and one clear, that have been fused so that the clear areas become milky when fired a second or third time, the picture of the process becomes easier to see. It is, of course, much more complicated than that, but for the sake of clarity, imagine the clear layer being pressed so that the second firing gives this opal milkyness to the outer edges, either to their designs or to the edges themselves, and the process becomes clearer. It is, of course, the skill of the glassmaker to control this opalescence so that it does what he wants. It is a fascinating process and anyone who has had the privilege of watching a glassmaker at work can testify to it being a near miracle.

Today, thousands of collectors seek opalescent glass, and each has his or her own favorites. Current markets place blown opalescent glass as more desirable, with cranberry leading the color field, but there are many ways to collect, and groupings of one shape or one pattern or even one manufacturer are not uncommon. When you purchase this glass, the same rules apply as for any other glass collectible: (1) look for any damage and do not pay normal prices for damage, (2) choose good color as well as good milky opalescence, (3) buy what pleases you! You have to live with it, so buy what you like. To care for your glass, wash it carefully in lukewarm water with a mild soap; never put old glass in a dishwasher! Display your glass in an area that is well lighted and enjoy it!

Opalescent Producers & Factory Sites

I believe there is a need for a brief history of the early makers of opalescent glass and their various factory locations. Often, a glass producer moved frequently to replace a lost factory site (factories burned because of the very nature of the heat used to produce glass) or to join other makers in new ventures. Gas supplies diminished, combines were formed, and workers moved on. Glassworkers, by nature, were a gypsy lot, moving after a winter season, camping out in good weather in some instances, and generally going where the jobs led them. It was not unusual for a worker to have been employed by every plant in their area at one time or another.

For these reasons, I've tried to put together a brief factory history that tells where the makers of opalescent glass were located in the years of major production. I include a brief history of England's best-known producers as well as those in America, and hope this is a helpful addition for beginning as well as seasoned collectors.

American Glass Company (1889 – 1890)
Anderson, Indiana

Opened in mid-1889 by John Miller and Andrew Gottschalk (former managers of the Buckeye Glass Company), American Glass Company produced fancy colored tableware, opalescent glass, and marblescent lamps, as well as other wares. Opalescent glass probably included its version of Reverse Swirl and a line of Chrysanthemum Swirl pieces. In early 1890 Mr. Gottschalk returned to Buckeye, and only months later, the plant closed and the factory site was sold (1891), becoming the Hoosier Glass Company (where prescription ware was made). John Miller went to the Eagle Glass Company, then to Riverside, and in 1901 became the manager of Model Flint Glass in Albany, Indiana, where opalescent glass was made.

Beaumont Glass Company
Martins Ferry, Ohio (1895 – 1902)
Grafton, West Virginia (1902 – 1906)

Percy Beaumont was the brother-in-law of Harry Northwood. He worked at the Northwood factory and left his position of shipping clerk there to begin a job at Hobbs, Brockunier & Company as a glass decorator. In 1893 he moved to West Virginia Glass (Elson's plant), where he was employed as a metalworker and chemist. He is credited with designing the Polka Dot pattern and the Fern moulds as well as the Daisy in Criss-Cross pattern. Opalescent glass seems to have been made before 1901, but not after the factory moved to the new site in Grafton, West Virginia. Beaumont sold his interests in this company in 1906, and the factory name was changed to Tygert Valley Glass. Beaumont later managed Union Stopper at Morgantown, and when this firm closed, he began a new firm that was first a decorating plant and later a lighting wares factory. Percy Beaumont died in the 1940s.

Buckeye Glass Company (1878 – 1896)
Martins Ferry, Ohio

Founded by wealthy entrepreneur, Henry Helling (a later investor in the Northwood Company), the Buckeye Glass Company opened in 1878 as a tableware company that introduced color into its glass line very early. The manager was John F. Miller (later associated with the Model Flint Glass Company). Buckeye produced opalescent glass and cased art glass in tableware, night lamps, cruets, syrups, and more. Patterns included Buckeye, Lattice, Reverse Swirl, Coinspot (cylinder lamps), Stripe, Big Windows, and possibly Chrysanthemum Swirl. The factory began to fail as early as 1891 and returned to tableware and opaque glass and oil lamps. Labor problems, a number of fires blamed on arson, and a large, consuming fire led to the closing of the factory in February 1896.

George Davidson & Company (1867 – 1987)
Gateshead, England

In 1888, eleven years after Sowerby produced its opal ware, the Davidson Company registered its Pearline opal ware in pale yellow (canary), soft blue, light green, and clear (white opalescent). Davidson's had been founded in 1867 by George Davidson, but his son, Thomas, became the firm's driving force in 1891. Davidson's Pearline patterns are numerous and include Brideshead (1889), Cane Rings, Chippendale (1887), Daisy and Greek Key (unconfirmed at this time), Pearline Epergne, Davidson's Shell (1889), Lady Caroline (1891), Linking Rings (1894), Lords and Ladies (1896), Princess Diana (1890), Prince William (1893), Queen's Spill (1891), Queen Victoria (plate #254027,

1895), Quilted Daisy Fairy Lamp, Quilted Pillow Sham (1893), Richelieu, Sea Scroll, Somerset (1895), Victoria and Albert (1897), War of Roses (1893), Whitechapel (not confirmed as Davidson), and William and Mary (1903).

Dugan Glass Company (1904 – 1913)
Indiana, Pennsylvania

Thomas E. Dugan, Harry Northwood's cousin, began his career at Hobbs, Brockunier, then moved to Buckeye Glass, to the Northwood Ellwood City plant, and then managed the Indiana, Pennsylvania, plant for National after Northwood's joining. In 1904, he gathered a group of financial backers to purchase the Indiana, Pennsylvania, plant from National, and the Dugan Glass Company was begun. Early production contained opalescent, but after 1910 iridescent glass became the mainstay. Opalescent patterns included Swastika, Diamond and Clubs, Daisy and Fern, Swirl, Coinspot (1903), Diamond Spearhead (1901), Victor or Jeweled Heart (1905), Circled Scroll (1904), New York (Beaded Shell), and many novelty items that include Waterlily, Corn Vase, and Palisades.

In 1913 Thomas Dugan resigned from the firm, and the company was renamed the Diamond Glass Company, with a trademarked "diamond with a D in the center." The Diamond Company remained in business until the plant burned in 1931. Thomas Dugan went on to be associated with a new Dugan company at Lonaconing and eventually became a minor player with Anchor Hocking.

Elson Glass Company (1882 – 1893), West Virginia Glass Company (1893 – 1896), West Virginia Glass Mfg. Company (1897 – 1899), National Glass Company (operating West Virginia Glass Works from 1899 to 1903)
Martins Ferry, Ohio

Readers may find this factory site a bit puzzling since no less than five companies operated here. First it was Elson, which is known to have made a castor set from Beaumont moulds in opalescent glass. The Elson Dewdrop pattern bears its name despite being made in 1893 as a design from West Virginia Glass Company. The owners of West Virginia Glass Company had reorganized Elson and then produced blown opalescent glass. Some patterns known are Polka Dot and Fern (in #203 optic moulds). The company made both blown and pressed glass until late 1895 when the plant was closed for nearly a year during a depression. The factory was then sold in 1896 and reorganized as the West Virginia Glass Mfg. Company, operating for nearly two years before joining National Glass in 1899. In 1901 the plant was operated by Crystal Glass Company (their second branch factory), but after Ed Muhleman offered his resignation in 1901 to begin building the Imperial plant in Bellaire, the factory declined and finally closed in 1903.

Fenton Art Glass Company (1907 – present)
Williamstown, West Virginia

In 1905 in Martins Ferry, Ohio, brothers Frank L. and John W. Fenton opened the Fenton Art Glass Company as a decorating shop using blanks from other glassmakers. Both had worked for other glassmakers. Soon another brother, Charles H. Fenton joined them. Two years later, they purchased a site in Williamstown, West Virginia, and not long afterwards produced their first glass. John was president, Frank, general manager, and Charles headed the decorating shop. Another brother, James E. Fenton, became maintenance supervisor in late 1908. Soon afterwards, John left Williamstown to form the famous Millersburg Glass Company in Millersburg, Ohio.

Early glassware included opalescent glass in topaz, blue, green, and in 1908, amethyst. By 1910, iridized glass had become the rage and the Fenton factory produced the first of this product, which is today called carnival glass. Over the years, the Fenton company has continued to produce opalescent wares both for itself and for other companies, including the L.G. Wright Company in the 1930s, 1940s, and 1950s. The Fenton Art Glass Company remains the only major glass plant that still makes hand-worked glass and has outlasted all its competitors in the field.

Fostoria Shade & Lamp Company (1890 – 1894), Consolidated Lamp and Glass Company (1894 – 1896)
Fostoria, Ohio

This firm was first known as the Fostoria Shade & Lamp Company and was managed by Nicholas Kopp and Charles Etz. The name was changed in 1894 to the Consolidated Lamp and Glass Company. A line of tableware was released in 1893 and the opalescent ware included Consolidated's Criss-Cross pattern. A new factory was built in 1896 in Coraopolis, Pennsylvania, after the firm merged with the Wallace & McAfee Company, with headquarters in Pittsburgh. The company then specialized in Kopp-cased colors and produced tableware, lamps, and shades. The factory produced Martele tableware in the 1920s, shut down in depression times, reopened in 1936, and closed for good in 1964.

Greener & Company (1871 – 1885), controlled by James A. Jobling (1886 – present)
Sunderland, England

Henry Greener worked at the Sowerby firm until 1857 when he began working in Sunderland. In 1871 he became head of the business and bought the land where James A. Jobling & Company stood. (Jobling was a chemical merchant who supplied Greener with chemicals for glassmaking and is later remembered for making Pyrex ware.) Greener renewed his Lion trademark in 1890, but Jobling was then the manager, I believe. Patterns were made in malachite (slag) and jet (obviously copying Sowerby's technique), and commemorative glass items were made. When Jobling took over the plant in 1910, he began to copy Rene Lalique's opal glass art and produced a product the company called "Jobling's Opalique." Examples of opalescent glass made at the Greener firm include Royal Jubilee, Contessa, and several small plate designs that resemble Lalique ware. Some of Greener's opal ware is found in strange colors like amber.

Hobbs, Brockunier & Company (1863 – 1888), Hobbs Glass Company (1888 – 1891),
U.S. Glass Company (Factory H 1891 – 1893)
Wheeling, West Virginia

An earlier glass plant controlled by James Barnes and John L. Hobbs operated at this site until it closed during the Civil War. In 1863 the firm of Hobbs, Brockunier & Company was begun at the plant. In 1887, the firm was reorganized and in 1888 became the Hobbs Glass Company. William Leighton Jr. left to join Dalzell, Gilmore & Leighton at Finlay, Ohio, and sales manager L.B. Martin departed to help forge the new Fostoria plant. Nicholas Kopp took charge and during this period, blown opalescent glass was produced. Absorbed by the U.S. Glass merger in 1891, the factory closed in 1893 during a strike and was finally purchased by Harry Northwood in 1903 (he had worked for Hobbs briefly as a glass engraver in 1882). The factory was refurbished and became the H. Northwood & Company Glass Works that year.

Jefferson Glass Company
Steubenville, Ohio (1900 – 1907)
Follansbee, West Virginia (1907 – 1933)

In an abandoned factory in Steubenville, Ohio, in 1900, the Jefferson Glass Company began its first production of glassware. The president, Harry Bastow, had earlier worked for Harry Northwood in Indiana, Pennsylvania, and the sales manager, George Mortimer, had also been associated with Northwood (oddly, both Frank and John Fenton were also associated with Jefferson for a time). Opalescent patterns from Jefferson were made in the 1901 – 1907 time frame and after that, the factory seemed to specialize in crystal. In 1908 Jefferson bought several patterns from the Ohio Flint Glass Company, including the Chippendale pattern, and the company's energies were put into the production of items with the "Krys-tol" trademark it had also purchased from Ohio Flint. In 1910 the firm was sold again and the factory turned to lighting wares. In the opalescent years, patterns at Jefferson were abundant and included Coinspot, Swirl, Buttons and Braids, and Swirling Maze, as well as several novelty bowl and vase patterns.

La Belle Glass Company (1872 – 1888)
Bridgeport, Ohio

La Belle Glass Company was established in 1872 as a tableware company. In 1884 Harry Northwood arrived, fresh from his position at the Hobbs, Brockunier factory, only to face a strike that closed LaBelle. Two years later with the factory back up and running, Northwood returned (after working at Phoenix) and opalescent production began with a copycat version of Hobbs' Hobnail pattern. The LaBelle factory burned in 1887 but the company leased new facilities in Brilliant, Ohio, while a new plant was built. The financial drain was too much, however, and brought on bankruptcy in 1888. The new plant was sold and then became the Crystal Glass Works where no opalescent glass was made to the best of my knowledge.

Millersburg Glass Company (1909 – 1912), Radium Glass Company (1912 – 1913)
Millersburg, Ohio

Founded by John W. Fenton upon leaving the Fenton Art Glass Company in 1909, this glass factory concentrated on crystal and carnival glass but did produce one pattern in an opalescent treatment: small bowls in two sizes (6" or 7½") in a pattern called Country Kitchen by carnival collectors and Milky Way by opalescent collectors. These were products of the last days of the Millersburg plant before it became the Radium Glass Company and few of these bowls exist today. They are desirable and very much collectors' prizes in either size. The Radium factory closed in 1913 and was purchased by Jefferson Glass. For a few years, they made lantern glass and glass parts for railroad lanterns but the plant closed permanently in 1916.

Model Flint Glass Company (1893 – 1899), National Glass Company (operating Model Flint, 1900 – 1902)
Albany, Indiana

First formed in 1888 in Findlay, Ohio, the company was moved to Albany, Indiana, in July 1893. Findlay production had been primarily tableware and this continued for the most part in Albany until the plant became part of the emerging National Company in 1900. In 1901 blown opalescent glass was produced; patterns include Wreath and Shell (Manila), Ribbed Spiral, Reverse Swirl, Stripe, Fern, Dolphin & Herons, Broken Pillar & Reed (Kismet), Ala-Bock, Calyx, Corolla, Diamond Stem, and Lotus. The factory was closed in 1902.

Nickel Plate Glass Company (1888 – 1893)
Fostoria, Ohio

Staffed with several men who had previously worked with other companies that made opalescent glass, Nickel Plate boasted such names as A.J. Smith, formerly with LaBelle, and J.B. Russell who had worked for Hobbs. Nickel Plate opened in 1888 and part of their production seems to have been in blown opalescent glass in Wide Stripe, Swirl, and other patterns that may well include Double Greek Key items. Opalescent colors run the gamut and included blue, white, cranberry, and canary. The company joined U.S. Glass in 1891 as part of the giant merger, and then closed abruptly in 1893.

Northwood Company (1888 – 1892), Martins Ferry, Ohio, The Northwood Glass Company (1892 – 1896), Ellwood City, Pennsylvania, The Northwood Company (1896 – 1899), Indiana, Pennsylvania, as part of National Glass Company, 1900 – 1904, H. Northwood & Company (1902 – 1924), Wheeling, West Virginia

Harry Northwood's career was full of twists and turns, opening one factory and a few years later, moving to another location. He never actually owned any of the factories that bore his name but either managed or controlled them.

The first Northwood Company was opened at an abandoned factory that had once been the Union Glass Company. Despite Northwood's production there, the venture was considered a failure. In 1892, the name of the company was changed slightly, and the Northwood Glass Company moved to Ellwood City, Pennsylvania, where production included opalescent, coralene, cranberry, and onyx treatments. The move in 1896 to Indiana, Pennsylvania, was partially financed by relatives and opalescent glass was again a featured item, primarily mould blown.

In 1902 and 1903 there were two factories with the Northwood name and Harry had established his last plant at Wheeling, West Virginia. Here, pressed opalescent became the norm along with all the other famous treatments including carnival glass (after 1907).

Phoenix Glass Company (1880 – 1940s)
Monaco, Pennsylvania

Founded in 1880 by Andrew Howard (president) and William I. Miller (secretary-treasurer) to make lamp chimneys and reflectors, the company made lamp shades from 1882 until the plant burned in 1884. The company then bought an abandoned chimney works that had been Doyle & Sons at Phillipsburg (and when a new plant was built, this became the Phoenix #3 plant). When the rebuilt plant opened in 1885 a second furnace was added. This plant eventually burned in 1893, but in 1883 the factories had begun to produce art glass when Joseph Webb, nephew of the famous English glassmaker, came aboard as plant superintendent. Mr. Webb had a great influence on the direction of Phoenix and was aided by Harry Northwood who came to Phoenix in 1885. Art glass and opalescent glass were made until 1892 when the firm tried to make cut glass. Then in 1900, they again added lighting wares, moulds from Co-operative Flint and Consolidated in the 1930s, and a line of sculptured artware in the 1940s. Today, Phoenix is part of the Anchor-Hocking Company.

Sowerby's Ellison Glass Works (1811 – 1957)
Gateshead-on-Tyne, England

Long one of England's three great glass firms from the country's northeast area, the Sowerby name is well known in the glass world. Richard Sowerby had been a partner in the firm of Robertson & Company. He died in 1811 and George Sowerby took his place, and in 1816 the firm became Sowerby and Lowry Glass. In 1824, George became the owner of the New Stourbridge Works and in 1857 the factory became Sowerby's Ellison Glass Works with John Sowerby in charge. Later, J.G. Sowerby, John's son, became the manager and the peacock head trademark was established. The company made slag or marble glass, jet (black) glass, and various types of Vitro porcelain. In 1879 the company began a limited production of opalescent glass. Patterns such as Diamond Pyramid, English Duck, Sowerby Swan, Victorian Hamper, and Paneled Cornflower are examples of their products.

In addition to the forementioned factories, others made smaller contributions to both pressed and blown opalescent glass. Here is a brief list of those I believe are in that group:

Dalzell, Gilmore & Leighton Company, Findlay, Ohio
King Glass Company, Pittsburgh, Pennsylvania
Central Glass Works, Wheeling, West Virginia
Belmont Glass Company, Bellaire, Ohio
Mount Washington Glass Works, New Bedford, Massachusetts
Burtles, Tate & Company, Manchester, England
Molineaux, Webb & Company, Manchester, England
Richardsons of Wordsley, Stourbridge, England
Stevens and Williams, Stourbridge, England
Thomas Webb & Sons, Stourbridge, England
George Baccus & Sons, Birmingham, England
A. Jobling & Company, Sunderland, England
John Walsh Walsh, Birmingham, England
Tygart Valley Glass Company, Grafton, West Virginia

Who Made It?

Confusion abounds over the Northwood/National/Dugan connection, as well as the Jefferson/Northwood connection. In 1896 Harry Northwood, Samuel Dugan Sr., and his sons Thomas, Alfred, and Samuel Dugan Jr. came to Indiana, Pennsylvania, operating the Northwood Glass Company there until 1899, when Harry Northwood joined the newly formed National Glass Company combine. In 1903, he moved his operation to Wheeling at the old Hobbs, Brockunier plant, and Thomas Dugan remained at the Indiana plant operating it as the Dugan Glass Company.

From 1896 on, several patterns were produced as first Northwood, then National, and finally as Dugan, patterns such as Argonaut Shell/Nautilus, for example. There were many others that have previously been classified as either Northwood or Dugan that are actually Northwood/National/Dugan or even National/Dugan.

In addition, certain patterns were duplicated by both Jefferson and Northwood, with little explanation as to why moulds that were once Jefferson's then became Northwood's. These companies were competitors, but examples of some patterns can be traced to both companies. It is also evident most patterns with a cranberry edging are really Jefferson, not Northwood as once believed.

Every answer raises new questions. Answers come in their own time and at their own pace. One day collectors will know most of what is questioned today and that is what drives us all. I learn every day, mostly by contact with other collectors and so, I'm sure, do all of you.

What Collecting Is All About

Sometimes I run across collections that are just too good to show piecemeal and I long for a way to display the entire collection so that other collectors may see just what one can do with a single pattern or a single shape. For this reason the next two pages include several group photos from the fine collection of Dave and Vickie Peterson. You will see various items from Davidson; a collection of marmalades, a nice grouping of Iris and Meander as well as various utilitarian pieces and a few whimsical pieces, all displayed in neat array.

I hope readers will enjoy seeing what a wonder this glass can be when arranged in such a fashionable display, and again I thank Dave and Vickie for sharing it.

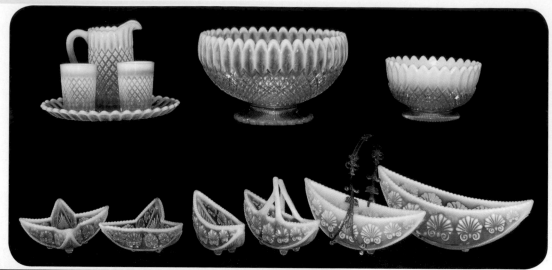

Abalone

Found only in bowls with small handles, the Abalone pattern is believed to be from the Jefferson Glass Company and dates from the 1902 – 1905 period. Colors are blue, white, green, and rarely canary opalescent glass. The design, a series of graduated arcs in columns separated by a line of bubble-like dots, is nice, but nothing special.

Acorn Burrs

Here is another of those well-known Northwood patterns that was made in the 1907 – 1909 era in very limited opalescent glass production. Acorn Burrs is found in carnival glass in many shapes such as table sets, water sets, and berry sets. In opalescent glass it is limited to the small berry bowl shape and possibly the larger bowl (though none has been confirmed to date). Opalescent colors are very rare, so consider yourself fortunate if you find an example of this rare pattern. These small bowls are known in white and blue.

Acorns

This lidded jar sports a banded group of acorns circling the lower half of the bottom with a bark-like pattern continuing nearly to the top. The top is covered with acorn caps around the outer edge and smaller acorns inside. This is one of the earlier Jobling "Opalique" pieces, with an Rd. #796182, which places it in 1934. Colors are white and blue opalescent. Photo courtesy of the Petrasichs.

Adonis Pineapple

Shown is a claret bottle (missing its stopper) from the Aetna Glass & Manufacturing Co., circa 1888. It can be found in either amber or blue with the opalescent design on the bottom portion. Thanks to the Petrasichs for sharing it.

Ala-Bock

From the Model Flint Glass Company and made around 1900, this very scarce pattern has been reported in a water set, the rose bowl, and a whimsied bowl (from the rose bowl mould). Colors reported are blue or vaseline opalescent glass, but don't expect to see any of this design in most malls; it seems to be more available in the rose bowl shape. I've never seen pieces of the reported water set. Also known as Galaxy.

Alaska

One of the early Northwood patterns, Alaska dates from 1897 and can be found in a wide range of shapes including table sets, water sets, berry sets, a cruet, banana boat, celery tray, shakers, and bride's basket. The tumblers and shakers are interchangeable with plain Fluted Scrolls and Jackson pieces. Colors are blue, white, vaseline, and emerald green, as well as plain and decorated crystal.

Albany Reverse Swirl

This was made by the Albany Glass Company in 1901 and 1902, and can be found in blue, canary, and white opalescent glass. Shapes include water set, table set, sugar shaker, syrup, celery vase, rose bowl, water bottle, toothpick holder, and 9" bowl. Albany was made by Model Flint Glass Company.

Albany Stripe

Made about 1900 and with the same moulds as the Albany Fern set, this beautiful water set is quite scarce. The pattern is also found in a barber bottle, sugar bowl, and a 4¾" vase. Colors are white, blue, and frosted vaseline, and here I show the white with an enameled decoration that is stunning.

Alhambra

Often confused with the Spanish Lace pattern, Alhambra is really an Albany Glass pattern. It is known in a rose bowl, tumbler, and a reported syrup jug. The confirmation of a tumbler suggests the possibility of a pitcher, but none is reported. Colors in opalescent glass are white, blue, or canary.

Alva

This very impressive oil lamp is found in several variations including a blue opal stripe with frosted base and a vaseline stripe with the same base treatment. Dating from the 1890s, this lamp is quality all the way.

Arabian Nights

Dating from 1895 or 1896, this Northwood pattern is confined to a water set and a syrup, and can be found in white, blue, canary, and cranberry opalescent glass. The design (swirls, blossoms, and dots) combines the best of both Spanish Lace and Daisy and Fern and is a very striking pattern.

Arched Panel

When I first showed this 9" bowl, I speculated about the maker but now I know it was made by Jefferson Glass in both large and small berry bowls. There are 12 wide panels around the bowl and the top is scalloped, and there is a many rayed star in the base. Colors are white, green, and blue opalescent. Heisey made a similar opalescent set called their #300 Peerless pattern.

Argonaut Shell (Nautilus)

Originally a Northwood pattern, the opalescent examples were made by National or by Dugan after Northwood left National. Colors are blue, white, and vaseline and the shapes include a water set, table set, berry set, compote, shaker, novelty bowl, and cruet.

Arrowhead

This John Walsh Walsh, pattern is similar in design to the Sharks Tooth pattern. It is found in a vase shape and a jar with lid and spoon (shown without the lid and spoon). The only color reported to me is vaseline. Thanks to Ruth Harvey for sharing it.

Ascot

This pattern was made in 1895 by the Greener Company of England as #262018 and can be found in blue and canary opalescent glass. A complete table set and a biscuit jar with lid are the shapes I've heard about. The design is one of arcs around a circle of file.

Astro

Primarily a bowl pattern, Astro was made by the Jefferson Glass Company about 1905. It is a simple design of six circular comet-like rings on a threaded background above three rings of beads that are grouped from the lower center of the bowl upward. Colors are blue, green, white, and canary.

Aurora Borealis

Made by the Jefferson Glass Company and dating from 1903, this vase pattern is very typical of stemmed vases in the opalescent glass era. Rising from a notched base, the stem widens with a series of bubbles and scored lines that end in a flame-shaped top. From the sides are three handle-like projections, giving a very nautical feeling. Colors are white, green, and blue opalescent.

Autumn Leaves

I am very drawn to this beautiful bowl pattern attributed to the Northwood Company from 1905. The colors reported are green, white, and blue opalescent. The design is quite good with large, well-veined leaves around the bowl, connected by twisting branches and a single leaf in the bowl's center.

Azzuro Verde

This pretty vase has a vaseline base and an azure blue top, hence the name from the owner Ruth Harvey. I do not know the maker but the treatment is similar to Hobb's formulas. I welcome any information about this treatment as well as the vase, which has an interior wide panel design.

Baby Coinspot

Shown is a 7" tall vase in a white opalescent color. I believe it is English and it has a polished pontil on the base. Baby Coinspot dates to the early 1900s and was previously shown in a syrup from Belmont Glass and an American vase shape. In addition, Fenton reproduced this pattern. Colors reported are white, green, and vaseline, but surely blue was made.

Ball Foot Hobnail

So very little is really known about this pattern. It may have been a product of New Brighton Glass Company of New Brighton, Pennsylvania, but this hasn't been confirmed. The date of production seems to be around 1889, and most items are crystal while only a few have opalescence. The distinguishing points of identification seem to be the scallops on the edges and while some pieces do indeed have ball feet, others are collar based.

Banded Hobnail

The owner of this strange dresser bottle believes it may be either English or from Europe (I believe the latter). It stands 5" tall and has a strange three-hobnail finial on the stopper. Bands of threading are found around the bottle in three places and at its neck and the hobnails go all the way under the base. The age is unknown to me.

Banded Lily Epergne

Similar to the Serpent Threaded epergne shown elsewhere, this is likely a European piece but I have no information as to the maker at this time. This ruffled-base epergne has one large ruffled center lily with a pinch banded application around the neck area. Vaseline is the only color reported to me to date. Thanks to Ruth Harvey for sharing this nice piece.

Banded Neck and Scale Optic

This very attractive small vase (5½" tall) is mould blown and has a pontil mark on the base. The scale optic pattern is on the inside and only the banding around the neck elevates this vase above the ordinary. I suspect it came in the usual colors but have only seen the white.

Barbed Wire

I've given this pattern a name and if anyone knows it by a previously established name I'd like to hear from them. Reported to me so far are a generous size shade and a vase, both in vaseline. I'm sure other shapes exist and possibly other colors. Any information on this pattern is welcomed.

Barbells

Barbells is found only on the bowl shape in opalescent glass and is credited to the Jefferson Glass Company in 1905. This design is identical to a previous Hobbs, Brockunier one called Mario (their #341). It is even possible Jefferson used the same 8" bowl mould. Barbells is found in blue, white, green, and canary opalescent glass. Bowls and a whimsey vase are known.

Beaded Base Vase

Very similar to a design by the Northwood Company and shown in an old Butler Brothers ad, this attractive jack-in-the-pulpit vase is enameled with sprigs of flowers and has dots painted on the stem and around the base. If anyone has more information about this piece, I'd appreciate hearing from them. I'm sure it came in the usual opalescent colors.

Beaded Basket

There seems to be some dispute over whether this pattern was made by Dugan Glass or after Diamond took over the plant. It is found mostly in carnival glass and since pink examples exist I know it was made very late into the 1920s (Dugan became Diamond in 1913). But here is the first reported example in opalescent glass putting it firmly in the Dugan time period, also.

Beaded Block

Made in 1913 by the Imperial Glass Company and found in crystal or carnival glass (called Frosted Block by carnival glass collectors), this pattern was also made in opalescent glass in limited amounts. Shapes include a rose bowl, creamer, sugar, 6" celery vase, celery tray, a plate, and a two-handled bowl called a nappy. Colors are limited but include blue, green, vaseline, and white. The blue is a darker shade called royal blue.

Beaded Button Arches

The nice compote shown, 4½" high and 5½" across the top comes from Greener and Company in Sunderland, England and the Rd. #304505 puts production in 1897. Shapes known are a compote, creamer and sugar, but other shapes may well exist. The colors are vaseline opalescent (primrose pearline) and blue pearline. Thanks to the Petrasichs for sharing.

Beaded Cable

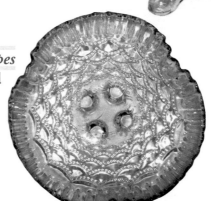

This well-known Northwood pattern can be found in several treatments including opalescent, carnival, and custard. In opalescent glass, the colors are blue, green, white, and canary. Both rose bowls and open bowls are from the same mould. The design is simple yet effective and dates from 1904.

Beaded Drapes

This very attractive pattern is thought to be from the Northwood Company although examples with cranberry edging like some Jefferson items can be found. Dating from 1905, the pattern can be found on footed bowls, rose bowls, and banana bowls in blue, green, white, and vaseline.

Beaded Fans

This pattern is found mostly on footed rose bowls from the same mould as the bowl shown. It is like Shell and Dots minus the dotted base. Colors are white, green, and blue, and the pattern dates from 1905. It has been credited to Northwood, but it is shown in Jefferson Glass ads as #211, so I know it is a Jefferson pattern.

Beaded Fleur de Lis

Attributed to Jefferson Glass, this stemmed compote can be found with the top opened out or turned in like a rose bowl. It was made in the 1906 era in blue, green, and white. The design is quite good, and the base is very distinctive with three wide feet and beaded rings on the stems.

Beaded Moon and Stars

This pattern is nearly the same as the Beaded Stars and Swag pattern shown elsewhere (both were made by the Fenton Art Glass Company) and is often called just Beaded Stars by carnival glass collectors. It's made in a small bowl, a short-stemmed compote, and a banana bowl from the same mould. In opalescent glass, the colors are the usual white, blue, and green.

Beaded Ovals in Sand

Originally called Erie, this Dugan/Diamond pattern is very closely related to two other designs from this company. It can be found in water sets, table sets, berry sets, shakers, a cruet, a toothpick holder, and a ruffled small bowl. Found in green, blue, and white opalescent colors, the pattern was also made in apple green glass, blue, and crystal (sometimes decorated). Opalescent pieces are rather scarce.

Beaded Ovals with Holly

I am pleased to be able to show this unreported Dugan/Diamond pattern, which has to be quite rare. This is the only example reported to me to date and is in a 4¼" spooner shape in white opalescent. If you'll take a look at the Beaded Ovals in Sand pattern you'll notice that it lacks the added holly berry and leaf design shown here. I'd be interested in hearing about other shapes and colors in this interesting pattern. Thanks to the Petrasichs for sharing this beauty.

Beaded Star Medallion

Although often credited to the Imperial Glass Company in carnival glass, a recent find of marked marigold carnival pieces confirms this to be a Northwood pattern. In opalescent glass, it can be found in white, blue, and green. The pattern dates from the 1909 era and was made for both gas and electric shades.

Beaded Stars

The opalescent version of this pattern was made by the Fenton Glass Company in 1907. Shapes reported are a bowl, rose bowl, and rare plate. The bowl and the plate are known in advertising items with "SOUVENIR LION STORE HAMMOND" and are quite rare. Colors found are white, blue, and green in opalescent glass, crystal, and carnival colors.

Beaded V's and Buttons

I have taken the liberty of naming this pattern and would appreciate hearing from anyone with solid information concerning it. This creamer is reported to me to date in blue only, but I would certainly think it came in other shapes and possibly other colors as well. It has an Rd. number which is illegible but possibly indicates a Greener and Company product. Thanks again to John and Mary Petrasich for sharing this nice piece.

Beads and Bark

Shown as early as 1903, this Northwood pattern was made in their Mosaic or purple slag treatment, as well as appearing in opalescent colors of white, blue, and canary, and limited amounts of green. Like on so many vases of the time, the theme was a rustic look with tree limbs forming the supports to the base. In the case of Beads and Bark, these supports generate into a bowl that is a series of inverted loops with beaded edging forming three rows of design.

Beads and Curlycues

This scarce short-stemmed piece, from the Northwood Company and advertised in Butler Brothers in 1906, has an open-edged top, much like that on the Shell and Wild Rose pieces. In the example shown, the top is fanned out evenly all around, but other pieces show a variety of tops. Colors in opalescent glass are blue, green, and white, but certainly vaseline may exist.

Beatty Honeycomb

The Honeycomb pattern was made by Beatty & Sons in Tiffin, Ohio, dates from 1888, and is also known as Beatty Waffle. Shapes found are table sets, water sets, berry sets, a cruet, toothpick holder, celery vase, salt shakers, mustard pot, individual cream and sugar, and the mug shape shown. Colors are white and blue opalescent. The pattern was reproduced in the 1960s by the Fenton Glass Company in blue and emerald green in vases, baskets, rose bowls, and a covered sugar.

Beatty Rib

The A.J. Beatty & Sons Company originally made glass in Steubenville, Ohio, until they merged with U.S. Glass and moved their operation to Tiffin, Ohio, in 1891. Beatty Rib dates from 1889 and was made in both blue and white in a vast array of shapes including table sets, water sets, berry sets in two shapes, a celery vase, mug, nappies in assorted shapes, salt and pepper shakers, a mustard jar, salt dips, sugar shaker, toothpick holder, finger bowl, match holder, and cracker jar.

Beatty Swirl

Like its sister pattern Beatty Rib, this popular design was produced in 1889 in blue, white, and occasionally canary opalescent glass. Shapes known are table sets, water sets, berry sets, syrup, mug, water tray, and celery vase. Other pieces might well have been made including shakers, toothpick holder, cruet, mustard pot, and sugar shaker, so be aware of this possibility.

Beaumont Coinspot

Beaumont Coinspot dates from 1900 and is found in the usual colors. The pitcher can be recognized by the squared top and slightly deeper coloring, especially on blue pieces. Thanks to Mary and John Petrasich for sharing this piece with me.

Beaumont Stripe

While one writer thought this was a Northwood pattern, the water pitcher shown has the same shape as that of the Stars and Stripes water set, first made by Hobbs and then by Beaumont in 1899. I believe it was actually made by Beaumont and have so named it, and I'll hear from collectors if I'm wrong. The set sits on a tray in the Beatty Swirl pattern.

Beaumont Swirl

I believe this pitcher in Swirl is from the Beaumont Glass Company but have no proof. It is speculated about in Heacock's Book 9, *Cranberry Opalescent from A to Z*, but that's the only reference I've found.

Berry Patch

This design, which was made by the Jefferson Glass Company as their #261 pattern in 1905, seems to be limited to small bowls and plates with a dome base. The design is a simple one, a trailing of vine, leaves, and small berry clusters that ramble around the inside of the bowl. The example shown is a flattened piece with the edges rolled up and is called a plate by some collectors. The pattern is accented in a goofus treatment of soft coloring, unlike most examples seen. Colors in opalescent are white, blue, and green.

Big Windows Swirled

Also called Big Windows Reverse Swirl, this Buckeye Glass Co. pattern is made in a variety of shapes and comes in white, blue, and green opalescent. Notice the difference in pattern design to the Windows pattern shown later in this book. Fenton later produced their Coin Dot pattern which is not to be confused with this pattern. Thanks to the Petrasichs for sharing it.

Bird in a Tree

This very unusual novelty piece was made by Burtles, Tate & Company in 1885 (Rd. #34196) and is found in the rose opalescent color shown. It is shown here through the courtesy of Mary and John Petrasich and I certainly thank them for sharing it with me.

Blackberry

While the pattern is sometimes called Northwood's Blackberry, I have no doubt it was produced by the Fenton Glass Company. It has been seen mostly in small sauce shapes but occasionally one of these is pulled into a whimsey shape. Colors in opalescent glass are blue, white, green, and a very pretty amethyst (another indication it is Fenton). It can be found in custard and opaque glass, and many times with a goofus treatment.

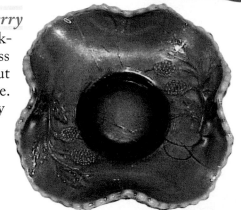

Blackberry Spray

Although very similar to the Blackberry pattern above, this Fenton design has less detail and more sprays. It is found primarily on the hat shape shown and usually in amethyst in opalescent glass, blue opalescent, or white. This same pattern and shape was made in carnival glass during the same time span and 1911 ads are known. It is also known in a jack-in-the-pulpit shape.

Block

Formerly called Northwood Block, this pattern is from Jefferson and was shown in their ads. It is found in a flared and ruffled vase, a hatpin holder whimsey, a JIP shaped whimsey, and flared bowls. Colors are white, blue, green, and canary, and some will have green or cranberry frit.

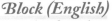

Block (English)

This Greener and Company pattern from 1891 has the Rd. #182002. It can be found on a pitcher, two sizes of tumblers, and a platter. The colors are blue and amber opalescent. It can also be found in non-opalescent colors as well. Many thanks to the Petrasichs for sharing it.

23

Blocked Thumbprint and Beads

While the history of this pattern tends to be confusing mainly because it is only one step in a series of patterns done by the Dugan/Diamond Glass Company over a period of time, the study of two closely designed patterns sets the picture in order. Blocked Thumbprint and Beads and Leaf Rosette and Beads (shown elsewhere in this book), are very much alike. When you add a Dugan carnival glass item called Fishscale and Beads (shown elsewhere in this book) to the picture, you can see that all three patterns came from the same maker. The latter is simply the original Blocked Thumbprint and Beads with an interior pattern of scaling. Opalescent colors are the typical white, blue, and green, but vaseline is a possibility.

Blooms and Blossoms

Also known as Mikado (if you'll look further in this edition at Northwood's Mikado you'll see why), this pattern is known in several treatments including frosted glass with enameling, ruby stained with gilt, the flowers painted in an airy transparent coloring, as well as a goofus treatment. In opalescent glass the usual shape is this square nappy with one handle. It has been called an olive nappy and can be found in white, green, and blue opalescent colors. And if two names aren't enough, it can also be found as Flower and Bud in some books.

Blossoms and Palms

Made by the Northwood Company in both carnival glass and opalescent glass first in 1905, some pieces like the one shown have a goofus treatment. Opalescent colors are white, blue, green, and vaseline, and some pieces have the Northwood trademark. The design consists of three acanthus-like leaves with a stem of flowers and leaves separating each of them.

Blossoms and Web

Advertised in 1906 in a Northwood ad as part of their Egyptian Art Decorated offering, this was one name for the goofus treatment over opalescent items. Blossoms and Web is a difficult pattern to find and is a collector's favorite. Colors are white (sometimes with goofus), blue (scarce), and a very scarce green. The design of six blossoms connected by a webbing of stems with one center blossom is simple but effective.

Blossom Top Caster Set

Shown is a four-piece set with metal stand. The owner says there are traces of gilt on the bottoms of the bottles and the opalescence is soft and covers most of the pieces. I chose the name because of the glass stoppers on the bottles. I believe this set is European. Anyone with more information is asked to contact me.

Blown Diamonds

I now have evidence this pattern may be from the Coudersport Glass Company (1900 – 1904) and may have a companion pitcher in the same shape with interior draping. This latter pitcher is in the Potter County, Pennsylvania, Historical Society Museum and is in white opalescent glass. Only time will tell if I can link these two water pitchers but for now I am convinced there will be such a link found.

Blown Drapery

This very beautiful tankard water set and a companion sugar shaker, made by Northwood as part of the National Glass combine in 1903, are mould blown and can be found in white, blue, green, canary, and cranberry opalescent colors. Please compare this set with the later Fenton Drapery set (shown elsewhere in this book) for a complete understanding of just how this pattern varies from blown to pressed ware. Also, be aware that Blown Drapery has been reproduced in a cruet shape by L.G. Wright.

Blown Rope

This vase is similar to the Twisted Rope vase shown elsewhere (I apologize for believing they were the same), but it is blown and not pressed. Blown Rope may well be from England but I have no proof and I'd certainly like any information readers may have about this piece.

Blown Twist

This pattern and its sister pattern (Blown Drapery) were made at the Northwood plant, when it was part of National Glass, date from 1903, and are shown in a Butler Brothers ad from that year. Besides the rare water set, a celery vase is known in canary or blue opalescent glass, and the water set is found in white, blue, green, canary, and cranberry. Note that the green shown is quite dark.

Boat with Wheels

This very interesting four wheel boat has a rather plain design of vertical ribbing on the side and is a characteristic "v" bottom boat. The color is vaseline and I can only assume it was used as a pickle or relish dish. Other than to say this is English, I have no information to offer at this time. Thanks to Steve and Radka Sandeman for sharing this interesting novelty.

Boggy Bayou

Boggy Bayou is often confused with another Fenton pattern called Reverse Drapery, and is found only on vase shapes. It can be found in opalescent colors of white, green, blue, and amethyst, in sizes from 6" to 13" tall. Production dates from 1907 in both opalescent glass and carnival glass. A Reverse Drapery whimsey vase is shown in the whimsey section, and a comparison of the bases will help distinguish one pattern from the other.

Bohemian Stripe

I'm told that this nice enameled piece is Bohemian (possibly Harrach), but I have no concrete proof to date. Nonetheless, it is a nicely done item and the enameled work is always pleasing to the eye. Blue is the only color reported to me at this time but I'm sure other colors as well as other shapes exist. Thanks to Donna Drohan for the nice photo.

Bough and Blossom

I believe this beautiful lavender rose bowl with squared top, gilded flowers, and an opal edging is English, but I have no evidence. It was shared by the Petrasichs and would grace any fine collection.

Brass Nailhead

This strange mug stands 1¾" tall and can be found in crystal as well as white opalescent glass. Some pieces are marked France, so I know the origin and the date (1890s). I certainly welcome any additional information. The example shown is from Mary and John Petrasich.

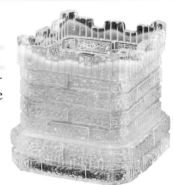

Brick

What a joy this little castle shape is. It was produced by Molineaux, Webb, and Company in 1885 and is marked Rd. #29780. The only color reported is white, but the Petrasichs report there are other shapes with the brick design.

Brideshead

This pattern was made by the Davidson Glass Works in England and bears their registration number, 130643, dated 1889. Shapes are numerous and include a water set, table set, celery vase (tall spooner), biscuit jar, compote, 5½" plate, handled fold basket, handled bride's bowl, cake plate (stemmed), fairy lamp, and various bowl shapes. Colors are blue and vaseline opalescent glass.

Bridesmaid

I am really taken by this exquisite pattern, shown here in amber in the pitcher and tumbler shape. Often mistaken for Davidson's Brideshead, this is actually a Greener and Company pattern, with the difference being it has no Rd. number, as Davidson pieces do. Reported shapes are various bowl sizes, large oval bowl, pitcher, tumbler, and tray. Colors are blue and amber, and all pieces and colors are hard to come by. Thanks to the Petrasichs for the information and photo.

Brilynacee Lace

Brilynacee Lace was made by Model Flint Glass of Albany, Indiana, and is very similar to Spanish Lace, Alhambra, and Ala-Bock. The blown pitcher is the first to be reported (surely there were matching tumblers) and the pattern was named by the owner, Kelvin Russell.

British Flute

I believe this pattern is from England, possibly by Davidson. It has a base pontil mark, 16 inside flute or wide panels, and is somewhat square in shape. The top has an interesting three-and-one ruffling much like that done by the Dugan/Diamond Company on some of their glass. This beautiful vaseline opalescent piece is 8" tall and probably came in other colors.

Broken Pillar

Called Kismet (#909) by some collectors, this pattern was made in the 1895 – 1900 era by Model Flint Glass. It was advertised in many shapes in crystal, decorated colors, and the one stemmed piece in opalescent glass. Colors are white, blue, and vaseline opalescent, and the piece is called a stemmed tray. The design is all exterior with a very heavily patterned stem.

Bubble Lattice

This pattern was called Plaid by Marion Hartung but is more commonly known as Bubble Lattice or simply Lattice. It was made in Wheeling by Hobbs, Brockunier & Company in 1889, and can be found in many shapes including water sets, berry sets, table sets, cruets, sugar shakers, syrups, toothpick holders, finger bowls, salt shakers, bowls, rose bowls, and bride's baskets. Colors are blue, white, canary, and cranberry, and the finish was occasionally satinized.

Bubble Lattice Lamp (Northwood's Paneled Mould)

The owner of this 4" tall lamp believes it was from Markham but the shaping of the glass is like Northwood's Paneled mould that is found on cruets and shakers, so I believe it is probably theirs. I'd certainly like any information about this lamp from readers.

Buckeye Bubble Lattice

The shape of this pitcher tells that it was a product of the Buckeye Glass Company of Martins Ferry, Ohio. This same shape is found in other opalescent patterns like Reverse Swirl and Big Windows. Besides the water set, a cylinder shade and a salt shaker are known. Colors include blue, white, canary, and cranberry.

Buckeye Coinspot

Often collectors have difficulty telling one maker's Coinspot pieces from another so I am showing several examples to help. Here is the Buckeye Glass pitcher, made in 1889, in the usual colors. Note that the top is round and the neck is short.

Bull's Eye

Seldom seen, this pattern (attributed to Hobbs by some writers) is found in the water bottle shown as well as a light shade and a bride's bowl. Colors are white, canary, blue, and cranberry opalescent. In addition, there seems to be some speculation this pattern was also made by LaBelle as well as Phoenix in other shapes that include lamp cylinders, oil lamps, and hanging glass shades.

Bull's Eye and Fan Variant

Apparently U.S. Glass must have done a lot of fiddling with this pattern. This was the second variation. The first is called Daisies in Oval Panels (see my *Collector's Encyclopedia of Carnival Glass*). Here is the first piece of opalescent glass reported and it has no bottom fan and no daisy motif in the bull's eye. Thanks to the Petrasichs for sharing it.

Bull's Eye and Leaves

At first glance this looks like the normal Netted Roses pattern from Northwood, but here I show a prototype bowl that was later retooled into that pattern. Notice the area that became roses is only circles or bull's eyes in this version. I truly thank the Petrasichs for this rarity.

Bushel Basket (Northwood)

This Northwood pattern was first made in 1905 in opalescent glass in colors of white, blue, and vaseline, and later in custard glass and carnival glass (carnival pieces have two different shapings and many color and mould variations). Some pieces have the trademark while others do not and a few items were gilded or decorated. This is a very popular pattern with most glass collectors.

Butterfly (Fenton)

This neat little compote is shown in the 1917 and 1918 Butler Brothers catalogs and is a product from Fenton. The only reported color in opalescent glass is white and the only shape reported is the small compote which can either be found in the round shape shown or a square shape. Thanks again to the Petrasichs for sharing.

29

Button Panels

This pattern was advertised as early as 1899 at the Northwood factory, shown in Dugan ads later, and also produced at the Coudersport Tile & Ornamental Glass Company sometime between 1900 and 1904. There it was called Shadow and it was made in white, blue, canary, and green opalescent, as well as transparent green glass. Shapes, all from the same mould, are a ruffled bowl, rose bowl, and straight-sided bowl that is called a nut bowl by most. Just who made what pieces is a real puzzle as is how three companies ended up with this pattern.

Buttons and Braids

Questions have come up as to the maker of this pattern. It was first credited to Jefferson in 1905, and was shown in old Fenton catalog ads from 1910. This pattern comes in water sets and bowls in blue, green, white, vaseline, and cranberry opalescent. Tumblers can be either blown or pressed and some can be found in a strange greenish vaseline that is like some Northwood pieces. I suspect that this pattern was also made by Northwood for National and may have even been a product of Dugan, once Northwood left the Indiana, Pennsylvania, plant.

Cabbage Leaf

Cabbage Leaf is like the Winter Cabbage shown elsewhere in this book, except it has three large leaf patterns over the twig-like feet. This piece is usually turned up to form a very neat vase. Both patterns are from the Northwood Company and date from its 1906 – 1907 period of production. Colors in the Cabbage Leaf pattern are white, green, and blue opalescent with canary a possibility.

Cactus (Northwood)

Made by Northwood, circa 1893, this is a reasonably hard-to-find item. The colors found on this shaker are blue, vaseline, and cranberry opalescent. Thanks to Ruth Harvey for sharing the photo.

Calyx

This pattern was made by the Model Flint Glass Company during their association with National and dates from 1899 or a bit later. This scarce vase can be found in crystal, canary opalescent, blue opalescent, white opalescent, and in opaque colors of blue, green, white, and yellow (shards) as well as some rare decorated opaque examples. A blue opaque vase with green painted leaves is shown in Ron Teal's fine book, *Albany Glass: Model Flint Glass Company of Albany, Indiana.*

Canary/Blue JIP Vase

This vase, like the Rubina Verde vase, is from Hobbs, Brockunier in the 1880s, but is even rarer. The bottom is canary opalescent glass while the top is blue opalescent glass. It is a blown item, 6½" tall, and a really beautiful piece of true art glass. Thanks to Connie Wilson for sharing this with me.

Cane Rings

This pattern can be found in several books that feature glass from England as a product of the Davidson Company, but has never been named as far as I can ascertain, so I've corrected that oversight. I know of bowls, a celery vase, a creamer, and an open sugar in this pattern, but more shapes were probably made. Opalescent colors are blue and vaseline.

Carousel

This was made by the Jefferson Glass Company in 1905 as their #264 pattern. Colors in opalescent glass are the usual white, blue, and green, occasionally with a frit decoration. The only shape I've seen is the standard novelty bowl shape, often with varied edge treatments. The design is a simple one with little imagination and low appeal to the collector.

Casbah

Now known to be a product of the Fenne Glassworks of Saarland, Germany, this pattern is found in the compote shape as well as a 10" bowl with candy-ribbon edge. I thank Siegmar Geiselberger of Germany for his glass research on this pattern.

Cashews

Cashew is attributed to the Northwood Glass Company and I suspect it was later continued by Dugan/Diamond. Shapes are bowls, plates, and a nice rose bowl, all from the same mould. Colors are white, blue, and green opalescent with some white examples found with a goofus treatment.

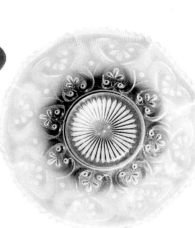

Centipede

This very unusual bowl gets its name from the strange feet that support it. The glass is delicate and has a cased edging. I believe this is another English pattern but have no proof. I welcome any information from readers about this pattern.

Cherry

Made by Bakewell, Pears, and Company about 1870, the Cherry pattern can be found in crystal as well as opalescent glass in many shapes including a scarce plate, goblet, berry set, table set, stemmed wine, open and covered compotes, and novelty bowls of several shapes. The cherry design is very realistic and the leaves form arcs.

Cherry Panel (Dugan Cherry)

Although better known in carnival glass, this Dugan pattern is often seen in peach opalescent glass. Other carnival glass colors are amethyst and marigold. In opalescent glass reported colors are white, blue, and canary. The example shown has a goofus treatment with the cherries done in red and the leaves in gold. Production dates from 1907 and the only shape reported in opalescent glass is the three-footed bowl, often shaped in a variety of ways, including a vase whimsey.

Christmas Pearls

Occasionally called Beaded Panel (it isn't the same as the Beaded Panels pattern often called Opal Open), this quite rare and beautiful pattern is most likely a Jefferson Glass design that dates from 1901 to 1903. The only shapes reported are the cruet shown and a salt shaker. The colors known so far are blue, white, and green opalescent.

Christmas Snowflake

This pattern was produced by the Northwood Company in 1888, and later continued by Dugan Glass after Northwood left the Indiana, Pennsylvania, factory. It was made in both plain and ribbed pieces in water sets (at least two distinct pitcher shapes are known), as well as oil lamps, a cruet, and possibly other shapes. In 1980 several reproduction shapes were sold by L.G. Wright including a plain water set, and new shapes that include a sugar shaker, barber bottle, syrup, basket, cruet, bride's bowl, milk pitcher, creamer, and rose bowls in two sizes. The original lamps were made in three sizes. Colors for old pieces are white, blue, green, and cranberry with the old cruet known only in the first color. Shown is a very rare green pitcher.

Chrysanthemum Base Swirl

This was first from Buckeye Glass then Northwood (speckled finish). Production dates from 1890 in white, blue, and cranberry (shown), sometimes in a satin finish. Shapes include water sets, table sets, berry sets, cruet, syrup, sugar shaker, toothpick holder, salt shaker, finger bowl, celery vase, mustard, and a beautiful straw holder with lid. Northwood's speckled pieces are in the same shapes.

Chrysanthemum Swirl Variant

Here is a very scarce variant pattern that is credited to the Northwood Company by some. It has even been called a mystery variant. In size and make-up, the tankard pitcher is much like Ribbed Opal Lattice, also credited to Northwood from 1888; however, if you examine the color of the pitcher here, you will find it anything but typical of that company. It isn't blue or even green, but a very strong teal. It can also be found in white and cranberry. It is possible the design was first made elsewhere and Northwood produced later versions.

Circled Scroll

This pattern was made in 1904 by the Dugan Glass Company and continued when the factory became Diamond. It is found in carnival glass, apple green glass, and opalescent glass. Shapes are a water set, berry set, table set, cruet set, jelly compote, and salt shakers but not in all colors or all treatments. In carnival there is also a whimsey vase pulled from a tumbler. Opalescent colors are white, blue, and green.

Cleopatra's Fan

After a series of names, the latest seems to be Cleopatra's Fan, so I'll settle on that one. Known in white, blue, and green opalescent glass, this pattern is actually a product of Dugan and was never a part of the Northwood line. It is quite scarce and collectible.

Coin Dot Lamp

There are three very distinct oil lamps known in the Coin Dot pattern. The largest lamp is called Inverted Thumbprint and Fan base and dates from 1890. It can be found in white and blue opal. The other table lamp is called Chevron Base and is shown in an 1893 U.S. Glass ad, made by King Glass of Pittsburgh. I strongly suspect the small hand lamp (shown in rare vaseline) was from the same company since they have the same font shape.

Coinspot (Jefferson)

I believe this previously unreported rose bowl was made by Jefferson from their salad bowl (Jefferson's #83). This company also made the water set (#180) in white, blue, green, and cranberry, which was later copied by Fenton. Please note the base which has been ground.

Coinspot (Northwood)

Shown is the Northwood water pitcher with a ruffled top in a different shape than was shown in the last edition. These water sets were made at the Indiana, Pennsylvania, plant and production was probably continued when Dugan took over the plant. Butler Brothers catalog ads show this pattern in 1903 – 1904 from the Northwood/National production. Colors are white, blue, green, and cranberry.

Coinspot and Swirl

Coinspot and Swirl was first thought to be from Hobbs and now is believed to be from the Northwood Company at Indiana, Pennsylvania. It was probably continued after the National Glass merger; production dates seem to be about 1898 – 1902. Colors in opalescent glass are green, white, blue, and cranberry. Shapes include a syrup (rare in cranberry) and a cruet (in the Parian Swirl mould). In addition, a rare amber has been reported but not confirmed by me.

Coinspot Syrup

While it is, at best, difficult to distinguish some moulds of one company from those of another, I truly believe the syrup shown is from the West Virginia Glass Company since the same shape can be found in their Polka Dot items where the dots are colored rather than opalescent. At any rate, I'm sure these pieces were made in white, blue, cranberry, and possibly other colors since some Coinspot items are also found in green, amber, vaseline, amberina, rubina, and even amethyst.

Colonial Stairsteps

Although mostly found on this toothpick holder shape, a breakfast set consisting of a creamer and sugar is also known. Colors are crystal and blue opalescent only and although the breakfast set has been reported with the Northwood trademark, none has been seen to date so the attribution is a bit shaky at this time.

Commonwealth

Shown is a standard tumbler, 3½" tall, with no pattern whatsoever. I believe this piece was used like the Universal tumbler and could be put with various pitchers to form a water set. Colors are blue and white opalescent, but certainly crystal, opaque, and carnival glass were made from this same mould. Opalescent pieces are known to have been enameled also.

Compass

This pattern was made by the Dugan/Diamond factory primarily as an exterior pattern on their Heavy Grape carnival glass pieces. It comes into its own in opalescent glass. It can be found on both 9" and 5½" bowls, as well as on 10" and 6½" plates. Some of these pieces are marked with the Diamond-D mark. Opalescent colors are white, green, and blue. The pattern is a good one with eight overlapping arcs and a marie (base) design of oversecting stars.

Concave Columns (#617)

As stated elsewhere (see Pressed Coinspot), this pattern was originally called #617 in a 1901 National Glass catalog and was later continued by Dugan/Diamond Glass in an ad assortment in the compote shape. For some strange reason, the vase has become known as Concave Columns. The compote in opalescent glass is known as Pressed Coinspot and in carnival glass it is simply called Coinspot. Shapes from the same mould are vases, compotes, goblets, and a stemmed banana boat. Colors in opalescent glass are white, blue, green, and canary.

Conch and Twig

This is another of those marvelous wall pocket vases the British made in opalescent glass. It was made by Burtles, Tate, and Company of England in 1885 with Rd. #39807. This one has the very natural look of a seashell with a twig-like holder or hanger. Colors are the usual ones of blue, white, and vaseline opalescent glass.

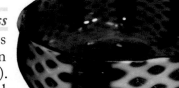

Consolidated Criss-Cross

Consolidated Criss-Cross was produced by Consolidated Lamp & Glass Company of Fostoria, Ohio, from 1893 to 1894. This pattern is found in white, cranberry, and rubina opalescent glass (either satin or glossy finish). Shapes include an 8½" water pitcher, tumbler, cruet, syrup, shakers, a table set, finger bowl, berry set, celery vase, mustard pot, sugar shaker, ivy ball, and a toothpick holder. This is a very collectible and scarce pattern.

Consolidated Shell

This beautiful rose bowl was made by Consolidated Lamp & Shade Company in 1894. It is often found in opaque glass or crystal, but here is a beautiful vaseline glass example with a rubina verde treatment and opalescent edges. The applied enameling of flowers and vines is very nice. The rose bowl is 5" tall. It is also known as Shell and Seaweed. Thanks to the Petrasichs for sharing it.

Constellation

This very scarce compote was shown in a 1914 Butler Brothers ad for Dugan/Diamond Glass Company and was reported to be available in both white and blue opalescent. Originally the mould for this piece was the S-Repeat goblet (the pattern was originally called National and was a product of Northwood/National Glass that dated from 1903). When Dugan obtained the National moulds, the exterior pattern became S-Repeat and the goblet was turned into a compote with a pattern on the interior called Constellation. In addition to the few opalescent items, many shapes were made in colored crystal with gilding, as well as a few shapes in carnival glass including the compote where the S-Repeat exterior is known as Seafoam! This is another example of name complication that plagues collectors.

Contessa

This hobnailed pattern, made by Greener & Company in England in 1890 and bearing Rd. #160244, can be found in several shapes including a pitcher, a two-piece footed breakfast set consisting of creamer and open sugar, stemmed cake plate, and the handled basket shown. (All other shapes are considered much rarer.) Opalescent colors include blue, canary, and a rare amber.

Convex Rib

This pattern was made by Jefferson Glass around 1905. The vase has 24 convex ribs running from the indented base to near the top. It was also made in green, white, and vaseline opalescent as well as the blue shown.

Coral

The Coral pattern, found only on bowls with odd open work around the edging, may well be a product of the Jefferson Company. Colors are the usual: white, blue, green, and vaseline. While it has the same name as a Fenton carnival glass pattern, the design is far different.

Coral and Shell

This large, 9½" bowl is a standout in any collection. Designed and made by W. H. Heppell, the molds for this pattern were acquired by George Davidson & Co. when Heppell went out of business in the mid 1880s. Any opalescent pieces found should be considered to have been made by Davidson, with other types of glass being by Heppell. The bowl shown is listed in an 1885 catalog as pattern #134. Although other shapes were made in crystal and slag, the bowl is the only reported shape in opalescent glass to date. Thanks to the Petrasichs for the information and photo.

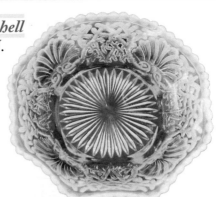

Coral Reef

While most collectors have lumped this pattern with Seaweed, it truly is a different pattern and it took a letter from a collector and an article by John D. Sewell to set the record straight. Seaweed has branches and distinct round dots while Coral Reef (Mr. Sewell's name) has a rambling line pattern with square-type extensions rather than dots. Coral Reef can be found in bitters bottles, barber bottles (round or square), finger bowls, rose bowls, lamps in four sizes including a mini night lamp, a stemmed oil lamp, a finger lamp, and a stemmed finger lamp.

Cornucopia

This novelty vase with handles, made by Northwood in 1905, can be found in white, blue, and green opalescent glass. Production continued for at least two years and despite there being rumors of this piece in carnival glass, none has ever surfaced. The design is almost like a wicker basketweave that rolls at the bottom to rest on a decorative base.

Cornucopia Vase

These little 4½" vases, 8" with the stand, are often attributed to Davidson but they don't actually match any known Davidson pattern. The closet resemblance would be to the Queen's Crown pattern, but still no match. They are fairly hard to come by, especially with the stand. Any new information about this piece would be appreciated. Photo courtesy of the Petrasichs.

Corn Vase

Despite having been reproduced by Wright Glass in the 1960s, this beautiful Dugan pattern is a collector's dream. Dugan made it in 1905 in white, blue, vaseline, and a rare green, as well as a super-rare marigold carnival. The mould work is fantastic and the open husks show real glassmaking skill.

Corolla

This pattern was probably made after National Glass took over the Model Flint factory at Albany, Indiana. It has appeared in the vase shape only. Colors are white, canary, and blue opalescent, with opaque pieces in white, blue, canary, and green glass. Production was likely from about 1900 to 1902, and some pieces have been found (shards) at the factory site. Production was small, for a short period of time I suspect.

Coronation

Here is another opalescent pattern from England, named by Heacock, and seen in both blue and canary opalescent glass. Shapes reported are a tankard pitcher, a tumbler, a creamer, a stemmed open sugar, cake stand, and oval platter, but I feel sure other shapes were made. The design is one of cane panels, separated by ovals of plain glass and topped by a fan shape of three elongated hearts. It was made by Greener (Rd. #136075) in 1890.

Counter Swirl

Although this vase is heavier than most pieces of English opalescent blown glass, I still feel it is a product of that country. The coloring is typically English and the wide and narrow random swirls that run in opposite directions have the English look. I'd appreciate any additional information about this pattern.

Country Kitchen

Here is the only reported opalescent glass version of this Millersburg pattern that is most often found in crystal or as a reverse pattern for some carnival glass bowls. If you compare it to the variant shown below, you will see the absence of the small stars and the addition of a file section.

Country Kitchen Variant (Milky Way)

I've re-titled this pattern as it is known to collectors and as it should have always been (it was misnamed in 1987). If you will compare it to the Country Kitchen pattern shown above, you see the difference. The former has a mid-section of file rather than the small stars.

Crocus

Since I first showed this fine vase, I've learned of an example that was marked "Made in Czecho-slovakia," so I can now say with authority where this vase was made. It stands 6½" tall and has a 2¾" base diameter and in design is much like the Daffodil pattern that was made first by Northwood and then by Dugan/Diamond. The example shown is a strong blue/green color.

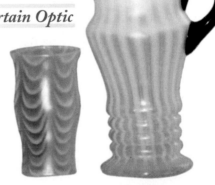

Crown Jewels

Since the last edition of this book I've learned this pattern was made by Greener and Company in 1892 (their Rd. #196641). It can be found in blue and canary, in shapes including a tankard pitcher, tumbler, plate, oval platter, creamer, and open sugar. Thanks to both John Petrasich and John Loggie for the information and the photo.

Curtain Optic

Fenton began making this very pretty design in 1922 and continued for several years, adding a medium wide striped opalescent pattern called Rib Optic. These patterns were made in several pitcher sizes and shapes along with iced tea tumblers, handled tall tumblers, and handled mugs. Even a two-piece guest set (small bedside pitcher and tumbler) can be found. Usually, the handles on both pitchers and mugs were of a darker glass. Some of these opalescent items were iridized.

Curvy

I have very little information at this time concerning this nice epergne except that it is almost certainly English. Vaseline is the only color reported to me and this is the only shape I've seen. Thanks to the Sandemans for sharing it.

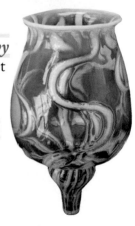

Cyclone

In previous editions I've shown this very scarce Northwood vase in vaseline (three reported) and blue (three reported), but here is the first white example I've seen. Cyclone measures about 7½" tall, and has a base that matches the Beads and Bark vase and a body like the Ocean Shell pattern.

Daffodils

Daffodils has been credited to Northwood and continued by Dugan at the Indiana, Pennsylvania, factory. This pattern is found in water sets (various shaped pitchers), two shapes of vases, lamps, and a bowl whimsey in white, canary, green, and blue. The example I show here is canary and has an enameled spider between the lower leaves, adding a real artist's touch to the piece.

Daffodils Oil Lamp

While both Northwood and Dugan/Diamond made this pattern in water sets, I believe this oil lamp shape was made by only Northwood about 1904 or 1905. Correspondence from their factory indicates they were making opalescent glass lamps, some with goofus base decorations and others with ruby staining on the base. Shown is a white opalescent glass table lamp with goofus on the base.

Daffodils Shade

I have no positive proof of the maker of this shade but highly suspect it to be English rather than from Northwood or Dugan. Richardson's, John Walsh Walsh, it's simply guesswork at this time. I'd like to thank the Sandemans for sharing it and encourage anyone with information on this pattern to contact me.

Dahlia

While I have questions about this piece shown (it sure looks like old glass), I know at least some of the opalescent pieces in this pattern (originally from Dugan in other treatments) are supposed to be new. L.G. Wright began marketing new Dahlia pieces in 1978, after their demise, and production has been continued by others. Shapes known are water sets (with a new tumbler mould) and table sets, but others may exist. Buy with caution.

Dahlia Twist

Dahlia Twist was made by the Jefferson Glass Company around 1905 as their #207 pattern. It is a typical cone-shaped vase on a circular base with a flared and ruffled top. The real interest comes in the ribbing that is twisted against an interior optic that runs in the opposite direction. Colors are the typical white, green, and blue opalescent.

Dahlia Twist Epergne

I am thrilled to show this very beautiful epergne as it was originally sold. Most collectors believe this Jefferson Glass lily had a glass dome-based bowl as a holder, but the lily was made expressly for decorative metal holders as shown in ads of the day. Most were silvered but a few were gilded as the one shown. The lily came in the usual opalescent colors. A similar lily and metal holder in the Fishnet pattern was sold by the Dugan/Diamond Company.

Duises Lamp

This nicely done English oil lamp sports a well suited marbled stem and platform just above the base and has a very complementary design on the metalwork as well. The only color reported to me is vaseline. Photo courtesy of Steve and Radka Sandeman.

Daisies in Pentagon

This lamp, although somewhat similar to the Daisies lamp, is a bit more sophisticated in appearance. With double green marble platforms separated by a band of fleur-de-lis in metalwork, this bracket footed lamp is a true piece of beauty. I feel certain it is English and do thank the Sandemans for sharing this nice vaseline opalescent item with me.

Daisy and Button

Believed to be from Edward Bolton (Oxford Lane Glass Works) in England, this pattern and shape were later copied by Hobbs in non-opalescent colors and even later made by the Fenton Company for L.G. Wright. Both English and Hobbs productions date from the 1880s and the reproductions for Wright began in the late 1930s. The piece shown is called an oval crown bowl or a bun tray. Old ones are found in blue and canary opalescent glass, as are the reproductions.

Daisy and Button with Diamonds

This small 4½" bowl in vaseline is the only shape reported to me at this time and the only information I can give at this time is to say it is likely English. Any information would be appreciated. Photo courtesy of the Petrasichs.

Daisy and Drape

Daisy and Drape was produced by the Northwood Company primarily as a carnival glass pattern. This rare piece is one of three known in vaseline opalescent. It stands 6½" tall, and has three rolled feet that carry the drape design from the vase on down. The pattern very much resembles a U.S. Glass pattern called Vermont, except for the ring of daisies that borders the top of the vase.

Daisy and Fern

This pattern was made at several factories including West Virginia Glass, Northwood (alone and as part of National), and the Dugan Company, and was later reproduced and sold by L.G. Wright as early as 1939. Colors for old items include white, blue, green, and cranberry. New items were made in white, blue, canary (not found in old pieces), and cranberry. Be especially cautious about rose bowls and barber bottles as well as cruets. All have been reproduced. Note: This same pattern is used on the three following molds from Northwood. The hard to find cruet in cranberry opalescent (shown) is courtesy of Sharron Lancaster.

Daisy and Fern (Apple Blossom Mould)

Northwood's Apple Blossom Mould line was never reproduced like many other Daisy and Fern items. It can be found in several shapes including a spooner (shown), creamer, sugar, and night lamp. Colors are blue, white, and cranberry. The spooner shape also doubled as a pickle caster insert. (This is the same pattern as Daisy and Fern, using a different mould.)

Daisy and Fern (Parian Swirl Mould)

This pattern is on Northwood's Parian Swirl mould just like the mould on the Christmas Snowflake cruet. A close examination reveals the swirl design in the mould, just below the handle on the cruet shown. (This is the same pattern as Daisy and Fern, using a different mould.)

Daisy and Fern (Swirl Mould)

This Northwood mould has a wide swirl in the glass. It can be found in several shapes including a water pitcher, tumbler, cruet, salt shaker, syrup, berry bowl, sauce, toothpick holder, spooner (caster insert), sugar shaker, covered sugar, covered creamer, and a covered butter dish. Colors are white, blue, and cranberry opalescent. (This is the same pattern as Daisy and Fern, using a different mould.)

Daisy and Greek Key

Recent evidence now confirms this pattern isn't from Davidson but was a product of Gerbruder von Streit of Germany in 1900. It was made in many shapes in crystal as well as opalescent glass according to Seigmar Geiselberger, a glass researcher in Germany. Colors in opalescent glass are white, blue, and green.

Daisy and Plume

While this famous design was made for years under the Northwood/National banner, the example shown comes from the Dugan Company, despite having no holes in the legs. The mould work is excellent and there is no Northwood marking. Colors are green, white, and blue opalescent glass and carnival glass. Dugan ads date from 1907 on this footed rose bowl.

Daisy Block Row Boat

This novelty piece was from Sowerby in England as early as 1886, and is found in crystal, carnival, and opalescent glass. The pieces originally had a stand. Sizes of 10", 12", and 15" are known (the largest size is shown). Colors in opalescent glass are limited to this very pale vaseline and green.

Daisy Dear

This exterior pattern was made by the Dugan/Diamond Company and is well known to carnival glass collectors, but not very imaginative. It is found in opalescent glass in white, green, and blue, on bowls of all shapes and plates like the ruffled example shown. Production began in 1907. The pattern shows four blossom-and-leaf sprigs around the bowl and a daisy design on the marie.

Daisy Drape

This well done creamer in vaseline opalescent is the only shape and color reported to me at this time. I'm certain it is of English origin. Any information on this pattern would be appreciated. Thanks to Kent with the Vaseline Glass Collectors Group for the name.

Daisy in Criss-Cross

Daisy in Criss-Cross is believed to be from Beaumont Glass Company, dating from about 1895. It can be found in water sets and a scarce syrup. Both the pitcher and the syrup have a ringed neck. Colors are mostly blue, white, cranberry, sapphire blue, and a strange pastel sapphire (shown), but there is also a scarce green set, which I am happy to finally show.

Daisy May

This design was made by the Dugan Glass Company, primarily as a carnival glass novelty called Leaf Rays. It is is found in opalescent glass on the spade-shaped nappy. It can be found in white, blue, and green (rare) opalescent glass. While the carnival design is interior, the opalescent pieces have the pattern on the exterior.

Daisy Swirl

I suspect the bowl shown is English, probably from Davidson, but have no proof. It is fairly deep and has a great vaseline color with strong opalescence. I'd certainly appreciate hearing from anyone who has additional information about this pattern.

Daisy with Panels

This interesting little bowl has 12 panels with daisy like medallions jutting out and downwards at a slight angle with additional daisies around the footed area. This piece in blue is the only reported shape and color to date. Thanks to the Petrasichs for sharing it.

Daisy Wreath

I am extremely pleased to show this very rare item from the Westmoreland Company. It is usually found in carnival glass on a milk glass base, but here is a rich blue glass with opalescent edges. The bowl is 9" in diameter and is the only example in opalescent glass I've seen without iridescence.

Dandelion Mug

This mug, which is rarer than even the Singing Birds mugs, also by Northwood, is found mostly in carnival glass in a host of colors. Here I show one of the ultra-rare blue opalescent versions (three or four are known) and its beauty is obvious. The carnival version dates from early 1912, so I believe the Dandelion opalescent ones were made at the same time. Thanks to the late Jack Beckwith for sharing this rarity.

Davidson Drape

I feel safe in calling this another piece from the Davidson & Company Glass Works of England. I'm surprised I haven't seen more of these. This one is vaseline and I'm sure blue was made. Thanks to the Petrasichs for sharing it.

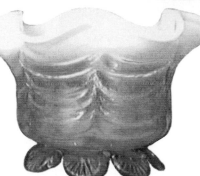

Davidson Germany Souvenir

What a nice little piece this is. The 5½" plate is labeled Strandschloss Kohlberg, which is a resort town on the German/Belgian border. This George Davidson pattern has the Rd. #340825 which places it from 1899. It is very similar to the Double Rib & Block shown later in this edition. This is not a transfer, but rather an example of where the usual star pattern on the base was replaced with a smooth disk, then the cardboard souvenir is placed in the center. Thanks to Dave Peterson for the photo and information.

Davidson Open Salts

I'm happy to be able to show several open salt dips from George Davidsons. The color on each is vaseline opalescent although blue should likely exist but I haven't received pictures of any yet. Most of these can also be found in metal holders on occasion. Thanks again to the Petersons for sharing glass from there nice collection.

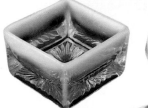

Davidson Pearline Epergne

This dramatic 14" tall four-lily epergne sits on a very deep well bowl with the same feet Davidson used on other items (see Lady Caroline). I believe this epergne was made in blue pearline also and possibly white which Davidson called Moonshine Pearline. The glass is thin and of very fine quality.

Davidson Shell

Here is the spill vase shape in this Davidson pattern advertised in 1889. It is found in opaque glass (blue, white, and ebony) as well as in canary and blue opalescent glass. Thanks to Ruth Harvey for sharing this piece with me.

Deco Lily

I have no information about this nice 7¾" vase. The Petrasichs who own it believe it is American and it certainly doesn't have the look of English or European glass. It is green opalescent but has a strong vaseline look. I welcome any information about it.

Decorated English Swirl

The Swirl pattern was made in England as well as America. Here is one in a beautiful rose bowl that shades from white to cranberry and has an enameled decoration of flowers and leaves. This piece has a pontil mark and is, of course, blown. Thanks to Kathy Gresko for letting me show it.

Desert Garden

This novelty dome-base bowl pattern can be found in white, blue, and green opalescent glass. The design of three sets of leaves bracketing a stylized blossom with a stippled background isn't very imaginative but does fill most of the available space. The example shown, like most, has a ribbon-candy edging that adds to the appearance. The maker hasn't been determined, but I lean toward Dugan/Diamond.

Diagonal Wave

Like the Waves pattern and the Diamond Wave pattern, this piece is very thin glass that has been mould blown. I suspect this piece may be British and probably came in blue as well as the vaseline shown.

Diamond and Daisy (Caroline)

Ads in a 1909 Butler Brothers catalog identify this pattern as part of the Intaglio line from the Dugan Company. It is clearly shown in a handled basket shape, so I know at least two shapes were made. Dugan first advertised the Intaglio line in 1905, and it included painted plain crystal as well as blue, green, and white opalescent. The pattern of Diamond and Daisy is very similar to the Wheel and Block pattern. It is known as Caroline in carnival glass.

Diamond and Oval Thumbprint

This very attractive design, found only on the vase shape, is from the Jefferson Glass Company, circa 1904. It can be found in white, blue, and green opalescent glass and may vary in size from 6" tall to 14".

Diamond Dot

This nicely done pattern appears to me to be a product of John Walsh Walsh, although I have no solid proof of such to date. Shapes are the compote shown and a shade and the only color reported to me at this time is vaseline opalescent. Anyone with information is urged to contact me. Thanks to Ruth Harvey for sharing this nice item.

Diamond-in-Diamond

What a beautiful pattern this is! It consists of smaller diamonds that are blocked into larger shapes. The opalescence is outstanding and it has the look of British glass but I haven't been able to pin the maker down yet. The blue glass has a slight aqua tint.

Diamond Maple Leaf

Attributed to the Dugan Glass Company (Dugan/Diamond), this hard-to-find two-handled bonbon can be found in green, white, and blue opalescent. The design shows rather realistic maple leaves flanked by very flowing scroll designs that give the piece a real artistic look. Diamond Maple Leaf dates from 1909.

47

Diamond Optic

I know very little about this attractive piece except it is from England. I base this on the finish and shaping. It may be known by another name also, but I felt this name summed up the configuration as well as any. The diamond pattern is all on the inside and runs from the outer rim to a middle diameter above the stem. It can be found in white opalescent also and may well have been made in canary and vaseline.

Diamond Point

This Northwood pattern dates from 1907. It is found only on the vase shape in white, blue, and green opalescent glass, and many carnival glass colors. Sizes range from 8" to a lofty 14" that has been swung to reach that size.

Diamond Point and Fleur-de-Lis

This pattern was made by the Northwood Company and illustrated in their 1906 ads. Most pieces can be found with the Northwood trademark. Novelty bowls with a collar base can be found, some shapes have been whimsied, and a nut bowl shape is known. Colors in opalescent glass are white, blue, and green, according to the ads, but certainly vaseline is a possibility. Thanks to Samantha Prince for the photo.

Diamond Point Columns

While many carnival glass collectors are familiar with this pattern and associate it with the Imperial Glass Company of Bellaire, Ohio, it was a product of the Fenton Company and is shown in Butler Brothers ads with other Fenton patterns. In opalescent glass, only the vase has been reported, and I am very happy to show an example of this. This opalescent piece stands 12" tall and was made in 1907.

Diamond Pyramid

Here is a better shot of the four-footed bowl shown in the previous edition. The pattern is unlisted as far as I know but certainly looks English and probably came from Sowerby, so I've taken the liberty of naming it. The color is a strong vaseline but it was probably made in blue as well and possibly in other shapes also. Anyone with information on this pattern is urged to contact me.

Diamond Rings

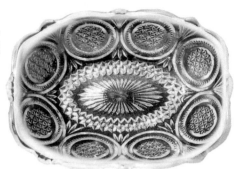

I have little information on this nice rectangular shaped bowl other than to say it is English. This is the only shape reported to me at this time and vaseline is the only color I've seen. Many thanks again to the Vaseline Glass Collectors Group for naming this pattern and thanks to the Sandemans for the nice photo.

Diamonds

Once thought to be from Hobbs, Brockunier or Northwood, and possibly later from Czechoslovakia (unconfirmed), this is now known to be a product of Phoenix Glass Co. of Monaco, Pennsylvania, circa 1888. Shapes include a water set, cruet, a sugar shaker, various bowls, and a handgrip bowl. Colors are white, blue, cranberry, and rubina opalescent glass. Pieces may be crackled as shown, or not. Thanks to the Petrasichs for the information.

Diamonds and Swags

This 8⅝" bowl shows characteristics from Greener and Co. but I have no proof that it was made at that concern. The name, given by its owner, certainly seems appropriate. This is the only shape I've seen to date, and vaseline is the only color reported so far. Additional information is appreciated. Thanks to the Petrasichs for sharing it.

Diamond Spearhead

This is Northwood's #22 pattern made when they were part of National in 1901. It can be found in crystal as well as opalescent glass. Shapes include a table set, water set, goblet, berry set, toothpick holder, mug, syrup, shakers, decanter, jelly compote, tall fruit compote, cup and saucer, 10" plate, water carafe, relish tray, and spittoon whimsey. The water pitcher and the creamer are found in more than one size. Colors are green, white, vaseline, blue, and sapphire blue in opalescent glass.

Diamond Stem

This very scarce vase from Model Flint dates from about 1900. It is now known to be made in three sizes, 6½", 8½", and 10½". Colors are canary opalescent, blue opalescent, green opalescent, transparent green, and blue, green, and white opaque pieces. Vases are found in straight, ruffled, or flared tops, as well as the familiar turned-in top. The name comes from the knob on the stem that has diamond facets.

Diamond Tree

This beautiful vaseline opalescent bowl is a real mystery. I haven't been able to locate it anywhere but strongly suspect it to be English. At any rate I've given it a name and welcome any information readers may offer. A tumbler is also known.

Diamond Wave

First found in amethyst opalescent glass and cranberry opalescent, here I show a pitcher with lid in vaseline. A child's or demitasse cup and saucer are also known in canary. This pattern was made in the Czech Republic, about 1880 – 1890. All items reported are mould blown. No new information has surfaced on this pattern since the previous edition, but I would certainly like to know more. Photo courtesy of Kelvin Russell.

Diamond Wide Stripe

A bit of a mystery, this pattern is credited to Nickel Plate, Hobbs, and others, but here is a pitcher that has the Northwood Swirl mould. The pattern is stunning with a diamond crosshatching added. Some call this Diamond Quilted Wide Stripe as well. The color is cranberry.

Dimple

Similar to the British Flute shaping but without the interior fluting, this British piece can be found with squared dimpling on each side or plain like the example shown. I suspect this piece is from Greener & Company, but have no proof. It is found in white, vaseline, and blue opalescent glass. The shape shown is called a spill and was used to hold matches (some refer to it as a toothpick holder). Thanks to the Sandemans for sharing it.

Dogwood Drape

I want to thank all those who pointed out the pattern I called Palm Rosette was really Dogwood Drape. The plate and the compote are still the only shapes I've heard about and I still suspect the design is English although I have no proof. Only white opalescent glass has been reported to date.

Dolly Madison

Originally called #271, this pattern by the Jefferson Glass Company was first produced in 1907. It can be found in crystal and blue glass, and opalescent colors of white, blue, and green. Shapes include water sets, table sets, berry sets, plates, and novelty bowls. The design uses flowers, stems, and leaves in every other panel.

Dolphin

Originally made by the Northwood Company as early as 1902, this beautiful compote has been widely reproduced in all colors, so buy only what you are confident with. Colors are white, blue, and vaseline. The older compotes have a stronger color and better glass clarity but those are about the only differences.

Dolphin and Herons

This rare and desirable pattern, made in Albany, Indiana, by Model Flint Glass, is found mostly in opalescent glass on a stemmed compote or the card tray shown. (A very rare crystal vase from the same mould is known and shown in my pressed glass book.) Colors in opalescent are white, blue, canary, and a very rare cranberry. The design has a dolphin for a stem with the bowl in its mouth with a herons design on the bowl. It is approximately 6½" tall.

Dolphin and Shell

The owner of this very nice spill tells me that the seller thought it was possibly a Sowerby piece but that it also looked somewhat like Westmoreland's Dolphin and Shell, although no opalescent pieces had surfaced in that pattern from Westmoreland. So, at this time it will remain as maker unknown. Either way, it is a very nice design. White opalescent is the only color reported at this time. Thanks to the Petrasichs for sharing it.

Dolphin Petticoat

Shards of these lovely candlesticks have been found at the Indiana, Pennsylvania, factory dump site and the pattern is shown in a National Glass ad, so I know the Northwood Company made these while a part of the National combine. Colors are white, blue, and canary. The mould work is outstanding, as is the design.

Dorset

According to recent information this pattern is a product of Greener & Company. Various size oval and round bowls, a creamer, and sugar are the only pieces reported to date. Colors reported are blue and vaseline. There was a bit of confusion as to whether the bowl shown was the same pattern as the creamer shown on the back cover of the previous edition but I am most certain they are the same pattern. Thanks to the Petrasichs and the Sandemans for photos sent to me in this pattern as well as providing the additional shapes to add to the list.

Dot Optic

Made by the Fenton Glass Company as early as 1910 in amethyst opalescent items, the pitcher shown dates from 1921. It is a tankard shape but the same design can be found in bulbous styles as well. Dot Optic is characterized by dots that recede into the glass and differ from the similar Coin Dot pattern in this respect. Colors found are white, blue, vaseline, and green. Shapes include pitchers, tumblers, vases, bowls, and handled tumblers.

Dotted Spiral

This English pattern can be found in a variety of vase shapes as well as a bowl in a metal holder with a handle. The only color reported at this time is vaseline opalescent. The maker is unknown.

Double Diamonds

This bowl has a pattern consisting of a series of diamonds within diamonds and a heavy opalescent treatment on the edge. The color is a nice vaseline opal. I'm certain it is English, although the maker has yet to be established. Thanks to the Sandemans for sharing it.

Double Dolphin

This is Fenton's #1533 pattern and the opalescent production was very limited, dating from the 1920s. The colors I've verified are blue and white (Fenton calls this French opalescent). This dolphin design was, of course, one of the company's favorites and has been used in many shapes and sizes for 75 years.

Double Greek Key

Double Greek Key was first a product of the Nickel Plate Glass Company of Fostoria, Ohio, and after 1892 from U.S. Glass. Shapes include a table set, berry set, water set, a celery vase, toothpick holder, mustard pot, syrup, pickle dish, and shakers. Colors in opalescent glass are white and blue, but the pattern can also be found on plain crystal. This is a very collectible pattern.

Double Panel

I know very little about this English bowl except to say it has an exterior paneling that is in two parts, hence the name. In addition it has a very attractive etched blossom and vine running around the upper bowl. I'd certainly appreciate any information about this bowl and am indebted to the Petrasichs for sharing it with me.

Double Rib and Block

The same process was used on this bowl as on the Davidson Germany Souvenir piece shown earlier in this book. This particular George Davidson & Co. 5½" bowl has the Rd. #340825 meaning it was made in 1899. The only color reported is vaseline. Thanks to the Petrasichs for sharing it.

Double Stemmed Rose

While this famous Dugan/Diamond pattern is very well known in carnival glass, the opalescent examples are very hard to find. The pattern dates from 1910, and I'm sure this bowl was an early product. As you can see, it has the very typical Dugan one-two-one crimp and may well show up in other opalescent colors including blue and green, and each of these would be equally rare. Thanks to Donna Drohan for the photo.

Dover Diamond

This pattern from England has appeared in more than one article about English opalescent glass. Shown is a creamer, but I know that an open sugar and other shapes exist including bowls. Colors reported are blue and vaseline opalescent. This piece is sometimes found with the Rd. #193365, making it a product of Davidson & Co. from 1892. It is sometimes referred to as Whitechapel.

Dragonfly Lamp

This is one of my favorite lamps and is a very classy item indeed. Although found mainly in carnival glass, here is an example with heavy opalescence in white with the very rare chimney. Some think this comes from Australia but I have no proof of such at this time. No matter where it comes from, if you find one of these consider yourself very fortunate, as they don't show up very often. Thanks to the Sandemans for sharing this wonderful item.

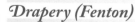

Drapery (Fenton)

While the Blown Drapery pattern was made at the Northwood Company, the Fenton example is mould blown and dates from 1910, five years later than Northwood's. In addition, the Fenton version has a shorter, ball-shaped pitcher while the Northwood version is tankard shaped. Fenton Drapery colors are the usual white, blue, and green opalescent, with amethyst being a possibility.

Drapery (Northwood)

Sometimes called Northwood's Drapery, this interesting pattern dates from 1904 and is usually marked. Colors are white and blue opalescent, often with gold decorated edges and ribbing. (The vase can be found in white, blue, green, and vaseline opalescent.) Shapes known are table sets, water sets, berry sets, vase, and some novelty items including a rose bowl. Some of the shapes were carried over into carnival glass production; these include rose bowls, candy dishes (from the same mould), and the vase shape.

Duchess

This seldom-found Riverside Glass pattern is known in a water set, a table set, berry set, toothpick holder, cruet, shakers, celery vase, and the light shade (not all shapes have been verified in opalescent glass). Opalescent colors are white, blue, canary, with non-opalescent treatments in emerald green (gilded) and frosted crystal. The date of production was 1903. Thanks to the Petrasichs for the photo.

Dugan Coinspot

Coinspot was made from 1906 to 1909 and shown in a Dugan/Diamond company catalog in 1907 as their #900 lemonade set. This very nicely shaped pitcher was made in decorated glass as well as opalescent glass in white, blue, and green. The almost-melon ribbing of the lower portion of the pitcher is the distinctive characteristic. The ad shows pitchers and tumblers on a tray that probably didn't match.

Dugan's #1013 (Wide Rib)

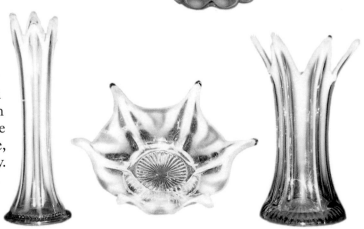

Shown in 1905 Butler Brothers ads along with other Dugan/Diamond products, this nice vase hasn't much in the way of design but is long on opalescence. It is often very widely flared at the top with opal running from the flames down between the ribs. Colors reported are blue, green, white, and canary, but I've never seen the canary. This vase was also made in carnival glass, often twisted.

Dugan's Diamond Compass (Dragon Lady)

As I said in the first edition of this book, this pattern has been confused with two other Dugan patterns, namely Reflecting Diamonds and Compass. There are differences and if you will compare the photos, you will see changes in both the collar base (marie) and the pattern designs. Green and blue, and white opalescent are the reported colors, but blue opalescent was surely made.

Dugan's Hexagon Base

This very pretty Dugan vase with the hex base and the jack-in-the-pulpit turned top stands 7½" tall. The coloring is very good and the mould work excellent. This vase was made in white and green opalescent, and perhaps with a ruffled top. It dates from the 1907 – 1910 period. Two sizes are known.

Dugan's Honeycomb

The mould for this pattern was made in 1905 or 1906. It is usually found in a rose bowl shape in carnival glass. A few pieces have surfaced in speckled treatments called Japanese or Pompeian, but only the bowl shown in white opalescent and one green opalescent bowl are known in this treatment (both have a ribbon-candy edge). I strongly suspect blue and vaseline opalescent examples may have been made, but all colors are rare in this pattern.

Dugan's Intaglio Acorn

Like the Intaglio Grape and the other patterns in the Dugan Intaglio line, this one is on white opalescent glass with a goofus treatment given to the pattern by applying it to the exterior within the recesses of the Intaglio pattern. Here I have a nearly square bowl that measures 10" across. The glass is very heavy and well designed. Thanks to John E. Wray for sharing this piece.

Dugan's Intaglio Cherry

Designed in 1904 for a line of mostly goofus ware, Dugan's Intaglio designs were primarily fruit patterns (very rare examples of flowers and birds exist) that had a gold and colored treatment added to the leaves and fruits while the rest of the glass remained crystal. Fruits found are cherries, grapes, strawberries, and plums, while flower patterns were mostly roses and poppies. Not all of these pieces had opalescence but a few did; I am showing a very pretty cherries bowl, which had red fruit and gilt leaves.

Dugan's Intaglio Daisy (Western Daisy)

In 1905 the Dugan Glass Company began producing a line of glass in crystal and opalescent white that had a goofus treatment. The following year they added colors to this line. It was advertised in 1909 as their intaglio line and it included the pattern shown, which is known in carnival glass as Western Daisy and in opalescent glass as Intaglio Daisy. Colors are blue, green, and white, often with a goofus treatment.

Dugan's Intaglio Grape

As I said in previous editions, this very well designed grape pattern was part of the Dugan Glass Company's Intaglio line (the pattern was incised on the exteriors of all pieces). Here is the super 13" chop plate but with the addition of the gold and red goofus treatment that looks so great with the opalescent edging. Many patterns are known in this treatment and all are very well done.

Dugan's Intaglio Peach

This design of peaches is a companion piece to the grape plate that is also 13" in diameter. Notice this piece still has the goofus treatment as well as opalescence and is just a super exterior design. Intaglio pieces came in all shapes including plates, baskets, bowls, and compotes, and in many sizes.

Dugan's Intaglio Pear and Plum

This is still another fruit pattern from Dugan's large Intaglio line from 1905. These large bowls were usually done with an opalescent edge and a goofus treatment on the fruit, which is all exterior and done in an incised or intaglio way. Thanks to Ruth Harvey for sharing this piece with me.

Dugan's Intaglio Rose

Like the other Intaglio patterns from the Dugan Glass Company, this one was developed for their goofus treatment, often with an opalescent edge. Shapes reported are large and small bowls but a plate shape is certainly possible.

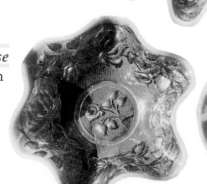

Dugan's Intaglio Strawberry

Like the other intaglio patterns made by the Dugan/Diamond Company beginning in 1905 and continuing for several years, this pattern was decorated with the goofus treatment on white opalescent glass. Shown is a rather large bowl but the same pattern is found on a stemmed 10" fruit holder.

Dugan's Junior

If you compare this Dugan vase to the stemmed Dugan Hexagon Base shown elsewhere in this edition, you will see both have a wide ribbed exterior and are similar in shape. This one is flat and measures 4½" tall while the hex-based one measures 7½" tall. The Junior is known in the usual opalescent colors of white, blue, and green.

Dugan's Olive Nappy

In a Butler Brothers 1906 ad, this piece is called a fancy handled olive and was listed as available in white, blue, and green opalescent glass from the Dugan/Diamond Company. It measures 4¾" across from handle to opposite edge and is on a flat base. Since there is no interior or exterior design, it relies on shape and glass finish for whatever appeal it has.

Dugan's Plain Panel

Dugan's Plain Panel is very similar to the Northwood Plain Panel vase shown elsewhere. This one has peaks between the ribbings at the top of the vase. There are six ribs and six peaked plain sections. This vase is found in white, blue, and green.

Eight Rayed Nappy

This purple nappy is from the Stourbridge region (most likely Stevens & Williams or Webb) and the pontil is finished off with a strawberry prunt. The spot mold that made this piece had eight vertical rays and the glass was then hand-finished into its present shape. This piece was purchased along with a sister piece in light green opalescent and both have attached vaseline glass handles and feet. They measure 1½" tall and 5" across. Thanks to Dave Peterson for the photo and information.

Elson Dewdrop

Once thought to be from Northwood, this is now known to have been made in 1887 by the Elson firm in colored glass, crystal, satin colors of blue or amber, and opalescent glass in white. The Elson Company was reorganized in 1893 as West Virginia Glass and this was their #90 pattern. Shapes in opalescent glass are a table set, a berry set, a mug, a two-piece breakfast set, and the tall celery vase shown.

Elson Dewdrop #2

This differs from the regular Elson Dewdrop pattern in that the #2 has dividing panels that come to points at the top. Shapes include a sauce, a spooner, cruet, salt shakers, and the punch cup shown. Elson was reorganized in 1893 as West Virginia Glass and this was from that production time.

Embossed Spanish Lace

Besides the American versions of Spanish Lace, there were pieces produced in England in the 1890s and here I show an example. This one is a 4½" tall vase and besides the usual design, it has an embossed vine that runs around the girth of the bowl.

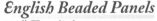

English Beaded Panels

I have no information concerning this 4½" English creamer and would appreciate anything readers may have regarding it. The color is blue opalescent and this is the only shape reported to me in this pattern. Thanks to the Petrasichs for sharing it.

English Drape

This nice vase can be found in various shapes and sizes, and I'm reasonably sure it is an English product that may have come in blue as well as the canary shown. Thanks to the Sandemans for sharing it.

English Duck

Slightly larger than the American Little Swan pieces from Northwood, Dugan, and Fenton, this one is marked Rd. #31844, indicating it was made in England in 1885. I believe it may be from Molineaux, Webb but I could be wrong. At any rate, I truly thank Jon Coppenbarger for sharing this beauty with me.

English Fern

This little 4¼" ruffled top vase is similar in design to other fern patterns and I'm told it is English. The color is green opalescent and the opal is very heavy. I'm sure other shapes and colors probably exist but haven't seen them to date. Photo courtesy of the Petrasichs.

English Lily Vase

Named by the owner, this nice looking English vase can be found in the cranberry shown as well as in vaseline opalescent. I feel it's likely that other shapes and possibly blue opalescent were made but they haven't been reported at this time. The maker is unknown to me to date. Thanks to the Petrasichs for sharing it.

English Oak Leaf

English Oak Leaf is found on this strange tri-colored bowl, a boat shape, and rectangular posy. This is from Bartles, Tate, and Company and has the Rd. #29106, dating it to 1885. It is patterned on the exterior with oak leaves. The exterior base is wedge-shaped. I've seen this piece in both the canary shown and blue opalescent glass, but white may have also been made.

English Optic Epergne

Standing 17" tall, this four-lily epergne with rigoree decoration, cranberry-throated lilies, and applied edging is about as decorative a piece of opalescent art glass as you are apt to see. It is English and probably dates from the 1880s or 1890s.

English Ripple

This is very similar to the Herringbone pattern, but has a softer rolling of the opalescent lines. I strongly suspect this is an English pattern. Please note that the base ends in panels that run from the top of the tumbler and these extend down and over the bottom. It was probably made in blue also but I haven't seen one. Thanks to the Petrasichs for sharing it.

English Salt Dip

What a fancy piece of table service this is! The vaseline opalescent salt dip, measuring 2¼" wide and 1⅜" tall, sits atop a silver tray that bears the marking: JH EPNS. The coloring of the dip (or fill) is typically English but I'm confident these came in other colors too. Made by Davidson, circa 1911, it has an Rd. #577153.

English Swan

This beautiful swan is the smaller (and the rarer) of two sizes made by Burtles, Tate & Company of England. These were made in 1885 and the example shown is 3½" long and 3½" tall. The larger size measures 4½" long, and has an Rd. #20086. These are mostly found in canary opalescent glass with a soft coloring but can also be found in white and blue opalescent.

English Swirl (Cased)

Reported to be from England, this water set is an opalescent reverse swirl design with an inner casing of cranberry glass. The pitcher is a squat ball-shaped one with an applied reeded handle. The owner describes this set as being like striped candy.

English Wide Stripe

This pitcher is a bit of a mystery. I believe it may well be an English version of the Wide Stripe pattern but I can't rule out others like Phoenix or LaBelle. As you can see, the coloring is cranberry with a distinctive amber reed handle. I'd appreciate any information readers may have about this piece.

Entangled Branches

The owner of this interesting oil lamp thought the design looked like branches so I incorporated her observation into the name and I hope she approves. This is the only example I've seen to date in this lamp and the color is a nice vaseline opalescent. Thanks to Ruth Harvey for sharing this interesting item.

Estate

This pattern, also called Stippled Estate, is known to have been made by the Dugan/Diamond Company in 1906 and by Model Flint in 1900 – 1902. In opalescent glass, colors are white, blue, and green, but it is also found in carnival glass and in green, amber, and speckled glass. Vases are of four sizes (2½", 3½", 4½", and 5½") and Model Flint also made a cruet shape.

European Lily Epergnes

These two epergnes with single lilies are from Sweden. They differ in size but both have similar lilies that are blown with a top twist and have interior ridges. The holders appear to be silver plate and are identical.

Everglades

This Northwood pattern was originally called Carnelian and dates from 1903. It was made in several treatments besides opalescent glass including custard and purple slag. Opalescent colors are white, blue, and canary, with some limited production in green. Shapes made are table sets, water sets, oval berry sets, cruets, salt shakers, and jelly compotes.

Everglades (Cambridge)

Everglades is a production name used by the Cambridge Company covering a line of items made from 1920 to 1958. The compote shown in white opalescent glass is simply one design from this line. It measures 7½" in diameter. In 1933, the Cambridge catalog listed 43 items in this line, including vases with flower patterns and a bowl with an Indian on horseback hunting buffalo.

Exterior Thumbprint

I've learned very little about this beautiful vaseline opalescent vase since I saw it. It measures 13¾" tall, has a 13-pointed star base, and six large thumbprints on the exterior just above the base. In addition there is a series of six vertical ribs that separates the thumbprints. I'd appreciate any input readers may have about this pattern.

Fan

Although long considered a Northwood pattern, Fan is actually from the Dugan/Diamond plant. Water sets, berry sets, and table sets in ivory (custard), and opalescent glass in colors of green, white, and blue were shown in a 1907 company ad. On a whimsey plate that was shaped from the spooner, the glass almost glows with opalescence. Fan was also made in emerald green and cobalt blue, sometimes with gold decoration, as well as limited shapes in carnival glass.

Fan and Shell

I am told by the owner of this beautiful vase that it may be from Greener & Company and I believe this may well be true. The base is shaped like a shell and another shell design extends up to the middle of the vase. I'd appreciate any information about this pattern. Thanks to Ruth Harvey for sharing it.

Fancy Fantails

While others credit this pattern to the Northwood Company, I'm convinced it is from Jefferson. As I've said before, research has convinced me most, if not all, of the cranberry decorated items came from Jefferson Glass. Fancy Fantails dates from 1905 and can be found in both rose bowls and candy dishes from the same mould. Colors are white, blue, green, and vaseline.

Feathered Hearts

No maker has been confirmed on this lovely English shade, shown in cranberry opalescent, but nonetheless it is a really nice item and I like the design. I've heard it called Peacock Eye but have elected to go with another name to avoid confusing it with other items of that name. I would think other shapes exist but haven't seen them to date. Thanks to John and Monica Vanspall for sharing this fine piece of glass.

Feathers

There's no question about the maker of this vase since most are marked with the Northwood trademark. Vases are the only shape, and the colors are white, blue, and green opalescent, as well as carnival glass colors. Sizes range from 7" to a pulled 13". I've seen a blue opalescent and a white opalescent vase with gold edging.

Fenton's #100 Ringed Bowl

Made first in 1929, this small bowl on stubby feet measures 7½" across and the plate from the same mould is ½" wider. Colors in opalescent glass are amethyst and vaseline and I suspect others were made. The only pattern is the exterior rings that extend from the feet up the sides of the piece. This pattern is called Hoops in carnival glass.

Fenton's #220 Stripe

This popular Fenton pattern, produced in 1929, is found in iced tea sets (both pitcher and tumblers have contrasting colored handles), creamer, sugar, and tumble ups (guest sets). Colors are blue, green, white, and vaseline, and there are two shapes and sizes in pitchers. Note that the one shown has a matching lid but not all shapes do.

Fenton's #260

This regal 7" tall compote was made by the Fenton Art Glass Company in all sorts of glass treatments including ebony opaque, stretch glass, Grecian gold carnival, and opalescent glass as shown, where the colors are white, topaz, and blue. Production of the compote dates from 1915 to the 1930s in ruby glass.

Fenton's #370

This beauty dates from the 1924 – 1927 period of Fenton production. The cameo opalescent coloring is a real treat and I'm happy to be able to show this example. This same coloring can be found in many patterns and shapes in the Fenton line including bowls, vases, nappies, and bonbons. The vase color of the glass is a strong amber and the opalescent is a rich creamy tint.

Fenton's Plain Jane

Usually seen on white opalescent glass, this completely plain design from the Fenton Art Glass Company is rarely seen on amethyst opalescent glass. A water set with tankard pitcher and a hat shape are known.

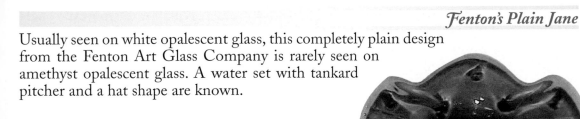

Fern

This pattern was made by several companies including West Virginia Glass, Beaumont, Model Flint, and probably Northwood. It is found in water sets, cruets, shakers, syrups, sugar shakers, toothpick holders, a table set, celery vase, finger bowl, mustard pot, a berry set, and a bitters bottle. Colors include white, blue, canary (rare), and cranberry. Shown is a rare celery vase in vaseline. Production of Fern dates from 1898 to 1906 and the Fenton Company reproduced this pattern beginning in the 1950s. Thanks to Kelvin Russell for the photo.

Fern Panels (Fenton)

Occasionally found in carnival glass, this is the very first piece in opalescent glass I've heard about. As you can see, it is a beautiful amethyst opalescent color. The shape is a hat that has been pulled in a JIP shape.

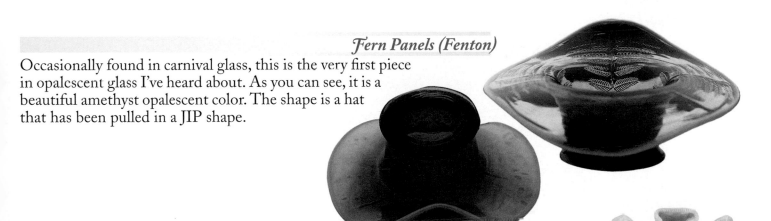

Festive Flowers

This very nicely done spill vase from England is decorated in coralene (frit) which gives the vase a very interesting look. I'm also told that it has a patent mark on the bottom. White is the only color reported to date and this is the only shape I've been made aware of. Thanks to Ruth Harvey for sharing it.

Field Flowers

In addition to the compotes in 7½" and 9" sizes, I am happy to report the opalescent bowl that measures 7¼" in diameter in this pattern. Many shapes are shown in the Inwald Glass Works of Czechoslovakia 1900 catalog in crystal so I may well expect other shapes to turn up in opalescent glass. Colors are blue and white.

Field of Flowers

I'm showing the interior of this nice compote in order to give readers a better look at the pattern for identification purposes. Ten flowers circle the outer edge of the compote (which has a totally stippled background) with many entangled stems going into the center. You'll also see two buds in the design. Blue is the only reported color at this time and the compote is the only shape known to me presently, although I feel other shapes and colors may exist. Any information on this nice pattern would be appreciated. Thanks to the Sandemans for sharing it.

File and Fan

Despite not locating this pattern in any reference sources, I feel this bowl may be foreign, possibly German or Czechoslovakian. I've given it a name but if any reader knows it by something else, I welcome your information. Thanks to the Petrasichs for sharing it.

Finecut and Roses

Early opalescent production of this pattern was at Jefferson's Steubenville plant; however, Northwood later produced it in their lines of custard and carnival glass. Colors in opalescent glass are white, blue, and green. Shapes (all from the same mould) are footed candy dishes, rose bowls, and a spooner that is slightly ruffled.

Fine Rib (Fenton)

I'm very happy to be the first to show this very rare Fenton vase pattern in opalescent glass. Until now, the Fine Rib vase was well known in carnival glass and scarce in plain colored pieces such as ice green and pink. But as you can see, the pattern was made in a beautiful vaseline opalescent treatment. This vase stands 11¼" tall with a 2⅞" base and a 3⅝" top opening. The opalescence runs well down the ribs and is just stunning! I believe this vase was made in the 1908 – 1910 era and there may well be white, blue, and green examples that exist.

Fine Rib (Northwood)

Opalescent glass collectors often refer to this as Many Ribs. Although not rare when found in opalescent glass, it is mostly found in carnival glass. Unlike the Model Flint Glass example with this name, the base of the Northwood pattern is not columnated and the design just rolls to an even finish above the straight base. Colors are white, blue, green, and vaseline, and the vases usually range from 9" to 13" in size.

Fine Rib Epergne

I know very little about this attractive epergne except the Fine Rib design is very close to the Northwood and Fenton vase patterns found mostly in carnival glass (the Fenton design is also shown in a rare opalescent vase). The metal work on this epergne isn't brass as on most shown but is a pot metal called speltzer, here with a silvered finish. Any additional information on this epergne would be helpful.

Fish-in-the-Sea

The speculation is now over concerning the maker of this well done piece of glass. Thanks to a monograph from the West Virginia Museum of American Glass, Ltd. (edited by Neila and Tom Bredehoft), it is now confirmed that this wonderful pattern was made by the Tygart Valley Glass Co. of Grafton, West Virginia. Colors are white, blue, and green. This vase is a very scarce item, much sought by collectors.

Fishnet Epergne

This four-lily epergne with a dome base is a puzzle. It has the fishnet lilies normally associated with the Dugan Company but it also has cranberry frit that suggests a Jefferson origin. In addition, the center lily is the same one found on the Strawberry epergne I see in carnival glass that was made by Dugan, so maybe I have to consider this company as a frit user too.

Fishscale and Beads

This pattern was actually misnamed by Heacock some years ago, it was originally named Scales by Marion Hartung in the 1950s (there is another carnival pattern she named Fishscale and Beads). The opalescent bowls were made by Dugan and predate the carnival items. Colors in opalescent glass are blue and white and the beads are exterior while the scales are interior.

Fleur-de-Lis

This 7¾" pitcher is unknown to me but the pattern has a similar look to some Northwood pieces, although I haven't found it in any catalog reprints to date and haven't seen this shape pitcher from Northwood. The interesting feature on this pitcher is the circle of teardrops on the base. This is the only shape I've seen and white is the only reported color to date. Thanks to the Petrasichs for sharing it and I do welcome any information readers might have concerning this pattern.

Fleur-de-Lis in Panels

I suspect this piece is a marmalade dish which was once in a metal holder, but have no proof of such. The design and color is very similar to items made in the Stourbridge region of England. (Note the similarities to the Striped Lemonescent set by Thomas Webb shown later in this edition.) The color is a combination of cranberry and vaseline. This is the only piece reported in this pattern at the current time. Thanks to the Petrasichs for sharing.

Flora

Dating from 1898, this Beaumont pattern can be found in a host of shapes including table sets, water sets, berry sets, shakers, cruets, syrups, toothpick holders, compotes, celery vases, and several bowl novelty shapes. Colors are blue, white, and vaseline with some items gilded. Other types of glass were also made in Flora including crystal and emerald green, which can also be found with gilding.

Floradine

If you will compare this piece with the Onyx one in this book, you will see they are the same pattern (both made in 1889 by Finley Glass) but have different treatments. The Floradine pieces are found in a satin treatment in ruby or autumn and shapes include a table set, water set, 8" bowl, cruet, shakers, 4" sauce, syrup, toothpick holder, and a sugar shaker.

Floral and Vines

This pattern consists of flowers and entangled vines. This English shade, possibly Richardson's or John Walsh Walsh (only speculation at this time), is reported only in vaseline to date and the shade is the only shape I've seen so far. This pattern is simple but very nicely done and would grace any collection. Photo courtesy of the Sandemans.

Floral Eyelet

Little is known about this very scarce pattern; it is believed to be a product of Northwood/ National or even Dugan at the Indiana, Pennsylvania, plant. The time of production has been speculated to be from 1896 to 1905. The only shapes are a water pitcher and tumbler in white, blue, and cranberry opalescent; the tumbler is shown here. The reproduced pitcher, made by the L.G. Wright Company, is shown in the second edition of this book. The new pitchers have reeded handles while the old do not.

Floral Freeze

Although unmarked, this is a Davidson pattern shown in publications from that concern. The only pieces brought to my attention are the creamer and open sugar in blue, although other shapes and colors possibly exist. Photo courtesy of the Petrasichs.

Flower Form

I have no idea what type of flower is represented on this English pattern but nonetheless it's a nicely done and well worth owning in any collection. The shapes reported to me are a toothpick and a bulbous single lily epergne in a metal holder. Vaseline is the only color I've seen to date. Any information would be appreciated. Thanks to Ruth Harvey and the Petrasichs for the photo submissions.

Flowering Vine

I'm using what I'm told to be the more commonly known name for this pattern in opalescent glass, although in non-opalescent glass it is referred to as Daisy Swag. It is not an easy pattern to find. The shapes reported are a butter, creamer, spooner, and sugar, all in blue opalescent only, although other colors are certainly possible. Speculation puts this as a Davidson pattern although no examples have been found in Davidson catalog reprints or other publications. Thanks to the Petrasichs and the Sandemans for the photo submissions.

Flower Starburst

The rather large flowers on this lamp font seem to provide total coverage, leaving little room for any other addition to the pattern. The ornate base and overall look of this lamp would make it a welcome addition to any collector's group of lamps or opalescent glass. The only color reported so far is vaseline. I have no confirmation on the maker and would appreciate any information available. Thanks to Steve and Radka Sandeman for the photo.

Fluted Bars and Beads

Once thought to be from Northwood, Fluted Bars and Beads is now known to be from Jefferson Glass, first made in 1904. Shapes are compotes and novelty whimsies from the same mould, and colors are white, blue, green, and canary. Many pieces have frit trim.

Fluted Scrolls

Made by Northwood in 1898 under the name Klondyke, this pattern is known today as Fluted Scrolls or Jackson. It can be found in crystal, custard, green clear glass, or opalescent glass in white, blue, and vaseline. Shapes include a table set, water set, berry set, cruet, shakers, puff box (also known as a baby butter dish), one-lily epergne, and various novelty bowl shapes. It has been reproduced for Rosso.

Fluted Scroll with Vine

Shown as early as 1899 in a Butler Brothers ad, this Northwood Glass Company pattern is one of my favorite vase designs. It is known in white, blue, and canary and may also show up in green one of these days. I am continually amazed at the colors and patterns that have been overlooked for years. The design of flowers, stems, and leaves winding around a fluted, cone-shaped vase is very pretty; when you add the base of spread leaves and the top rim of scalloped blossoms, the whole piece becomes a real work of art.

Footed Stripe

With feet resembling roots as well as the overall look of this piece it most certainly has to be English, although no maker is confirmed at this time. The only noticeable pattern is the rather wide stripes, hence the name. This is the only shape reported and vaseline opalescent is the only color. Other shapes and color may exist but I haven't seen them or had them reported to me at this time. Thanks to Ruth Harvey for the photo.

Forked Stripe

If you look at the base of this barber bottle, you'll see the stripes end in points, so I've given it this name. This piece is white opalescent, measures 7" tall, and has a base diameter of 3½". It is marked on the base "PAT-PENGING." The maker isn't known at this time, but a pitcher from a very limited Imperial Glass production in 1930 has this same pointed finish to its stripe except it is reversed and faces upwards. Other colors may exist.

Fountain with Bows

In previous editions this was listed as Jack-in-the-Pulpit. Being as the JIP name primarily describes a shape, I decided to change the name to better suit this particular pattern design, although I'm sure I'll hear about doing so. The pattern has a distinct bow at the bottom of what looks like a fountain spraying up into the air. Shapes are lamp shades and various vases. Colors are vaseline opalescent and cranberry opalescent. It is likely made in England although no specific maker is reported at this time. Thanks to Ruth Harvey for sharing it.

Four-Footed Hobnail

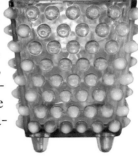

This pattern is now confirmed to be a product of LaBelle Glass of Bridgeport, Ohio, in 1886. The only shapes are the butter, creamer, sugar, and spooner. Colors are white, dark blue, and canary, but it was also made in crystal, blue, and vaseline glass without the opalescent treatment. Thanks to the Petrasichs for sharing it.

Four Pillars

Four Pillars was made in opalescent glass by Northwood and later in carnival glass by both Northwood and Dugan/Diamond. This vase is also found with advertising on some Northwood carnival pieces. Opalescent colors are white, blue, green, and vaseline. The four columns or pillars run from top to bottom and end in four rounded feet. Sizes range from 9" to 14" tall, and some pieces from Dugan/Diamond have gilding.

Frosted Leaf and Basketweave

This pattern was a product of the Chicago Flint Glass Company of Chesterton, Indiana (it was long thought to be from Northwood). It is found in table set pieces and the spooner can be found whimsied into a vase shape. It was made in crystal and opalescent colors of white, blue, and vaseline.

71

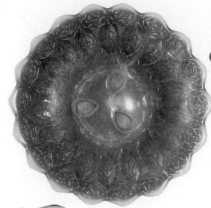

Garland of Roses

Garland of Roses is found primarily in crystal or vaseline glass. This is a small cake stand or card tray, flattened from a jelly compote shape. This is the only shape reported to me at this time. Colors are white and blue. I'd like to hear from anyone having other shapes or colors of this pattern in an opalescent treatment. The piece shown measures 6⅝" across and stands 2" tall.

Gonterman (Adonis) Hob

Like the Swirl pattern with the same titles, this is an Aetna Glass pattern dating from 1886 (despite bearing "Pat d Aug 4, 1876," on the base). Unlike the Swirl pattern, there doesn't seem to be a blue version, only the amber. Needless to say, since only the cruet shown has been reported, it is extremely hard to find and has to be considered rare.

Gonterman Swirl

Found on both frosted and opalescent pieces, this pattern is attributed to Aetna Glass by most collectors (the patent was issued to Hobbs, Brockunier & Company for the joining process). One writer believes Hobbs may have licensed Aetna to do the pattern. At any rate, pieces are known in blue and amber with opalescence in table sets, water sets (rare), berry sets, cruet, syrup, celery vase, lamp shade, and a toothpick holder (sometimes in a metal frame). Pieces are marked "Patented August 5, 1876," but this refers to the joining process and not a production date, which is a decade later.

Grace Darling

Grace Darling was a heroine during the early nineteenth century in England who helped rescue a group of people who had been shipwrecked. Books have been written about her. She was about 12 or 13 years old when she helped her father rescue the stranded boaters. Grace Darling is actually embossed inside this boat, both in the bottom and the stern. The Rd. number is 39414. There is a second number which is just for the inscription of Grace Darling Boat, which was a registered wording: Rd. #23527. The piece was made by Edward Bolton and the design was registered on December 11, 1885. The version shown is 11¼" in length. There is also a 13" version. It is uncertain to date if other sizes exist. Vaseline is the only reported color. Many thanks to Dave and Vickie Peterson for the photo and information.

Grape and Cable (Northwood and Fenton)

Very little of this pattern in opalescent glass is found besides the very rare bonbon (shown) and several shapes of the large footed fruit bowl (some are turned like a centerpiece bowl). The bonbon has been reported in vaseline only, while the footed bowl has been seen in white and vaseline and is suspected in blue. The bonbon may have been made in white also. All carry the famous Northwood basketweave as the exterior pattern. In addition, the Fenton Company made a Grape and Cable large fruit bowl nearly identical to Northwood's and it can be found in white opalescent. Photo courtesy of the Petrasichs.

Grape and Cherry

Grape and Cherry is known in both carnival glass and opalescent glass. Old opalescent pieces are known in white, blue, and canary, and these, or course, came from Sowerby. Several shapes can be found, including deep round bowls, ruffled square bowls, and oval banana bowls, all from the same mould. It was reproduced in blue opalescent for L. G. Wright in 1978 and is known as simply Cherry.

Grape Cluster

This interesting little square bowl (5 ⅜" by 2" tall) is most likely a Fenton product, although I haven't located it yet. The pattern design as well as the candy ribbon edge treatment all point to Fenton. This is the only piece I've seen in this pattern to date. The color is a light blue opalescent. Any information is appreciated. Many thanks to the Hollenbachs for sharing it.

Grapevine Cluster

Made by the Northwood Glass Company in 1905, this very realistic vase pattern is found in white, blue, aqua, canary, and green (rare) opalescent glass as well as a treatment of purple slag the company called Mosaic. The design features heavy grapes and leaves, grapevines supporting branches, and a grape leaf base. The pattern is a collector's favorite and always brings a high price when sold. Some of the blue examples tend toward a soft aqua color.

Grecian Urn

The owner of this small pretty vase (4¼" tall with a 2" base diameter) named this piece and it seems to fit. I believe this piece may be English, but I could be wrong. The opalescence is outstanding. I'd be interested in hearing from anyone who knows more about this pattern or of other colors.

Greek Key and Ribs

This Northwood bowl pattern from 1907 is similar to the Greek Key and Scales bowl shown below. The dome-based bowl can be found in white, blue, green, and canary, as well as the host of carnival colors. Just why one company would create two moulds so similar is a mystery, but it seemed to happen frequently, especially in opalescent and carnival glass. Perhaps competition forced so many variations, but I can't be sure. At any rate, it makes collecting more interesting for all of us.

Greek Key and Scales

This often-marked pattern, made by the Northwood Company in 1905, is well known in both opalescent and carnival glass. The bowl shape has a dome base and is usually ruffled. Opalescent colors are white, green, and blue.

Greener Boat

This nice 7" boat shape piece (a 5" boat is also known) is reported to me in blue only to date. The interior transom bears the Greener & Co. logo (lion holding an axe) which was used from 1885 to 1890. Other sizes and colors may exist but haven't been brought to my attention. Thanks again to the Petrasichs for sharing this piece from their collection.

Greener Dewdrop

I've now seen two pieces of this pattern from Greener and both have been in amber opalescent glass typical of that company. The first was a stemmed cake plate and the second is the 5" bowl shown. Other shapes and colors wouldn't surprise me and I welcome any information. Thanks to the Petrasichs.

Greener Diamond Column Epergne

Made by the Greener Company, this beautiful 13" tall epergne is a standout in pressed glass. It is amber opalescent with a glass bowl and matching lily and the metal base and fittings. Again, I have to thank the Petrasichs for sharing this fine item with me.

Harlequin

Since I showed this pattern in the last edition, I've learned it is found in cranberry with vaseline, blue with vaseline, plain vaseline, as well as other treatments and occasionally decorated with enamel work. Shapes are a rose bowl, ewer, and many different vase sizes and shapes, in both flat and footed. The pattern is Bohemian and also known as Quadruple Diamonds.

Harrow

This English pattern has been unnamed to the best of my knowledge so I've taken the liberty of calling it Harrow. It stands 6" tall and bears an Rd. #217749. A stemmed wine or cordial has been seen, and the possibility exists that a table set could have been made. Blue is the only reported color to date, at least to me, but vaseline is very likely to have been made.

Heart Handled Open O's

While this is primarily the same pattern as the Open O's I show elsewhere, the handled ring basket has always been shown on its own and I will keep it that way. It is a Northwood pattern from 1905 – 1906. Colors are white, blue, and green, with canary a strong possibility.

Hearts and Clubs

This Jefferson Glass Company pattern was originally their #274 and was produced about 1905. As you can see, the footed bowl shown here has a goofus treatment, but it can be found on blue and green opalescent glass as well. The three feet of the bowl are shaped like those on the Daisy and Plume pieces made by Northwood and later Dugan, but are solid without any portholes.

Hearts and Flowers

This well-known Northwood pattern can be found in carnival, custard, and opalescent glass. In the latter, it is seen on compotes and bowls in white, blue, and very rarely, vaseline. Production dates from 1908, when the maker added several well-known patterns to their opalescent production on a limited basis, including Singing Birds, Peacock on the Fence, Rose Show, Grape and Cable, Three Fruits, Bushel Basket, Acorn Burrs, Beaded Cable, Finecut and Roses, and Daisy and Plume. All were made mainly in white and blue, with a few vaseline items.

Heatherbloom

This seldom-discussed pattern, Jefferson Glass's #268, circa 1905, is found only on vases. Colors in opalescent glass are the usual white, blue, and green with the latter hardest to find. The design has a tendency to blur as the vase is swung to taller sizes, and only the shorter ones really show the pattern at its best.

Heavenly Stars

I am told this bowl is from England. As you can see, it is rather large and has three brass legs. The pattern consists of a series of double bands that form areas for the stars. I believe this is a Sowerby product that was made in canary, blue, and white opalescent glass.

Helen Louise

This is a creamer from Davidson that is reported to have been made in 1885. It is 3⅞" tall. John Petrasich reports an open sugar to match.

Heron and Peacock

While I have very little information about this child's mug known as Heron and Peacock, I believe it is an old example. I've been told it has been made in many glass treatments over the years and is listed in one book on children's collectibles as having once been made in crystal and cobalt blue, but this is the first I've actually seen. It may well have been made in other opalescent colors, and a blue or canary one would be outstanding. The design has a peacock on one side and a heron on the other, with floral sprays dividing them. The opalescence is quite good. It is currently being reproduced by Boyd Crystal Art Glass, Cambridge, Ohio.

Herringbone (Plain)

Since shards of this pattern were found at the Indiana, Pennsylvania, plant, I can be confident one of the makers of Herringbone (both plain and ribbed) was the Northwood Glass Company. Shard colors were white, yellow, and blue, but of course, cranberry items are also known. Shapes known are water sets, cruets, syrups, and crimped salad bowls. Some treatments are cased mother-of-pearl in a satin finish. The plain Herringbone dates to 1885, when Harry Northwood was at Phoenix Glass.

Herringbone (Ribbed)

As I said in the narrative about Plain Herringbone, this is most likely a Northwood pattern, found on water sets, cruets, syrups, and crimped salad bowls, in white, blue, cranberry and canary opalescent glass. The Plain Herringbone came first and dates from Northwood's days at Phoenix, the Ribbed Herringbone is believed to date from about 1902, at the Indiana plant. Since I felt the two treatments were so different, I chose to discuss them as separate items.

Herringbone and Crocus

This interesting 4½" herringbone vase with applied crocus has a rough pontil on the bottom suggesting an English origin, although the Phoenix Art Glass Co. has also been known to have made various pieces using the herringbone pattern. Green is the only color reported to me at this time. Thanks again to the Petrasichs for sharing the photo and information.

Hidden Hearts

This interesting little hat shaped item is normally seen in a metal holder with a handle. I'm showing it here without the holder simply to display the pattern better. Several designs come to mind when viewing this pattern; Butterfly Wings, Spear Points, but I've elected to go with the assigned name and hope the owner doesn't mind. If you'll look closely you can see the heart designs throughout the pattern. This is the only reported shape to date and cranberry opalescent is the only color I'm aware of. Many thanks to Ruth Harvey for sharing it.

Hilltop Vines

This unusual compote is shown in Northwood ads as early as 1906. It can be found in white, blue, and green opalescent glass and stands roughly 5" tall. The outstanding features are the leaves that overlap, making up the bowl of the compote; the branch-like legs that form the stem; and the domed base covered with tiny bubble-like circles.

Hilltop Vines Variant

This example is like the regular Hilltop Vines pattern from Northwood except the leaves are veined and stippled. I believe this variant was a later mould recutting and is somewhat harder to find than the regular one. Thanks to John Loggie for sharing it with me.

Hobbs Polka Dot

This Hobbs pattern was made in many exotic colors (shown is a green to sapphire bowl) and dates from 1884. It is found in bar bottles, a finger bowl, shell-footed bowl, celery, covered cheese dish, creamer, sugar, shakers, cruet, syrup, water set, lemonade mug, bowls, a sugar shaker, and a custard cup.

Hobnail (Hobbs)

Here is Hobnail from Hobbs, Brockunier. Shapes made in this well-known pattern are water sets, table sets, berry sets (square shaped), cruets, shaker, syrup, finger bowls, celery vase, barber bottle, water tray, bride's basket with frame, and five sizes of pitchers. Production of the Hobbs Hobnail design began in 1885 and lasted until 1892. Colors reported are white, blue, rubina, vaseline, and cranberry. It is also known as Hobbs Dew Drop.

Hobnail and Paneled Thumbprint

Most collectors credit this pattern to Northwood but I know of no proof it was made at that concern. The pattern dates from 1905 or 1906 and can be found on berry sets, table sets, water sets, and vases that have been pulled from the spooner shape. Colors are white, blue, and canary in opalescent glass. It is a shame no toothpick holder, cruet, or salt shakers are known.

Hobnail-in-Square

This Aetna Glass and Manufacturing Company of Bellaire, Ohio, pattern dates from 1887 and is often confused with a recent pattern called Vesta made by the Fenton Company since the 1950s. Colors of the original pattern are primarily white but it was also made in crystal. Shapes are water sets, table sets, berry sets, a celery vase, salt shakers, and compotes.

Hobnail Toy Mug

I have no idea who made this tiny 2" mug in vaseline and can only guess that it might have been used either as a child's mug or a toothpick holder. Either way, it has to be the smallest piece of opalescent glass I've seen and is really a conversation piece. Thanks to the Sandemans for sharing this cute miniature piece.

Hobnail Twist

This very nice vase, or lily if you will, comes in a metal holder which has a design of grapes and leaves circling about the metal stand. The vase consists of rows of hobnails and is twisted in a diagonal spiral with a ruffled top. This is the only shape reported to date and the color is Rubina Verde. Thanks to the Sandemans for sharing this nice item.

Hobnail with Bars

Hobnail with Bars was made by U.S. Glass and can be found on a berry set, a table set, and the cruet shown, mostly in crystal. Here is the cruet in a white opalescent treatment, which I believe is on the scarce side. Thanks to Mary and John Petrasich for sharing it.

Holly and Berry

Primarily a carnival glass pattern from Dugan/Diamond, the nappy shape has surfaced in opalescent glass in white only (surely blue and green were also made). The design is a good one with a center cluster of holly berries and leaves and the same design in a wreath shape around the rim with three strings of leaves and berries. The nappy is a large one, measuring 7" across the top, from handle to pouring lip.

Holly Berry Lamp

In past editions this wonderful lamp was shown with a Rubina Verde shade, but finally, here is an example with the correct shade. The pattern is one of holly berries, hence the name. Of English origin, this oil lamp (drilled for electric use later on) was made between 1880 and 1890. Thanks to the Steve and Radka Sandeman for sharing this beauty.

Honeycomb

This pattern is called Hobbs Honeycomb or Opal Honeycomb by some collectors. Actually there is no evidence this was a pattern from Hobbs, Brockunier and the more I see of this pattern, the more I am convinced it was made by someone else. All the shapes reported are from the same mould and consist of a vase or a bowl that has been pulled from the vase. Colors are white, blue, and green opalescent. Besides the honeycombing, the only other design is the ribbed-skirt base.

Honeycomb and Clover

Honeycomb and Clover was made by the Fenton Company in carnival, opalescent, and gilt decorated glass. Production in opalescent glass dates from 1910. Colors known are the usual white, blue, and green; however, amethyst is a definite possibility and would be a real find. The exterior pattern consists of an allover honeycombing with clover and leaves twining over it. Shapes in opalescent glass are water sets, berry sets, table sets, and novelty bowls.

Horse Chestnut

Until now this pattern has only been reported to me in a compote shape, but here is a nice ruffled vase shape in vaseline opalescent, courtesy of Steve and Radka Sandeman. This pattern was first credited to Richardson's of England in 1916 and then to Thomas Webb in 1936.

Idyll

The Jefferson Glass Company's Idyll is found in a water set, table set, berry set, toothpick holder, cruet, shakers, a bowl, and a tray. Colors are blue, green, and white in opalescent glass, as well as crystal or gilded crystal. Idyll was first made in 1907. It is well-done and pleasing to the eye for collectors. Sometimes the opalescent pieces are decorated with gilding.

Imitation Cut #1

This basket from Greener & Co. bears three different Rd. numbers, which is somewhat unusual. The first number is 96775, which I'm told is for the handle. The second and third numbers are 95935 and 98551, all three being from 1888. I believe one of the second numbers would be for the pattern design but I'm not sure what the other is pertaining to. The only color reported to me is blue opalescent. Thanks to the Petrasichs for the photo and information.

Imitation Cut #2

Here again we see the same situation as in the previous pattern, Imitation Cut #1. This also has three different Rd. numbers and they are the exact same numbers seen on the first piece, although the handle and design show obvious differences. This particular piece is in white opalescent and the pattern design shows somewhat of a Japanese Art look. Thanks again to the Petrasichs for the photo and information.

Infinity

The owner of this 8" by 5½" bowl gave it this name and I think the figure-eight elongated loops which resemble the infinity symbol can be noticed with little trouble and I do like the name. Although this blue opalescent piece has some characteristics of Davidson it isn't found in any of their catalogs, thus leading the owner to believe it may be a Greener product and I won't argue with that observation. Photo courtesy of the Petrasichs.

Inside Ribbing

Beaumont Glass of Martins Ferry, Ohio, made this very pretty glass in the early 1900s, and while it isn't plentiful, many times it is overlooked. Colors are white, canary, blue, and possibly green; the shapes are berry sets, table sets, water sets, toothpick holders, a cruet, a syrup, salt shakers, a cruet set, and a celery vase. Some pieces have enameled decoration adding to the interest.

Intaglio

Intaglio was one of Northwood's earlier patterns dating from 1897 in custard production. It was made in a host of shapes including table sets, water sets, berry sets, a cruet, salt shakers, a jelly compote, and many novelty shapes. Colors made in opalescent glass are white, blue, and occasionally canary, but other treatments such as gilded emerald green, and of course custard, are available.

Intaglio Holly (Dugan's)

Like the other Intaglio patterns from the Dugan Company, this one had goofus treatment when it was sold. The pattern is very similar to Dugan's Holly and Berry design. Intaglio Holly is found in large bowls, small bowls, and possibly a compote shape.

Intaglio Lattice

The Petrasichs named this bowl and I believe the name is fitting. I've been able to learn nothing about the pattern and certainly hope readers can offer something more. I believe the piece may be either English or European, but can't be sure.

Intaglio Morning Glory

Morning Glory, another of Dugan's 1907 patterns in their vast Intaglio line, is a standout. It is found on both large and small bowls and possibly a short-stemmed compote. The white opalescent glass is decorated in a goofus treatment of red and gold.

Intaglio Panels

This pattern, which was named by the owner, can be found in a small 4¾" bowl and a celery vase (or according to the owner a tumbler). The only color reported so far is white opalescent. Thanks to the Petrasichs for sharing it.

Interior Flute

Interior Flute has wide panels that are about twice as far apart as Fenton's Interior Panel pattern. Shown is a 5½" vase in lavender opalescent glass with a jack-in-the-pulpit top. I believe this is a Dugan/Diamond pattern but can't be sure at this time. It probably came in blue, white, and green opalescent glass as well.

Interior Panel

This very nice Fenton vase dates from the early 1920s. Besides this fine example in amber opalescent, I've seen it in Cameo opalescent and iridized stretch glass in Celeste Blue, Velva Rose, and Florentine Green, all from the 1921 – 1927 era of production. The same mould was used to make several different whimsey shaped vases also. The example shown is 8" tall and has a fan spread of 5".

Interior Poinsettia (Pressed)

Unlike the blown Poinsettia pattern, this one is pressed and seems to be found only on the tumbler shape. It is known in marigold carnival glass, on clear glass, and in blue, green, and white opalescent glass. The pattern is credited to the Northwood Company, and a trademark can be seen on the inside of the tumbler.

Interior Swirl

Interior Swirl is much like the Inside Ribbing pattern but with a twist. This very pretty rose bowl is perfectly plain on the outside and has a ribbing that has been twisted on the interior. Notice the cranberry frit along the top indicating this pattern is most likely from Jefferson Glass. One writer dates this pattern from the 1890s, but I'd place it closer to 1904 or 1905. The canary coloring is quite good and the base prominent.

Interior Wide Stripe

If you look closely at this tumbler, you will see the exterior is flat and the opalescent wide stripe is on the inside. I believe this water set may have been made by LaBelle Glass but I could be wrong (one writer says it may be from Phoenix Glass).

Inverted Chevron

This very attractive vase is sometimes confused with Fenton's Plume Panels vase, a pattern well known to carnival glass collectors. But on close examination, it is very different. I suspect it may be from Jefferson Glass and I've named it Inverted Chevron. While blue and green are the only colors I've seen, I'm sure it must have come in white.

Inverted Fan and Feather

This well-known pattern was made first by Northwood in custard glass and then by Dugan in opalescent glass. It is found in berry sets, table sets, water sets, punch sets, jelly compote, toothpick holder, cruet (rare), shakers, many whimsies including a pulled vase from the spooner, a rose bowl, and a spittoon. Colors include white, blue, green (rare), and canary. Shown is a blue gilded footed sauce.

Iris (English)

I apologize for lumping this pattern with Daffodils in previous books, but they are so very much alike I overlooked the differences. Iris is found in a water set (lidded pitcher is shown), a hand lamp, and a vase (there may be additional shapes I haven't heard about). Colors are white, blue, green, and vaseline. Many thanks to Kelvin Russell and Debra Jennings for sharing this beauty.

Iris (Northwood)

This Iris design is similar to the Daffodils pattern that was made by both Northwood and Dugan, but it shows a different flower. I believe it is from Northwood, but I could be wrong. Shapes reported so far in Iris are a water set, a vase (shown), and a lamp, but there are surely more. Colors are white, blue, green, and vaseline.

Iris with Meander

Iris with Meander is also known as Fleur-de-Lis Scrolled and is a product of Jefferson Glass, dating from 1902 or 1903. It was made in table sets, water sets, berry sets (two sizes of sauces), toothpick holder, salt shaker (very rare), jelly compote, vase, pickle dish, and plate. Colors are flint, blue, canary, green, and rarely amber opalescent, as well as crystal, blue, green, and amethyst glass with decoration.

Ivy Ball

I have little information to offer on this swirl pattern piece other than to say the color is white opalescent, the stand doesn't look old to me, and it may in fact be a late Fenton piece. I simply don't know. Any information would be appreciated. Thanks to Judy Parker for the photo.

Jazz

While I can't find this pattern pictured in any Dugan/Diamond ad, I feel sure it came from that company. The base has two levels and the unusual treatment of the top is sassy and bold, so I've named it Jazz and feel that is certainly a descriptive title. Shown in blue, it probably came in white and green also. Date of production should be in the 1906 – 1909 time frame, I'd bet. It is 6" tall.

Jefferson #270 (Jefferson Colonial)

At first glance this looks like another Jefferson pattern called Iris with Meander. Indeed, the moulds may have been the same, but this design is missing the fleur-de-lis at the base and the beading in the slots. Shown is the master berry bowl in blue, so I know the berry set was made. Colors are surely the usual Jefferson ones of white, blue, green, and canary, and I'd like to hear from anyone who has additional information about shapes and colors.

Jefferson Shield

This is Jefferson Glass Company's very rare #262 pattern. It is a dome-based bowl found in green, white, and blue opalescent. It has a series of 13 shields around the center of the bowl. If you are the owner of one of these bowls, consider yourself very lucky, for less than two dozen in all colors are known.

Jefferson Spatter Vase

This vase was made on the same mould shape as the Convex Rib vase from Jefferson. It has a spatter decoration and the ribs can actually be felt on the inside, Ruth Harvey tells me. The coloring is a good vaseline but this piece may have been made in other colors as well.

Jefferson Spool

This very unusual hyacinth vase from the Jefferson Glass Company looks as if it were turned on a lathe. It stands approximately 8" tall and was made in 1905. Colors reported in opalescent glass are white, green, blue, and vaseline. No other shapes have been seen, but it could easily have been opened into a compote.

Jefferson Stripe

This is Jefferson's #33 Lily vase shown in their 1902 ad. This nice vase (shown in amber) can be found with a variety of top shapes and is 7½" tall. Colors known are white opalescent, blue opalescent, green opalescent, and amber opalescent. Pieces may be found with or without the cranberry glass frit on the top edge. The green tends to be a bit dark, almost an emerald green shade. Thanks to Janine Patterson for the nice photo.

Jefferson Wheel

This very attractive bowl dating from 1905 is, as the name implies, another pattern from Jefferson Glass. It was originally Jefferson's #260 pattern and can be found in white, blue, and green opalescent glass. It has been reported in carnival, but I have yet to see an example.

Jewel and Fan

Jefferson made a lot of opalescent glass and this was originally identified as their #125. It is found on bowls and an elongated banana bowl in white, blue, green, and rarely, canary. The design is simple but very effective.

Jewel and Flower

This very attractive pattern was made by the Northwood Company in 1904, and originally called Encore. It can be found on water sets, table sets, berry sets, cruets, and salt shakers. Colors are white, blue, and canary, often decorated with gilding. Incidentally, there is a variant with the design going all the way to the base and eliminating the beading and threading band.

Jeweled Heart

Although long credited to Northwood, Jeweled Heart (or Victor, as it was originally called) was first made by Dugan in 1905. Shapes available are table sets, water sets, berry sets, a syrup, sugar shaker, a condiment set consisting of cruet and salt and pepper shakers, and toothpick holder on a round flat tray or plate. Colors in opalescent glass are white, green, and blue, but the pattern is also found in carnival glass, crystal, green, and blue decorated glass, and very rarely, ivory or custard glass. Some items are marked with the Diamond-D marking.

Jewels and Drapery

This very pretty Northwood vase dates from 1907 and can be found in ads from that year. As you can see, the drapery is very well done with a tiny tassel ending between the folds. Around the base is a series of jewels or raised dots. Strangely, in a Northwood ad in a 1906 Lyons Brothers catalog, there is a similar vase shown that has an additional row of pendants below the jewels. The ad is labeled the Fairmont opal assortment.

Jewels and Drapery Variant

As I said earlier, this pattern is exactly like the Jewels and Drapery pattern except for the row of pendants that hang like fringe below the row of jewels. This pattern was shown in a 1906 glass ad called the Fairmont opal assortment.

Jolly Bear

Jolly Bear was made by the Jefferson Glass Company in 1906 or 1907. It is found in opalescent glass in white, blue, and green. The white pieces (and occasionally blue) sometimes have gilding on them, leading to the possibility they were also used with a goofus treatment. Shapes are round, ruffled, or even tri-cornered. The bear is very much like that on the U.S. Glass pattern called Frolicking Bears. It would be an excellent companion piece.

Jubilee (Hickman)

Jubilee was originally made by McKee & Brothers in crystal, so this blue opalescent bowl is a bit of a mystery. It has fewer fans than the original pattern and is opalescent glass. I do question its age, but will show it here and hope readers can shed some light on it. Thanks to the Petrasichs for sharing it with me.

Keyhole

The keyhole pattern is shown in 1905 Dugan Glass Company ads. It can be found on opalescent glass on bowls that have a dome base in white, blue, and green, and with a painted or goofus treatment on the white. A few years later, it was adapted for use as the exterior of carnival glass bowls with the Raindrop pattern as an interior and on a very rare marigold bowl where the exterior is plain and Keyhole became the interior pattern.

King Richard

More recent information now places this pattern, which is also known as Waffle and Vine, as a product of the short-lived Coudersport Glass concern (1900 – 1904). All pieces are considered rare and besides the blue, white, and green opalescent ones, factory shards are known in non-opalescent colors as well. The scroll-supported stem and the interior design of vines and a scroll filled with waffle or file are very well done.

King's Panel

Besides the bowl I showed in the last edition, I now know of a creamer and open sugar. The pattern is all interior ribs or panels. Colors are both canary and blue opalescent. It was made by Davidson.

King's X

This 3¼" spill is from Greener & Co. and is quite rare. It bears the Greener logo which dates it between 1875 and 1885. Blue is the only reported color at this time. I'd appreciate hearing of additional shapes or colors. Thanks to the Petrasichs for sharing it.

Kittens

Kittens was from the Fenton Company (their #299) and is primarily found in carnival glass. Rare cups and saucers are known in crystal, royal blue, and these two items in amethyst opalescent glass that date from 1908 production. The saucer is really a 4" plate since all Kittens pieces were toy items, intended for children. I once owned this one of a kind set and wish I still did. Probably other pieces in this opalescent treatment were made but none have been reported.

LaBelle

This is the name given to me by the owner and I'm happy to honor it. It is a vaseline opalescent toothpick holder; the only color and shape I've had reported to date. It resembles the Inside Ribbing pattern but without the ribbing. I have no indication as to the maker at this time. Thanks to the Sandemans for sharing it.

Lady Caroline

Lady Caroline was made by Davidson in 1891 as their Pearline pattern in blue and canary opalescent glass. Shapes are an open sugar and creamer (shown), baskets, a two-handled spill, and several novelties from this mould.

Lady Chippendale

This is now known to be from Davidson and Company in England (incorrectly labeled Greener in pervious editions). Some additional shapes have been found including baskets, compotes, pitcher, salt holder, bowl, tumbler, an open sugar, and the creamer shown, as well as advertising and promotional pieces. The pattern dates from 1881 and is found in either blue or canary opalescent glass, all marked Rd. #176566. Thanks to the Petrasichs for the new information.

Lady Finger Spill Vase

Like other patterns with these feet, I strongly suspect this spill vase is English from George Davidson & Company. I've seen it in vaseline as well as the blue shown.

Lady Slipper Vase

Here is another of those English vases with a flair that can only be found on glass of the Victorian age. It was made by Davidson and is only 4½" tall. It is shown in canary but was also made in blue and white opalescent glass. It was probably made in other sizes as well.

Late Coinspot

Here is a Fenton version of the famed Coinspot. This one dating from the 1925 – 1929 era was called an iced tea set in advertising and had a taller tumbler with it. Colors were white, blue, and green. As you can easily see, it has a semi-cannonball shape and the handle is rather thick. In 1931 Fenton made this same pitcher with a dark, contrasting handle, and teamed it with mugs with the same handle treatment.

Lattice (English)

The owner of this nice vase in vaseline tells me it's English and I have no reason to believe otherwise. This cylinder shaped vase with bulbous base has an interesting pattern of elongated lattice work throughout the entire piece. This is the only shape reported to date. Thanks to the Sandemans for sharing it.

Lattice and Daisy

This tumbler is likely a Dugan product before it became Diamond Glass Co. in 1913. It is a bit tough to find, especially in vaseline. No opalescent pitchers or other shapes have been reported to date but the pitcher would certainly be a welcomed sight to see. Thanks to the Sandemans and Ruth Harvey for the photo submissions.

Lattice and Points

This Dugan pattern is pulled from the same mould that produced the Vining Twigs plates, bowls, and vases that were made in carnival glass. In opalescent glass, the vases are usually short and haven't been pulled or swung as most vases are. Colors are white, mostly, but scarce blue examples are known and I suspect green was made also. Production of the opalescent pieces dates from 1907.

Lattice Medallions

This very graceful pattern is from the Northwood Company and is sometimes marked with the famous "N." Lattice Medallions, found primarily in bowl shapes, often very ruffled and ornately shaped, can be found in the usual opalescent colors of white, blue, and green. Shown is a very pretty white opalescent bowl with the tri-corner shape.

Laura (Single Flower Framed)

Here is another example of poor naming. The Laura name is from Rose Presznick but the pattern has long been called Single Flower Framed by carnival glass collectors. It is a Dugan pattern, found only on the exterior of nappies, bowls, and this very rare ruffled plate. Colors previously reported are white and blue opalescent, as well as carnival colors (especially peach opalescent). These scarce items date from the 1909 period of Dugan production.

Laurel Swag and Bows

While I've searched every reference I could find about this pattern, it doesn't seem to be shown anywhere. I know it was made by the Fenton Company about 1908, for they made the only amethyst opalescent glass around that time. As you can see, there are laurel swags tied with a ribbon and bow, as well as cosmos-like flowers and an unusual bull's eye with a swirl of connecting leaves. I would appreciate any information about this pretty gas shade.

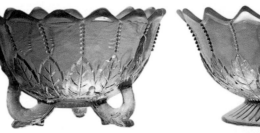

Leaf and Beads

Just why Northwood made two variant treatments to this pattern is unclear, but both are shown here. One has twig feet and a few changes in leaves while the other has a dome base. The latter should be called a variant. Production of the twig-footed bowl began in 1905, but by 1906 both styles were being advertised. Colors are blue, white, and green opalescent plus custard glass and carnival pieces.

Leaf and Diamonds

This pattern was first made in 1907 and was shown in a 1908 Butler Brothers ad that included other Jefferson Glass items. Leaf and Diamonds can be found in white, blue, and a scarce green opalescent treatment, and may well be a companion pattern to Jefferson's Hearts and Clubs opalescent bowl pattern. Bowls have three large spatula feet and show an interior design of three diamond patterns separated by three fans of leaves, with a leaf circle in the center of the bowl.

Leaf and Leaflets

Here is another of those patterns that appeared first in Northwood's lineup (1907 ads) and later became part of the Dugan production line. The opalescent examples in blue, white, and goofus are Northwood; however the same mould turns up later as a Dugan carnival glass pattern called Long Leaf in a beautiful peach opalescent iridized bowl. In addition, Long Leaf can be found as the exterior design for bowls and baskets of the Stippled Petals design in peach opalescent, also made by Dugan.

Leaf Chalice

Leaf Chalice was made by Northwood while a part of the National combine. It appears in a May 1903 Butler Brothers ad that featured three shapings of the piece. Colors usually found are white and blue, but green was also made and is considered a rare color in this pattern.

Leaf Garland

This 4½" tall by 6" wide compote in blue opalescent is from Greener & Co. and has the Rd. #176239 (1891). This pattern is also known in a small bowl in vaseline opalescent. I'm sure other shapes may exist but they haven't been reported to me to date. Thanks to the Petrasichs for the name and photo.

Leaf Garland and Ribs

Although it isn't marked I feel that this little 3" creamer may be a product of Davidson (compare it to the Lady Caroline pattern) judging by the looks of it. Vaseline is the only color and the small creamer is the only shape reported at this time. Thanks to the Petrasichs for sharing it.

Leaf Rosette and Beads

Made by the Dugan/Diamond Company beginning in 1906, this pattern seems to be a cousin to Blocked Thumbprint and Beads with the addition of the chain of leaves. And if you take a look at the Single Poinsettia pattern, you will see just how similar these patterns are. Leaf Rosette and Beads is a scarce pattern and was most likely made in the usual colors, but the only ones I've seen are white and green.

Leafy Stripe

Measuring 9" long, 7" wide, and 4½" tall, this beautiful honey-amber bowl was probably made to fit into a bride's basket or to be a hanging bowl. It has a pontil on the base and I strongly suspect it is from England. Besides the opalescent stripe design, there is a mould pattern of leaves around the bowl.

Lily Pad

Other than to say it's English, I have no other information to offer on this beautifully done epergne at this time. I will say that it is probably one of my favorite epergnes. I really love the way it is arranged and can picture water flowing out of the lily down into the bowl, perhaps with flowers floating in the water. Vaseline is the only reported color at this time. I do thank the Sandemans for sharing this super piece of glass with me.

Lily Pool Epergne

This item is not a one-piece item as I originally thought; the lily pulls loose from the bowl base. It was just a matter of my misunderstanding the owner's description and I'm happy to get it straightened out. At any rate, it appears to be an American product and I'd guess from the Northwood Company. Other colors probably exist but to date I've seen only vaseline.

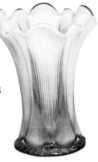

Lined Heart

This 1906 Jefferson Glass Company vase pattern can be found in white, blue, and green opalescent glass. The examples shown haven't been swung as many are and are about 7" tall; some range to 14".

Linking Rings

Linking Rings was made by Davidson in 1894, and most pieces bear Rd. #237038. Shapes in opalescent glass are a water set, oval 8½" x 7" tray, juice glass, bowls, a compote, 7½" plate, 3" creamer, and an open sugar. Colors in the opalescent treatment are a deep blue, a softer blue, and canary (vaseline). Thanks to the Sandemans for the nice pitcher photo.

Little Nell

Despite being very plain, this vase is still a very cute item. Except for the threading above the collar base, there is no design at all and whatever the vase has going for it comes from the shaping and fine opalescence. The maker isn't certain at this time, and I'm not sure it really matters. Colors are white, blue, and green opalescent.

Little Swan (Dugan)

Dugan's version of Little Swan is slightly larger than the Northwood swan shown elsewhere. It came along in 1909 and can be found in white, green, and blue opalescent glass and various carnival glass colors. The Fenton Company also made a version, but the breast feathering is quite different from the two versions here, more like flower petals than feathers.

Little Swan (Northwood)

The Northwood version of this pattern is virtually the same design as the Dugan Little Swan, but came first and is slightly smaller. It can be found in blue and white; green may be a possibility but I've only seen Dugan ones in that color. Some examples have been gilded on the head, along the rim of the opening, and down the tail.

Lords and Ladies

Lords and Ladies was made by Davidson in England (their Rd. #285342) and can be found in blue and canary (vaseline) opalescent glass. Shapes include a 2¼" salt, covered butter dish, a 3" creamer, small sugar, one-handled nappy, cake plate, creamer and sugar on feet, a celery boat, platter, a 4" x 6" oval bowl, and possibly a water set. The date of manufacture is October 2, 1896.

Lorna

This should be called the traveling vase since it was first made at Model Flint in 1900, then at Northwood as their #562 the same year, then by Dugan/Diamond when Northwood left the plant, and finally by West Virginia Glass! Most stand about 6½" to 7" tall and can be found in white, canary, and blue opalescent.

Lotus

This Albany Glass pattern is found only in a rose bowl shape with an attached underplate shown. It was made from 1900 to 1902 in white, canary, and blue opalescent glass as well as opaque glass colors of blue, green, white, and yellow. Speculation is this was made by Model Flint during their last years at Albany. It is also called Lotus Blossom by some collectors.

Love Flower

I've had this photo for a year or two but hadn't been able to track it until someone told me it was called Love Flower and was English. It has three handles like a loving cup, so that may be the source of the name. The flowers that wind up the center are somewhat like Dugan's Windflower pieces as well as the Tree of Love pattern. Thanks to Richard Petersen for sharing this piece with me.

Lustre Flute

Northwood's Lustre Flute, also called Waffle Band or English Hob Band, is found sparingly in carnival glass and decorated glass. The opalescent colors reported are white and blue. Opalescent production began in 1907. Shapes include a water set, table set, berry set, a custard cup, and a vase shape. The pattern is a bit on the plain side and certainly not one of the better remembered ones from this company.

Many Diamonds

This likely European ruffled candy ribbon edge bowl on a metal stand is heavy opalescent with a sapphire colored crest. It is very similar in appearance to the Peacock Tail bowl, also on a metal stand. Any information would be appreciated. Thanks to Marty Vogel for sharing it.

Many Loops

Jefferson Glass Company's #247 pattern was confined to novelty bowls, rose bowls, and banana bowl shapes all from the same mould. This spirograph-like pattern of overlapping loops bordered by zig-zag threading is a distinctive design. It is found in crystal, and opalescent colors of white, blue, and green.

Many Ribs

This very distinctive vase with a columnal base was made by the Model Flint Glass Company of Albany, Indiana, in 1902. It can be found in white, blue, and the very attractive canary. This particular vase measures nearly 8" and has the typical slightly flared top.

Maple Leaf

Maple Leaf was apparently first a Northwood pattern (at least in custard glass), and then a Dugan product in opalescent and later carnival glass. The opalescent glass dates from 1908 to 1910. Colors in this glass are green (scarce), white, and blue, with a very rare example in vaseline. The only shape reported in opalescent glass seems to be the jelly compote, but others may certainly exist.

Maple Leaf Chalice

This very pretty vase is a naturalistic piece from the Northwood Company made in purple slag and opalescent glass. Ite dates from the 1903 – 1905 era. Opalescent colors are white, blue, green, and vaseline. The design is much like Leaf Chalice, also from Northwood, and the two are often confused.

Markham Swirl Band with Opal Cobweb

What a name! Actually there are other Markham Swirl designs with various opal designs in white, blue, cranberry, and possibly canary. The piece shown is a finger lamp but examples in standard oil lamps are also known.

Mary Ann

While this vase is well known to carnival glass collectors, it comes as a surprise to many who collect opalescent glass. It came from the Dugan Company and received its name from Fanny Mary Ann Dugan, sister of Thomas E.A. and Alfred Dugan. In carnival, the vase is known in an eight-scallop and ten-scallop top, and a three-handled, flat-topped example called a loving cup. Carnival colors are marigold, amethyst, and a lighter lavender shade. There is also an amber glass example in satin finish. In opalescent glass, the only colors reported are white and blue, and both are considered rare. This pattern has been reproduced.

Mary Gregory

Normally I wouldn't consider this small lidded piece as opalescent, but if you look closely at the lid you will see it has an opalescent stripe in the glass. The piece stands only 4" tall and I suspect it is from Europe where most of the Mary Gregory type enameling was done.

Mavis Swirl

This 1901 Model Flint Glass pattern is sometimes called Opal Swirl but the correct name is as I list it. It's found in water sets, barber bottles, a toothpick holder, shakers, trinket dishes, and a rose bowl. Colors are clear, green, white opaque, frosted, or speckled blue.

May Basket

Jefferson Glass Company's May Basket was shown in ads as their #87 pattern. For years some collectors thought this was a Northwood pattern since it has the same design as the Pump and Trough pieces. May Basket can be found in white, blue, green, and the scarce vaseline opalescent shown, in three sizes.

Meander

The moulds for Jefferson's #233 were obtained by the Northwood Company after its move to the Wheeling location. The opalescent pieces in white, blue, and green are attributed to Jefferson, and the carnival bowls with Three Fruits Medallion as an interior pattern are strictly Northwood.

Medieval Arches

This 4" square bowl has so much opalescence in the bottom that it gives the appearance of having skim milk in it. Vaseline is the only color and this is the only shape reported to me so far. I have no idea of the maker at this time although the owner states it is flint glass and dates to the mid 1800s. Thanks to the Sandemans for sharing it.

Melon Optic Swirl (Jefferson)

This very beautiful, tightly crimped bowl has a melon rib exterior that has been shaped into a swirl with cranberry edging. This bowl appears to be quite close to a series of pieces shown in a 1902 Jefferson ad, showing Stripe, Swirl, and Coin Dot items. The ad lists colors of white, blue, green, yellow (vaseline), and cranberry.

Melon Swirl

Having done a great deal of research and soul-searching, I'm convinced this very beautiful water set may well be from the Indiana, Pennsylvania, plant at the time of early Dugan production. Examples of handles just like the one on the water set shown are found in 1904 ads showing decorated sets. In addition, the enamel work is very similar to that found on several Dugan sets made between 1900 and 1905. These sets, more elaborate than most in this enameling, are consistent with Melon Swirl. I certainly hope someone out there can shed more light on this fantastic pattern. It is one of the prettiest I've ever seen.

Mermaids and Shells

What a beautiful design this piece is. It is from Burtles, Tate, and Company and is reported in white opalescent and the vaseline opalescent shown. It measures 7½" long and 3" deep. Thanks to John and Mary Petrasich for sharing it with me.

Mica Spatter JIP Vase

This 4½" vase is shaped just like the Rubina Verde JIP vase shown elsewhere, is on clear glass, and has a beautiful spatter treatment with flecks of mica in the pattern. Hobbs, Brockunier & Company used this treatment on vases, tumblers, and pitchers, and I suspect the vase shown is theirs. Dates of production were from 1883 to 1885. This glass was later produced at Northwood and Bonita Art Glass Company.

Mirror Frame

This rather interesting round frame looks like flower petals surrounding a border of beads. The color is a nice vaseline opalescent, which is the only reported color at this time. Additional information would be appreciated. Thanks again the Steve and Radka Sandeman for sharing this nice piece.

Monkey (Under a Tree)

This 1880s pattern is found mostly in crystal, but occasionally turns up in white opalescent glass. Shapes known are water sets, a finger bowl, waste bowl (shown), a toothpick holder, a mug, a pickle jar, a jam jar, a celery vase, and an ashtray; not all shapes have been found in anything but crystal. Opalescent pieces are very collectible and expensive.

Murano Floral Vase

This squat vase has applied rigoree and opalescent glass flowers and is typical of this famous Italian' sproducer's work. The vase has a hammered look in clear glass. I appreciate Ruth Harvey sharing this item with me.

Mystic Maze

This blown vase of very thin glass is similar to Jefferson's Swirling Maze. The color is a soft canary yellow. I certainly welcome any information about this vase from readers. I thank Ruth Harvey for sharing it.

National's #17

This rather scarce 8" vase was created at the Northwood plant in Indiana, Pennsylvania, for the National glass combine. It was shown in a 1901 catalog ad, called a bouquet vase. It can be found in dark blue, dark green, and canary opalescent glass. Here I show two of the three colors and all are equally scarce.

National Swirl

As I said in an earlier edition, I have no proof this pitcher is from National but a similarly shaped pitcher appeared in their ads in 1900 in a G. Sommers & Company catalog. A vase with this same shape, known as Fenton's #39 Swirl, is shown in Fenton ads in 1939. I've never seen a Fenton ad picturing a pitcher however. As for National, their ad showed reeded handles and listed colors of crystal, blue, and green, so perhaps these pitchers evolved from this earlier treatment.

Nesting Robins

In the second edition I said the bowl shown was marked EZAN as well as Made in France, but I now know of a bowl in this pattern that is marked Sabino, also a French company, making glass in the 1920s and 1930s. The quality of workmanship is quite good, and only time will tell more about this piece. The bowl shown measures 10" across and was purchased in France.

Netted Cherries

While I have no proof, I feel confident this pattern was made by Dugan/Diamond. It is found only on bowls in crystal or opalescent glass where the colors are white and blue. Shapes include round, tri-cornered, and banana shape, but all are from the same mould. Goofus examples have been reported too.

Netted Roses

This 1906 Northwood Company bowl pattern is another of those with one name for opalescent glass and another for carnival. In carnival, the pattern is called Bull's Eye and Leaves and it is an exterior pattern also. In opalescent glass as Netted Roses, the colors are blue, green, and white, often with a goofus treatment.

Northern Star

This very nice 1908 Fenton geometric pattern is most often found in carnival glass or crystal but can rarely be found in large plates in white, blue, and green opalescent glass. Just why the small bowls and plates were not made in an opalescent treatment is a mystery since 5" bowls, 7" plates, and 11" plates are all known in crystal.

Northwood's Mikado

Perhaps this should be called Northwood's Poppy since that is the interior design, and most pattern names originate from the interior design unless there is only an exterior pattern. If you'll compare this very rare nappy to the Blossoms and Blooms pattern earlier in this edition you'll see that only the exterior is the same. The difference in this piece, besides it being round and vaseline, is that it carries a Poppy interior pattern and the base has a full flower in the center as opposed to the rayed base seen on the Blossoms and Blooms pieces. This could possibly be a prototype due to the design and since it's the only reported example to date. Nonetheless it is considered a very rare variant to any of the designs seen on these pieces regardless of the name used.

Thanks to Dave Peterson for sharing this rare and interesting item.

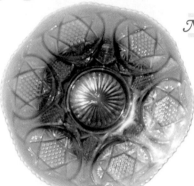

Northwood's Poppy

Northwood's Poppy is found primarily in carnival glass but it was also made in custard glass. This is the first example of this pattern in opalescent glass that I've seen. The shape is called an oval pickle dish. It does not carry the Northwood trademark. It is possible other colors were made in the opalescent treatment, and all would be rare and desirable.

Northwood Swirl

Since Northwood Swirl is found primarily in carnival or decorated glass, it was a bit of a surprise to see this tumbler in opalescent glass. It has also been reported in vaseline opalescent glass. It is 3⅞" tall and the ribs are all interior. Thanks to the Petrasichs for sharing it.

Ocean Shell

Ocean Shell is another of the naturalistic compotes. It has three variations of twig-like supports for stems. Some go all the way to the bowl, others are short and not connected, while still others are longer but remain unattached at the top. Ocean Shell was made by the Northwood Company circa 1904. Opalescent colors are white, blue, and green, and purple slag glass is also known.

Ocean Wave

Shown is a very beautifully ruffled bowl in a pattern I've named Ocean Wave. I believe this piece was made by Jefferson for the Oneida Silver Mfg. Company since the bowl is labeled: O.S.M. CO. — NY — ONEIDA. It was obviously made to go into a bride's basket or some sort of holder for the silver company. If anyone has additional information on this item, I'd like to hear from them.

Ohio State Seal

This lettered 3⅜" white opalescent cup plate is embossed "The Great Seal Of The State Of Ohio" around the outer edge. It shows a bright sunrise coming up between a mountain range. White is the only reported color and the small cup plate is the only shape reported to me at this time. It is a nice addition to any opalescent glass collection. Thanks to the Petrasichs for sharing it.

Oktoberfest

This very attractive German ale glass may have another name but I haven't found one. It has a very active pattern of birds, people, flowers, crowns, and German writing. The coloring is a very good vaseline with a fine opalescent edging (the lip tilts as you can see). I'd appreciate any information on this item.

Old Man Winter

This Jefferson pattern, shown in the two sizes made (the larger one is footed), was advertised as #135 (small) and #91 (large). Some are marked Patent 1906 and Patent March 18, 1902. I've seen the baskets in white, blue, vaseline, and green. The very interesting handle treatment is a design giveaway and harkens back to Victorian baskets with decorative handles.

Onyx

This well-known Findlay Glass treatment, first made in 1889, isn't often thought of as opalescent ware but it really is (just look at the handle of the pitcher shown). The base glass is white or tannish with a white casing inside. The floral design can be silver lustre, gold lustre, ruby lustre, or bronze lustre. A similar design from the same mould is known as Floradine but it isn't considered Onyx ware. Onyx shapes include bowls, a butter dish, tall celery vase, creamer, cruet, lamp, pickle caster, pitcher, shakers, sauce, spooner, covered sugar, sugar shaker, syrup, toothpick holder, and a tumbler.

Opal Bull's Eye

I've yet to learn the maker of this pattern but I'm reasonably certain it is English and do hope someone has additional information to share. The only color reported to me is vaseline opalescent. The shapes known are a mustard with lid and spoon, and a 1½" tall open salt in a metal holder. Thanks to Joan and Wayne Jolliffe for the photo.

Opal Daisy

These two strange pieces are a real mystery. The smaller is 2" tall and the larger 3½". Both have brass bound tops and both slant. At this time I have no idea who made them or even what they were used for. I certainly welcome any information readers may have on these pieces.

Opal Dot

This generous size vaseline water tray is the only reported shape and color I've heard about at this time. I certainly would think that at least a pitcher and tumbler would exist and possibly other shapes but none have been reported to me yet. I believe this to be English in origin but have no proof of such. Additional information would be appreciated. Thanks to the Sandemans for sharing it.

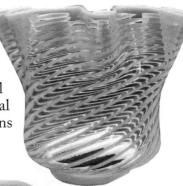

Opalescent Swirl

This shade, which I am assuming is English, can be found in at least two different shapes, but is reported only in vaseline at this time. All of these diagonal swirl patterned shades that I've seen have been ruffled. I urge anyone with additional colors, shapes, or information to contact me. Thanks once again to the Sandemans for sharing with me.

Opal Floral

I suspect the maker of this nice little compote to be John Walsh Walsh or possibly Richardson's. This is the only shape and color reported to me but I wouldn't be surprised to see other shapes in this pattern. Additional information would be appreciated.

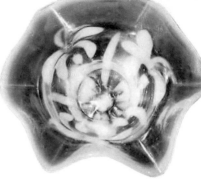

Opal Flower

This English cylinder shade (maker unconfirmed) is very well done, with large and small flower groupings and vines throughout the pattern. The color seems to be a white opalescence with a cranberry top, but may in fact be rubina verde (I have no information on the actual color). Either way, it's a very nice shade. This is the only color and shape reported to me to date. Thanks to Steve and Radka Sandeman for the photo.

Opal Loops

I understand this pattern was made by one of the smaller English glass companies in the 1880s. Pieces known are a decanter, a flask, a vase, and a glass pipe. Pieces like the one shown are mistakenly called Nailsea glass by some collectors, but they were made in Sunderland or Nailsea or Newcastle plants perhaps.

Opal Open (Beaded Panels)

Carnival glass collectors have long known this pattern as Beaded Panels. Opalescent glass collectors call it Opal Open. It is shown in a Northwood ad in 1899, so I know they made it. But it later shows up in Dugan ads after 1907, and I know the iridized items are Dugan. To add to the complication, Westmoreland made a reproduction in the 1940s and 1950s that has a solid stem rather than one pierced like the originals. Old pieces in opalescent glass were made in white, green, blue, and canary.

Opal Stripe

This striped vase in vaseline has applied feet and beautifully applied flowers in a rose pink color. It is obviously of European origin (no maker confirmed to date). This would enhance any opalescent or vase collection. Additional information would be appreciated. Photo courtesy of the Sandemans.

Opal Urn Vase

I now know this fine 7½" vase is Jefferson Glass's #18, made in 1902. It is found in white, blue, and green opalescent glass, and the distinctive feature is the flaring above the 2½" base and the ending of the striping before it reaches the base.

Open Blossom Vase

This pale green opalescent vase stands nearly 6" tall and has the shape of an open blossom, hence the name. The owner feels it is from England (as do I). If readers have additional information, I'd like to hear from them. This is another fine pattern from the Petrasichs.

Open Edge Basket (Fenton)

Introduced into the Fenton line in 1910, this novelty item has been made in opalescent glass, carnival glass, stretch glass, milk glass, opaque, and all sorts of clear colors. Shapes are bowls of three sizes, plates, candleholders, and vase whimsies. Carnival items sometimes have interior patterns. Early opalescent production colors are white, blue, green, and canary, but later production offered cobalt or royal blue and emerald green. These later examples date from the 1930s.

Open O's

Open O's was advertised by Northwood as early as 1903. This very unusual pattern is known mostly in short, squat vase shapes, but it was also made in novelty bowls and a handled ring bowl. Colors are white, blue, green, and canary. It is possible Dugan continued production of this pattern once Northwood moved to Wheeling, but I can't confirm this at this time. The ring bowl is known as Heart Handled Open O's.

Optic Basket

This mould blown basket has a ten-panel interior optic pattern, six crimped ruffles, and a twisted vaseline handle that is one piece of glass doubled. It measures 5" tall, 5½" across, with a base diameter of 3". The glass is quite thin and there is a pontil mark. I suspect this is from an English glassmaker.

Optic Panel

This beautiful vase is truly a work of art with its applied cranberry edging. It is 6" tall with a 2¾" foot. It is mould blown and has eight optic panels that run from the applied base to the top. The color is a superb vaseline, but I feel confident it was made in other colors. I believe this pattern dates from the 1890s and may well be British.

Orange Tree

I was very surprised to see this well-known Fenton pattern showing up in the mug. It is very much like the Wild Daffodils mug shown elsewhere in this book in that it has a custard-like opaqueness with a good deal of opalescence. Needless to say, it is a real rarity, and one can only speculate if other shapes in this pattern were made in opalescent glass since both bowls and plates are found in carnival glass with opalescent edges.

Oscar's Legacy

This Art Nouveau vaseline opalescent glasier tile is in the shape of an iris, but other shapes and colors were also made. This tile was made by Oscar Haase, who lived in New York City and made these glass tiles for stained glass windows sometime between 1905 and1915. The tiles were exported to Italy and one of those tiles was found at an old window company with a paper label still attached. All of the shapes and colors have been named in honor of the maker, who was a contemporary to Louis Comfort Tiffany. This particular iris-shaped tile measures 4¾" left-to-right and 4½" top-to-bottom. Special thanks to Siegmar Geiselberger and Dave and Vickie Peterson for this research.

Oval Windows

I haven't found this pattern in any Hobb's or Beaumont catalog reprint, so I can't say it came from either factory, as the regular windows patterns did. It's possible that this could be English but this is pure speculation at this time. The piece shown has oval windows rather than the round ones seen on the regular windows pattern shown elsewhere in this edition. The particular piece shown is in vaseline opalescent and has a metal flower frog lid. This is the only shape and color reported to me at this time. Many thanks to Ruth Harvey for sharing it.

Over-All Hobnail

I mistakenly called this pattern a Nickel Plate pattern, but it is A. J. Beatty's #100 pattern, later made by U.S. Glass. The pattern can be identified on most shapes by the small feet (tumblers are the exception). Colors are white, blue, lavender, and canary opalescent, and amber, blue, and clear in crystal. Shapes known in opalescent glass are water sets, table sets, berry sets (sometimes triangular), a celery vase, toothpick holder, finger bowl, mug, bone dish, nappy, and two sizes of plates.

Overlapping Leaves (Leaf Tiers)

While it has been reported as a Northwood product, this pattern has long been known by carnival glass collectors as a Fenton pattern called Leaf Tiers. In opalescent glass the colors are white, blue, and green, but amethyst is a strong possibility. Shapes are the rose bowl, a bowl, and a plate, all footed and from the same mould.

Palisades (Lined Lattice)

Here is yet another pattern first credited to the Northwood Company but now known to be a Dugan/Diamond product. Carnival glass collectors call this pattern Lined Lattice where it can be found in stretched vases and even a light shade for a table lamp called the Princess Lamp. Colors in opalescent glass are white, blue, green, and canary. Vase and novelty bowls are from the same mould.

Palm and Scroll

Although credited to the Northwood Company in 1905, Palm and Scroll is actually a product of the Dugan Glass Company. It was produced in opalescent glass beginning in 1906, in blue, green, and white. Shapes are various bowls on feet and a neat rose bowl from the same mould. The design is easily recognized, three palm leaves over the curled and ribbed feet and three very artistic feather scrolls between these designs.

Palm Beach

Palm Beach is a U.S. Glass pattern that can be found in crystal, carnival glass, and opalescent glass where berry sets, table sets, water sets, a finger bowl, sauce, and a compote are known. Colors are white, blue, and canary. The opalescent pieces date from 1906.

Pan American

This interesting vase is found with "Pan American 1901" embossed on the front in the emblem. All examples have applied rigoree surrounding the neck. It was made by National Glass at the Northwood factory in Indiana, Pennsylvania. Colors are blue and vaseline opalescent. The shape of the tops will vary. These are quite hard to find, so consider yourself fortunate if you locate one. Thanks to Dave Peterson for the photo and information.

Paneled Acorn Vase

This is a tiny 3" tall English vase with root-like feet and an acorn cup in the middle with a paneled top. I can't pin the maker down but strongly suspect it was Thomas Webb. The color is a strong canary. Thanks again to Ruth Harvey.

Paneled Cornflower

Shown in an 1882 ad from the Sowerby Glass Works of England, this two-handled bowl is typical of the opalescent glass produced by this company. The Paneled Cornflower design was also used on bowls with knob feet and on a vase shape in other types of glass, as well as opalescent ware.

Paneled Fronds

This 5¾" basket is likely a Greener and Co. product. The pattern consists of a series of panels with a frond at the top of each panel. The rustic handle has two open sections with the usual bumpy protrusions sticking out from around the handle edges. Blue is the only color reported to me. Photo courtesy of the Petrasichs.

Paneled Holly

Paneled Holly was made by the Northwood Company in crystal, decorated emerald glass, limited shapes in carnival glass, and opalescent glass (often decorated also). Shapes in opalescent glass include a water set, table set, a berry set, novelty bowls, shakers, and some whimsied pieces from the table set items. Opalescent colors are white and blue, and either can be found with gilding.

Paneled Lattice Band

This beautiful tumbler has a band that is similar to that found on Dugan's Lattice and Daisy tumbler shown elsewhere, but I have no information to link this pattern to that one. The Paneled Lattice Band tumbler is about 4" tall and has a many-rayed base with panels from the base to the banding. Any information on this pattern would be appreciated. Thanks to the Sandemans for this piece.

Paneled Sprig

This 1894 pattern was made by Northwood and perhaps later by Dugan. It is found in white opalescent glass only. Shapes known are a cruet, toothpick holder, and salt shakers. In non-opalescent glass table sets, water sets, berry sets, and table accessories in both cranberry and rubina were made, but these have been widely reproduced.

Panels with Spiral Band

This paneled vase with rigoree applied in a spiral fashion, and with various crimpings to the top is almost certainly European. The only color is vaseline and a vase is the only reported shape. Thanks to Ruth Harvey for sharing this nice piece.

Peacock Feathers

I don't know the maker of this bowl but it certainly has a European flavor and somewhat resembles some of the carnival glass Aurora Pearls pieces from Austria. This bowl on a metal stand has a peacock tail feather design and is shown in white opalescent with a rose pink edging. Any information would be appreciated. Thanks to Marty Vogel for sharing it.

Peacocks (on the Fence)

One of Northwood's best known patterns, especially in carnival glass, Peacocks on the Fence is found only on bowls or plates. Besides opalescent glass and carnival, a rare example of opaque or marbleized glass that was iridized is well known. The pattern dates from 1908. In opalescent glass it can be found in white, blue, and cobalt. (I suspect canary will eventually show up.) All these opalescent colors are quite scarce, as small amounts must have been made.

Peacock Tail

This rare Fenton tumbler is quite different from the pressed Drapery. Note the octagon base and design that ends about ¾" below the lip. Just why the Fenton Company decided to make only this one item in opalescent glass is a mystery since many shapes are known in carnival (but no tumbler!). I have seen a white opalescent example also and certainly green is a strong possibility.

Pearl Flowers

This aptly named Northwood Glass Company pattern from 1903 or 1904 isn't appreciated as much as it might be. All shapes are from the same mould with short knobby feet that are nearly ball-shaped. Shapes include bowls, plates, nut bowls, rose bowls, and even ruffled plates. Colors include white, blue, and green opalescent, but certainly a vaseline example wouldn't surprise me.

Pearline Rib

This Davidson Company bowl has no flat base so it has to sit in a holder. I have seen these in a chain ring and hung by windows as a bulb bowl. In the middle of the ribbing is a standing line of scallops that holds the piece in the holder. This was part of Davidson's Pearline run and can also be found in blue opalescent glass.

Pearls and Scales

This often seen pattern is now known to be from the Jefferson Glass Company from 1905 – 1906. It appears on stemmed pieces all from the same mould. Shapes include a compote, a scarce rose bowl, and even a banana bowl shape, and colors include white, green, blue, emerald green, and vaseline opalescent. Sometimes a cranberry frit edge is present.

Petals with Cupped Pearl

This piece looks English to me, perhaps Richardson's or John Walsh Walsh, but I have no proof of such at this time. The design has several five petal flowers which go up as well as down toward the base, along with a "U" shaped cup which holds a pearl. Vaseline is the only reported color so far. If anyone knows this by another name or has additional information I urge you to contact me. Many thanks to Ruth Harvey for sharing this interesting pattern with me.

Phoenix Coinspot

The owner of this exciting pitcher has been told this was a Phoenix Glass product and I've found nothing to contradict that statement. The shape of the pitcher is very unusual as is the ruby throat treatment of casing. The glass color is a strong canary and the whole piece is about as pretty as this pattern ever gets.

Phoenix Drape

This pattern was by the Phoenix Art Glass Co. in the mid 1880s. It has been reported in blue and cranberry opalescent. Shapes reported are a butter dish, celery vase, punch cup, pitcher, and tumbler. I suspect other shapes were made as well. Thanks to the Petrasichs for the photo and information.

Phoenix Honeycomb

If you'll compare this pitcher with the Phoenix Coinspot pattern earlier in this edition you will notice the same edge crimping as well as the same style reeded handle. Both I'm told were made by Phoenix Glass and I'll agree unless proven otherwise. This blue opalescent pitcher is the only reported color and shape to date. Thanks to the Petrasichs for sharing it.

Piasa Bird

After reviewing a copy of Cyril Manley's *Decorative Victorian Glass*, I can say this pattern is English, probably by Sowerby. Manley shows it in a ruby glass with applied decoration, but the feet and design above them can't be mistaken for anything else. In opalescent glass, it is found in both white and blue but certainly vaseline was made. Shapes are bowls, vases, and several whimsey shapes, all footed, from the same mould.

Picket

This very well done square vase is English, credited to the King Glass Company of London (1890) by Heacock, but is part of the Pearline ware from George Davidson according to Sheilagh Murray. I can report it is certainly from England, and found in canary, white, and blue opalescent glass. It can be found in two sizes.

Pilgrim

The information I was given is that this flint candlestick in white opalescent was made by the New England Glass Co. in 1868 – 1869. I'm also told that reproductions were done for the Metropolitan Museum of Art and that all are marked MMA. Thanks to the Petrasichs for the photo and information.

Pineapple

This English compote (or open sugar) measures 5¼" tall by 5¾" wide and is blue opalescent (other colors and shapes may exist). Additional information would certainly be appreciated. Photo courtesy of the Petrasichs.

Pineapple and Fan

This A.H. Heisey Company pattern from 1898 is well known in crystal, ruby stain, gilded, and green glass. This was their #1255 pattern and in opalescent glass is a very rare item indeed. Here I show the extremely rare vase in vaseline opalescent glass. I want to thank Douglas S. Sandeman for sharing the photo with me.

Pinwheel

I have no information about the maker of this very attractive stemmed 12" cake plate but suspect it may be English because it has that soft look. The stem is short and the whole piece is only 2" tall. I'd appreciate any further information. Thanks to the Petrasichs for sharing it.

Pistachio

This 8" vaseline opalescent pitcher is believed to have been made in the 1890s by Harry Powell of James Powell and Sons, London (which later became Whitefriars Glassworks). Only the pitcher and tumbler shapes have been reported at this time and only in vaseline opalescent. Thanks again to the Petrasichs for sharing their nice glass with me.

Plaid

Here is the first opalescent bowl in this Fenton pattern that previously had only been reported in crystal or carnival glass. It is shared with me by Ruth Harvey. This pattern is also known as Granny's Gingham by some carnival glass collectors. The example shown is a ruffled 8½" bowl.

Plain Jane

I'm relatively sure this pattern came from the Dugan Company. This assumption is based on shape, color, and similarity to other Dugan pieces, chiefly nappies. Over the years I've seen several Dugan Leaf Ray nappies with exactly the same shape. Shown is the Plain Jane nappy in blue, but white and green were made. Production was most likely from the 1906 – 1909 period.

Plain Opal

Other than a slight scalloping around the top, this pattern has no mentionable features. The color is a light vaseline and the creamer shown is the only reported shape to date. Thanks to the Sandemans for sharing it.

Plain Panels

Plain Panels was made by Northwood in crystal, colored glass, carnival glass, and opalescent glass, and later by Dugan/Diamond in carnival glass. The opalescent production by Northwood dates from 1908. Colors are white, blue, and green, but certainly vaseline may have been made. There are six ribbed panels with plain panels between each one. The ribs run from near the base to the top, forming knobby flames. Sizes range from 9" to 14" tall.

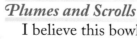

Plumes and Scrolls

I believe this bowl may be American but have no proof. In fact, I have no information on this bowl at all, not even the size. The only thing I can positively say is that it's a ruffled bowl in blue opalescent. I can't even find any records as to who sent me the photo, so I guess its open season on any information readers can supply me on this mystery pattern.

Poinsettia

Northwood's Poinsettia, also known as Big Daisy, is found mainly on water sets but is also known on syrups, bowls, and sugar shakers,. The pitcher shapes vary from a semi-cannonball type to three other tankard styles, and even a ring-necked one. Poinsettia dates from 1902 and can be found in white, cranberry, blue, green, and rarely canary. The tumblers are found in both pressed and blown examples. The bowl, which was made for use in a bride's basket, is most often found without a metal frame. Both the shaker and syrup are quite rare in any color and the tall tankard pitchers are very desirable.

Poinsettia Lattice

This very beautiful Northwood bowl pattern is known in carnival circles as Lattice and Poinsettia, where it is a somewhat rare and very prized pattern. In opalescent glass the colors are limited to white, blue, and vaseline. Production at the Northwood factory dates from 1907. The latticework is exactly like that of a sister pattern called Cherry Lattice that followed a few years later in other types of glass.

Polar Medallions

I'm told by the owner that this milk pitcher is German in origin and I currently have no information indicating it isn't. I feel certain that other shapes were made but none have been reported to me at this time. Vaseline is the only color found so far. Information on additional shapes and colors is appreciated. Thanks to the Sandemans for the photo and to "gbarnm99" for the name.

Polka Dot

This West Virginia Glass Mfg. Company pattern, shown in an 1899 ad, was copied by Northwood and reproduced by L.G. Wright. Shapes in old glass include a water set, cruet, salt shaker, syrup, finger bowl, barber bottle, toothpick holder, sugar shaker, oil lamps in several sizes, and a celery vase. Colors are white, blue, and cranberry opalescent. The pitcher shown is called the West Virginia mould.

Polka Dot with Thorn Handle

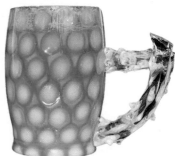

The 5" tall mug shown was purchased in the Czech Republic so I believe it may be from that area, Germany, or even England. The most interesting feature is, of course, the thorn handle, making it more an object to see rather than to hold. The date of production is unknown.

Popsicle Sticks

This is Jefferson Glass Company's #263 pattern. The design is a simple series of wide unstippled rays that fan out from the center of the bowl. Colors are white, blue, and green opalescent glass, and it is found on large bowl shapes with a pedestal base. Shapes include ruffled edges, a banana bowl shape, and even a squared shape.

Poseidon

I suspect the maker of this very well done pattern is either German or English. The shapes reported to me are bowls of various sizes and shapes, butter dish with lid and a plate. I suspect other shapes certainly exist. All pieces reported so far have been in vaseline opalescent, with the exception of one bowl in white opalescent. Anyone having additional information is requested to contact me. Thanks to the Sandemans for the photo and to Thom from the Vaseline Glass Group for giving this pattern its name.

Poseidon Shell

This rather large bowl with a beaded shell design from Greener and Co. measures a whopping 8½" x 4¾" and is of very thick glass. It has two scroll type handles at each end and sports four bracket style feet. The Rd. #113896 indicates a production date of Nov. 15, 1888. This is the only color and shape reported at this time. Thanks to the Petrasichs for sharing this very nice piece.

Pram

Here is a really neat novelty piece from Greener and Co. that should be considered fairly tough to find. It measures 6½" long by 3" wide. It has Rd. #150277 which indicates a production date of June 3, 1890. The pattern is also known as Carriage. This interesting carriage is certainly a piece that would cause much conversation in any collection. This is the only size known and blue opalescent is the only reported color to date. Many thanks to the Petrasichs for the photo and information.

Prayer Rug

In previous editions the Prayer Rug bonbon came as quite a surprise since it was made mostly in custard glass and iridized custard glass. Now I'm pleased to finally show the vase. Both are Fenton pieces dating from 1914. While the bonbon can be found in either blue or vaseline opalescent, the vase has only been reported to date in vaseline opal. Thanks to Donna Drohan for sharing it. (Please note that most of these pieces once had paint or gilding that has mostly worn off.)

Preakness

In this edition I've eliminated some of the single lily epergnes shown in previous editions since the lily was interchangeable with various metal holders and they could mostly be lumped together, which I've done in the price guide under Universal Epergne. However, this is one I felt should be shown because of its uniqueness. The design is an allover diamond pattern and this particular one has a cranberry edge treatment. Thanks to Marty Vogel for sharing this nice piece.

Pressed Coinspot (#617)

This compote (advertised as a card tray) first showed up in a 1901 National Glass catalog and then showed up in a Dugan ad for an Oriental assortment, labeled #617. The vase shape later became known as Concave Columns and in carnival glass it is simply called Coinspot. Shapes from the same mould are tall vases, compotes, goblets, and a stemmed banana boat shape. Colors in opalescent glass are white, blue, green, and canary.

Pressed Diamond

The owner of this 13" x 5" boat shaped bowl tells me that Central Glass is the maker and I have no reason to doubt that attribution at this time. This very large piece has only been reported to me in white opalescent but certainly other colors and shapes are possible. Thanks to the Petrasichs for sharing it.

Primrose Scroll

This is another beautiful pattern from England. It has flowers and a scroll as well as occasional filler dots. It has a 6" diameter and a glass applied ring to fit in a holder of some sort. Additional information would be appreciated.

Primrose Shade

This rubina verde shade with opalescent treatment is a wonder to behold. I've also seen a water pitcher in this same design in canary opalescent. Hobbs, Brockunier introduced this process (vaseline and cranberry with opalescence) in 1884 and I suspect this may be their pattern. The pattern is similar to the Daffodils pattern shown elsewhere.

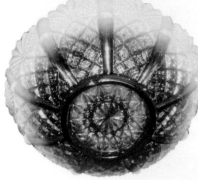

Prince Charles

This English pattern is similar to both Princess Diana and Queen's Crown. It can be found in amber as shown, an indication it may have been made at Greener & Company. The 4" bowl shown has a metal holder. Photo courtesy of Mary and John Petrasich.

Princess Diana

This Davidson of England pattern was from 1890 and is also known as Suite 1890 or Queen Anne. Shapes include a crimped oval plate (8", 10", and 12"), crimped round plate (7", 8½", 10½", 12"), crimped round dish (6", 7½", 9", 10½"), crimped oval dish (10½"), covered butter dish, creamer, footed sugar, biscuit jar and plate, water set (pitcher in both pint and half-pint), salad bowl, and water platter. Colors in opalescent glass are the usual blue and canary.

Prince William

This pattern, made by Davidson in 1893, carried an Rd. #217752. It is found in an oval plate, a creamer, open sugar, child's water set, and the rare handled basket shown. This piece is 6½" long and stands 3½" tall. Colors are either blue or canary for pieces in this pattern as far as I know.

Prism Hobnail

This nice little creamer is interesting in that each hobnail has a distinct scoring added to it. The color is vaseline and I believe it to be English but have no concrete proof to date. Additional information would be appreciated. Photo courtesy of the Petrasichs.

Pulled Coinspot

These mugs are a puzzle in a couple of ways. First the design has been pulled into ovals rather than the usual dots and then the coloring blends from a cranberry glass at the base to a clear glass above. The maker is unknown and I welcome any information about these pieces. Thanks to Mary and John Petrasich for sharing them.

Pulled Loop

This 1906 Dugan/Diamond opalescent glass vase pattern is well known to carnival glass collectors too. Opalescent pieces are limited and found in white, green, and blue. Sizes range from 9" to 14" in height and there are at least two base sizes, 3" diameter and 5" diameter. There are six ribs with very extended tops and six rows of panels that contain the loops. The Pulled Loop pattern was advertised as #1030.

Pump and Trough

This pattern was shown in a 1900 Pitkin and Brooks catalog along with other North-wood Glass Company items. The very interesting Pump and Trough pieces are listed as #566 and #567, respectively. Colors listed are white, blue, and canary. The design of these items typifies the trend toward naturalism in so many Northwood glass products (Grapevine Clusters, Ocean Shell, Leaf Chalice, and even the Dolphin compote), a trend that continued into their carnival production to some degree with the famous Town Pump. Of course, as with many good things, the Pump and Trough has been widely reproduced, so beware of pumps with flat tops!

Pussy Willow

This little vase stands 4½" tall. The shape is somewhat like one in the Dugan/Diamond Pompeian and Japanese assortment advertised in 1906, but this one has an opalescent design of ovals on the diagonal, connected by a fine line of opalescence. Other colors were probably made and there may be another name for this piece, but this name is what the owner calls it.

Queen's Candlesticks

Queen's Candlestick is now known to be from Greener & Company (Rd. #17637). It is very similar to the Queen's Spill shown elsewhere. These date from 1891 and stand 2½" tall. They were probably made in blue opalescent also.

Queen's Crown

This very scarce pattern is from England, made by Davidson in 1898 as their #320124 registered design. It is found in either small bowls or a low standard compote (certainly other shapes may have been made). Colors are blue and the canary shown here (the view is of the interior of the compote).

Queen's Spill

This very pretty Greener & Company spill vase stands 4" tall and is 3¼" wide at the top. It was part of the Pearline glass production of 1891. Colors are blue and canary opalescent. If you will compare the Quilted Daisy Fairy Lamp to this piece, you will see they are similar.

Queen Victoria

The pattern on this Davidson ruffled plate is actually one I show elsewhere in this book called Somerset. Here, the pattern was registered in 1895 as #254027. This piece with Queen Victoria's portrait was obviously made to honor the Golden Jubilee of her reign in 1887. The portrait seems to be a form of photo transfer. Since Somerset was made in blue opalescent also, surely this piece was offered in that color.

Question Marks

It is difficult to use only one name for this well-known Dugan pattern, for it actually is not one but three patterns. The interior is called Question Marks, the exterior pattern is known as Georgia Belle, and the stem has a pattern called Puzzle! These compotes are mostly known in carnival glass, but here is a beautiful blue opalescent glass. I suspect it may have been made in white opalescent also, but no examples have been verified at this time. It was reproduced in vaseline.

Quilt

This 5¼" bowl is a real mystery. Only the opalescence gives a clue that it is probably a Sowerby product. It is oval (many English bowls are), has an oversized collar base, and the opalescence is almost uniform over the piece rather than on the high spots as on American glass. I'd appreciate any information on this pattern.

Quilted Daisy

Anyone who doesn't appreciate this beauty just doesn't like opalescent glass. It is English, I'm sure, and has a superb canary color. The base is hard to see since it is a plain color without any milky finish. The design is diamonds bordered by sections of daisy filler with a skirt of points below a similar band of points. This piece was made by Greener in 1891 in white and blue as well as canary.

Quilted Phlox Lattice

This Northwood piece is on a Quilted Phlox mould but has the lattice opalescent treatment. It was probably an experimental combination, dating from the 1895 – 1905 era. It may have been made in blue and cranberry as well. Shown is a sugar shaker, but the pattern is also known on a syrup, toothpick, and salt shaker as well.

Quilted Pillow Sham

Quilted Pillow Sham, also known as Pattern 900, was made by Davidson in 1893. This pattern is found in canary and blue opalescent glass. Shapes include a creamer, handled open sugar, and a covered butter dish. The design is distinctive with a petticoat base, an allover diamond quilting, and a collar of glass below the top of each piece.

Quilted Rose

I've learned very little about this interesting pattern except that it is probably European. The pattern is an allover one on the tumbler shown. I must assume there is probably a matching pitcher. I welcome any information from readers about this design.

Rainbow Stripe

This strange flared blown glass compote (it has a pontil) is believed to be from England. It has an unusual shading of opalescent striping that varies from vaseline to cranberry. I thank Ruth Harvey for sharing it and welcome any information about its origin.

Raised Rib

This was Fenton's #857 pattern, made in the cameo opalescent treatment in 1929. Shown is an 11" flared bowl on a dome base, but ads show a deep cupped bowl from the same mould. Thanks to the Petrasichs for this piece.

Raspberry Prunts

This interesting creamer is the first of its kind I've seen. It is believed to be from Stuart and Sons Limited of England, although positive proof of such has not been established. The applied handle, rolled feet, and application of the prunts make for an unusual design. This is the only shape I've seen and vaseline is the only reported color. If anyone knows of other shapes or colors I'd appreciate hearing from them, as well as any additional information about this piece. Photo courtesy of the Sandemans.

Ray

I now know this pattern was from Co-operative Flint Glass. It was advertised in crystal and gilded crystal in 1904, but this company isn't known for making opalescent glass until the 1920s. I've seen this vase in a dark blue, a dark green, and white opalescent glass. The example shown is 13" tall and has a 3½" base diameter.

Rayed Heart

Although often credited to the Dominion Glass Company of Canada, the opalescent pieces certainly came from Jefferson Glass in this country before the moulds traveled north. This pretty compote dates from 1910; came in blue, green, and white in opalescent glass; and can be found in crystal, probably Canadian. I know of no other shapes or colors.

Rayed Jane

This Dugan nappy is like the Plain Jane stemmed nappy shown elsewhere in this book, except it has scalloped edges and interior rays. Just why a glass company would make two such similar pieces has always been a mystery, but both are quite attractive. The Rayed Jane nappy comes from the 1909 – 1914 era and was made in white and green opalescent too.

Reeds and Blossoms

The Petrasichs have given this bowl its fitting name. It has the look of English glass with a collarless base and the design extending below it. The pattern is a simple one with waving stems and leaves and small flowers.

Reflecting Diamonds

Let me say again, while they were both Dugan patterns, Reflecting Diamonds is not the same pattern as Compass. Reflecting Diamonds appears on bowl shapes only and has been found as early as 1905 in Butler Brothers ads featuring Dugan/Diamond patterns. This geometric pattern, like so many others, has a series of diamonds filled with a file pattern bordered by fan shapes standing back-to-back between the diamonds. The base has the exact overlapping star design as that found on the Compass base.

Reflections

This Dugan design is a difficult pattern to locate. It is found on footed novelty bowls, sometimes round or sometimes squared, like shown. Colors are white, blue, and green opalescent. The pattern was continued from Dugan into Diamond production (it was signed with the Diamond-D mark on some pieces). Thanks to John Loggie for sharing it.

Regal

This pattern is certainly rightly named for it has a regal look. It was made by the Northwood Company in 1905, and some pieces are marked. Regal can be found in table sets, jelly compote, water sets, berry sets, salt shakers, and cruets in white, green, and blue opalescent glass as well as in crystal and emerald green glass with gilding. The pattern was also known as Blocked Midriff, but the Regal name is more widely used.

Reverse Drapery

This Fenton pattern (also called Cut Arcs in carnival glass) is sometimes confused with Boggy Bayou from the same maker. It is found on bowls as well as vases (shown in a regular and a pulled vase). Opalescent colors are white, blue, green, and amethyst.

Reverse Swirl

This well-known Buckeye Glass, and later Model Flint Glass pattern dates from 1888. It is found on lamps, berry sets, table sets, water sets, sugar shaker, salt shaker, syrup (shown), cruet, custard cup, toothpick holder, mustard pot, water bottles, a finger bowl, night lamps, a caster set, a rare tall salt shaker, and lamp shades for tall metal or hanging lamps. Colors are white, blue, canary, and cranberry in opalescent glass. Items may be satin finished on some places too.

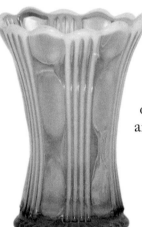

Rib and Big Thumbprints

This vase was shown in a Butler Brothers ad in 1906 for Dugan/Diamond and in a 1908 Jefferson ad in the same catalog! The design of four ribs in five columns with spots of opalescence between must have been a popular one for both companies. It appears to be another example of copying what sells. Colors are green, white, and blue opalescent.

Ribbed Beaded Cable

This is just like the regular Beaded Cable pieces made by the Northwood Glass Company in 1904, except it has added interior ribbing. Found on both opalescent pieces and carnival items, this ribbed version is much scarcer than the plain interior pieces. Colors in opalescent glass are blue, green, white, and canary.

Ribbed Coinspot

Ribbed Coinspot was made by Northwood in 1888, in white, blue, and cranberry opalescent glass on water sets, table sets, a syrup, shakers, and a celery vase. It is actually the Coinspot pattern blown into a ribbed mould. Thanks to the Petrasichs.

Ribbed Epergne

I can only imagine the original cost of this exquisite five-lily epergne in its very fancy base. I can see it as being a centerpiece to grace any table, and certainly a focal point in any collection. It is most certainly European. This is the first time I've seen these particular ribbed lilies. Vaseline is the only reported color. Thanks to Dennis Crouse for sharing this wonderful epergne.

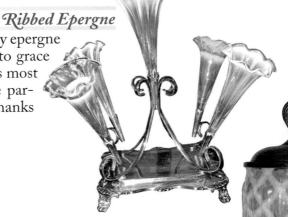

Ribbed (Opal) Lattice

This is probably a Northwood Glass pattern but may have been an earlier LaBelle Glass product. It is found in water sets, a cruet, salt shakers, syrup, table set, berry set, toothpick holder, sugar shakers in two sizes, and a celery vase. Colors are white, blue, cranberry, and vaseline.

Ribbed Opal Rings

Ribbed Opal Rings is sometimes called Ribbed Opal Spiral. The pattern is believed to be from the Northwood Company. It is found on water sets and a sugar bowl. Colors are white, blue, and cranberry opalescent.

Ribbed Optic

The Fenton Company made this pattern in 1927 in the bedroom set or tumble-up (the tumbler is missing) in green, vaseline, blue, and the light cranberry shown. The water bottle is 6" tall and has a base diameter of 3½".

Ribbed Pillar

This Northwood pattern is also called Northwood Pleat by some collectors. Like the Apple Blossom mould, the name of this pattern refers to the mould shaping. It was Northwood's #245 pattern, found in crystal spatter or acid etched. Shapes include a berry set, water set, table set, sugar shaker, cruet, syrup, salt shaker, and a celery vase.

Ribbed Spiral

This was #911 from Model Flint Glass (1899 – 1902). It can be found in crystal as well as white, blue, and canary opalescent glass. Shapes include 4", 7", 8", 9", and 10" bowls (either round or square), a table set, celery vase, 7¾", 9¼", and 11" plates, a salt and pepper, toothpick holder, water set, custard cup, jelly compote, lemonade glass, and vases that range from 4" to 21" tall.

Ribbed Triangle and Fans

Although this pattern resembles Davidson's Victoria and Albert pattern, it is a registered Greener and Co. piece with Rd. #284639. This gives it a date of 9/23/1886, which was 11 months before the Victoria and Albert pattern was in fact registered. This oval 9½" x 7½" bowl is the only reported shape to date and blue opalescent is the only color I've seen. Anyone having additional shapes or colors is urged to contact me. Thanks once again to the Petrasichs for sharing it and I hope they approve of the name.

Ribbon Wave

This nice salt in metal holder is likely from England, and dates from 1880 to 1890. It has a wave band applied around the center and the only reported color is the rubina verde shown. Any information would be appreciated. Photo courtesy of the Sandemans.

Richelieu

Richelieu was made by Davidson of England with Rd. #96945 or #96943. Shapes include a jelly compote, creamer, divided dish, biscuit jar, handled basket, handled fold basket, oval bowl, oval dish, square basket, salad bowl, handled nappy, footed sugar, tumbler, pitcher, and probably a water tray. Colors are blue, white, and canary in opalescent glass.

Ric-Rac

This unusual blown vase in vaseline stands 8¼" tall and has a pontil mark on the base. The glass is very thin, and I suspect it is English. If anyone knows it by another name, I'd be interested in hearing from them. It may well have been made in other colors, including white and blue.

Rigoree

This very attractive sauce bowl is probably English, made in the 1890s. It is a ribbed optic stripe opalescent piece in rubina verde with a vaseline rigoree (ribbon) ring applied. I don't need to tell anyone this is opalescent glass art at its best and the piece shown would be a standout in any collection.

Rigoree Spill

This beautiful spill vase has just a touch of rubina at the top and ribbons of rigoree along the sides and top. I suspect it is English but can't determine the maker. I certainly welcome any information and thank Ruth Harvey for sharing it.

Ringed Barrel

The owner of this piece (it is either a toothpick holder or a spittoon shape) pointed out its similarities to the Triangle piece from Sowerby I show elsewhere in this book. I believe they are both from that concern (both have three ball feet and little decoration). This piece has no RD number but surely dates to the 1890s.

Ringed Flute with Beaded Medallions

The owner of this nice basket tells me it is likely Greener and Sons and I can't disagree at this point. The basket stands 5¾" tall by 6" at the widest point. Blue is the only reported color at this time. I like the design of this basket and would love to hear from anyone who has additional information about it. Thanks again to the Petrasichs for sharing it.

Ring Handled Basket

This fine center-handled basket has the same basic design as Opal Open (Beaded Panels). The same design is found on salt shakers. Colors are white, blue, green, and vaseline, and the white opalescent may sometimes have a clambroth effect. The Ring Handled Basket measures 7½" wide. It was made by Dugan/Diamond, I believe, but may have also been a Northwood product.

Rings and Arches

I have no information on this bowl but believe it to be English. The design consists of two sets of fine cut rings within double arches and the base is a star pattern. This is the only shape reported to me at this time and blue opalescent is the only color I've heard of. I urge anyone with information on this pattern to contact me. Thanks to the Petrasichs for sharing it.

Rings with Wave Band

With its applied wavy band, rings circling the stem from top to bottom, and the finecut pineapple look to the base, this 5¾" vase certainly has an English flavor to it. Vaseline is the only reported color. Thanks to Joan and Wayne Jolliffe for sharing this very nice vase with me.

Ripple

This scarce Ripple vase, made by Imperial, has a many rayed base and is more flared at the top. Colors reported so far are blue, vaseline, and green, but surely white was also made. This was a very popular carnival glass design, made in at least four base diameters and many carnival colors.

Rococo

Thanks to the research of Siegmar Geiselberger of Germany, I can now say this pattern was a product of the Fenne Glassworks in Saarland, Germany. Pieces known are a bowl that fits a bride's basket and the 10" ruffled plate shown. There are some variations to the design and the Casbah pattern seems to be one of these. Photo courtesy of the Sandemans.

Rolled Wide Stripe

This interesting tumbler from England is only 2½"tall and may really be a spill vase. I do not know the maker and would appreciate any information from readers. Thanks to Ruth Harvey for sharing it.

Rose

This pattern, also called Rose & Ruffles, was first made at Tiffin and later at their U.S. Glass factory. It is seldom seen in opalescent glass but shapes known are candlesticks, a cologne (shown), vase, powder jar (two sizes), pomade jar, covered bowl (large), small bowl, dresser tray, and tall compote. Colors in opalescent glass are blue and canary. This pattern has been copied by Fenton in several shapes and treatments so beware of reproductions and look for the Fenton logo.

Rose Bush

This extremely well done 5¼" wall pocket with flowers, leaves, and twig handle has been reported on white opalescent only, although other colors may exist. This was probably made by Burtles, Tate & Co. or Molineaux Webb & Co. in the 1880s. Anyone with additional information is urged to contact me. Thanks to John & Mary Petrasich for sharing this nice piece with me.

Rose Show

Although known primarily as a carnival glass pattern, this very beautiful bowl can be found in limited amounts in white and blue opalescent glass. Rose Show is reputed to be a Northwood pattern. The bowl has a reverse pattern of Woven Wonder, a spin-off design of Frosted Leaf and Basketweave.

Rose Spatter

While I still feel the water set I showed in a previous edition is either Buckeye Glass or Beaumont, I feel the Northwood Company had a try in this same coloring. Here is a ruffled vase that certainly looks like Northwood. It is the first reported and I'm happy to show it.

Rose Spray

Although found mostly in carnival glass, this Fenton compote can be seen on rare occasions on opalescent glass. Colors are white (French), blue, and amethyst, and all are scarce. Production dates from 1910 to 1914. The design of a stem, leaves, and a rose is little more than a line drawing and is very hard to see.

Roulette

Roulette was made by the Northwood Company and shown in one of their ads in a Lyon Brothers 1906 glass catalog. This is not one of their better designs, consisting of a series of ovals that are bordered by beading, with a stylized three-petal flower between each. Opalescent colors are the usual white, blue, and green. All pieces are dome based and from the same mould, despite a variety of shapings.

Royal Fan

This small whimsey posy has an overall coverage of overlapping fans. Other than the top being ruffled, it has the look of a ladies' cuspidor in some respects. Vaseline is the only color reported to me and this is the only shape I've seen to date. I feel certain it is English and would love to hear from anyone having additional information on this piece. Photo courtesy of the Sandemans.

Royal Jubilee

This British pattern, which is credited to Greener & Company, can be found in blue, vaseline, and amber opalescent glass. The shape is a footed novelty basket (other shapes probably exist) with a scroll curling on each end of the elongated piece. The pattern somewhat resembles a zipper design.

Royal Scandal

This superb English wall pocket vase is one of four designs I've seen, and all are well above the ordinary in the glassmaker's art. Royal Scandal has no Rd. number but most of these pieces were made in the 1880s or early 1890s by various makers. The design is a series of rope-like strips over a shell and flower pattern. Royal Scandal is known in blue, canary, and white opalescent glass and some are found with felt-backed mounting pieces.

Royal Sunburst

I'm certain this is English but haven't found any information about it to date. Only the bowl shape has been reported to me at this time and vaseline is the only color. I do suspect other shapes were made and blue is a possibility. Any information about this pattern would be appreciated. Thanks to the Sandemans for the photo and name.

Rubina Diamonds

I'm not sure that this pattern was made by Hobb's like the regular rubina verde pattern shown next. I'm not even certain of its age. The pattern is an overall coverage of diamonds and the shape is a jack-in-the-pulpit with ribbon candy edge (notice the twist at the bottom of the edge treatment). If anyone knows anything about this piece I urge you to contact me. Photo courtesy of Marty Vogel.

Rubina Verde

Rubina Verde was made by Hobbs, Brockunier & Company in the 1880s. It is actually a combination of canary and ruby glass, with the ruby plated over the canary or portions thereof. Some pieces are acid finished. Shown is a 6½" tall jack-in-the-pulpit vase with opalescence on the reverse of the throat. Other patterns such as Dewdrop (Hobnail) were made in this formula. All are truly fine pieces of art glass at its best.

Ruffles and Rings

Ruffles and Rings is another of the Jefferson Glass patterns that came into the Northwood production orbit. The opalescent version appears to have been made in 1906 and after. In carnival glass, the pattern has been found as an exterior one with such designs as Rosette and even on a rare flint opalescent bowl with no interior pattern, marigold iridizing, and an added floral border edging. Colors in opalescent glass are white, blue, and green, with various shapes existing.

Ruffles and Rings with Daisy Band

Just why the Northwood Company decided to do this variant of the Ruffles and Rings pattern is a mystery, but here they've added a classy banding of daisies along the outer edge. Since both Jefferson and Northwood are credited with Ruffles and Rings, perhaps the unbanded pieces are Jefferson's that were later made by Northwood who then added the band. At any rate, Northwood later made both versions in carnival glass and a very rare example of marigold with an opalescent daisy band exists. Opalescent colors are the usual white, blue, and green.

Salmon

According to Cyril Manley in his book *Decorative English Glass*, this fish bowl was made by Molineaux Webb Glass Works in 1885 with a registry number of 29781. It is found in white opalescent glass as well as the canary opalescent shown. Manley calls it a posy bowl. It is also known as Pink. Molineaux Webb was a glass factory in Manchester, England.

Scheherezade

While the maker of this very pretty pattern has not been confirmed, I really believe I need look no further than the Dugan/Diamond Company. Found primarily in bowls, the opalescent colors are white, blue, and green. The design of file triangles, finecut triangles, and hobstars is a close cousin to Dugan's Reflecting Diamonds, but it has more than enough difference to distinguish it from any other pattern. Scheherezade is a rather scarce pattern but well worth looking for.

Scottish Moor

This pattern is attributed to the West Virginia Glass Company by some collectors. It is found in only a limited number of shapes (pitcher, tumbler, cruet, cup, celery, cracker jar and vase). It was made in the usual opalescent colors of white, amber, and blue, as well as in cranberry, rubina, and a light amethyst color. Here I show the water pitcher and you will note the handle is reeded. Production may have been as early as 1890 or as late as 1900, but I have no evidence of an exact date.

Scroll

This 4½" high by 6⅛" bowl is very light vaseline opalescent and the glass is quite thin. The design is similar to Buttons and Braids but without the buttons. I certainly don't think it's a Fenton product, but believe it is possibly English in origin. It does have somewhat of a Model Flint Glass look, but this is only guesswork. Any information is welcomed on this pattern. Thanks to the Petrasichs for sharing it.

Scroll with Acanthus

Credited to the Northwood Company, Scroll with Acanthus can be found in water sets, table sets, berry sets, a jelly compote, salt shaker, toothpick holder, and cruet. Colors are white, blue, and canary opalescent glass with some novelties in green opalescent, crystal, and purple slag, as well as decorated green and blue crystal. Production dates from 1903.

Scroll with Buttons

For the lack of a better name I've given this pattern one. The intricate pattern on this white opalescent 4⅜" creamer is very nicely done and I only wish I knew more about it. Additional information is requested. Photo courtesy of the Petrasichs, and I certainly thank them again for sharing so much of their nice collection with me.

Scroll with Cane Band

This pattern was made by the West Virginia Glass Company in crystal, ruby stain, and possibly gilded glass. I was very surprised to see this wonderful green opalescent bowl. This pattern dates to 1895 and could possibly have been a treatment testing, but no other pieces have been reported. Thanks to the Petrasichs for sharing it with me.

Sea Scroll

I've seen this piece in a book section devoted to Davidson glass so I now know it was made by that company in England. Pieces include the compote shown as well as one on a very short stem that would be called a dessert in this country. Colors known are white, blue, green, and canary in opalescent glass and all are beautiful. The compote shape measures 4¾" tall, with a base diameter of 2⅝". The shorter piece is 3¼" tall.

Sea Shore

This blue opalescent bowl looks to be American to me but I have yet to find it in any old catalogs or other reference material. The pattern reminds me of waves rolling on a sandy beach with a shell inside a shell being the center of attention. This is the only shape and color I've heard of at this time. Thanks to the Sandemans once again for the nice photo.

Sea Spray

This is Jefferson Glass Company's #192 pattern from 1906 – 1907. The only shape reported is the very attractive nappy (round or tricorner shaped). The colors are the usual white, green, and blue opalescent. The design is somewhat similar to the S-Repeat but has an interesting beading added.

Seaweed

This pattern was first made by Hobbs, Brockunier in water sets, a salt shaker, a syrup, table sets, berry sets, a barber bottle, a sugar shaker, a pickle caster, a cruet, and two sizes of oil bottle. It has become confused with a pattern called Coral Reef. The differences lie in the shaping of the small bulb and line patterns and if you will make a comparison of both, you will be able to instantly tell them apart. Hobbs made both patterns and Coral Reef was also made by Beaumont and possibly Northwood a few years after the Hobbs production. Colors in Seaweed are white, blue, and cranberry.

Seaweed Variant

This is somewhat different than the regular Seaweed pattern, and I believe it to be American. I think this is a very nice looking vase and do love the top shape with its candy ribbon edge and the way the opposite sides are turned down. Some may consider this rubina verde (and they may be right) but in my opinion it is white opalescent with cranberry edging. I hope someone can shed more light on this nice pattern. Photo courtesy of the Sandemans.

Serpent Threads Epergne

This stately epergne stands 23" tall. The glass is very thin and fine, and each lily fits into a brass holder. This epergne was made in vaseline opalescent with or without cranberry frit on the edges, and can be found with a ruffled or a candy ribbon edged base. The lilies are decorated with glass banding. It is probably European and possibly from Italy, but I have no proof. Thanks to Marty Vogel for sharing this beauty.

Shamrock

This is the first one of these lamps I've seen. The font is vaseline opalescent and shows what certainly would pass for a shamrock design. The base is black glass. This is the only color reported to me and I've seen no other sizes of this lamp at this time. Again, thanks to the Sandemans for sharing this nice oil lamp with me.

Sharks Tooth

Reported to date in this pattern is a spooner and oil lamp in vaseline opalescent and smoke shade in rubina verde; a process which combined vaseline and cranberry with opalescence added. Hobbs, Brockunier introduced this treatment in 1884 but I have no proof that this rare shade is from that company. John Walsh Walsh is another possibility. It was also known as Christmas Trees in previous editions. Thanks to the Sandemans for the photo and the name.

Sheldon Swirl

These Buckeye Glass Company lamps (shown in two sizes) are of course, Reverse Swirl pattern, and are highly desirable to collectors. Colors are white, blue, canary (shown), and cranberry, and are sometimes found with a satin finish or with a speckled treatment. The distinctive stem design gives this lamp its name.

Shell

These two shell dishes (blue: 4½" long, vaseline: 5½" long) were made by Geo. Davidson. They both appeared in a 1912 catalog that featured various items for the soda fountain. (I am told these are ice cream dishes but haven't confirmed this to date.) It is not known if the blue came in the long size and the vaseline in the short size as they are so rare. Thanks to David Peterson for the photos and John Bell for the catalog reference source.

Shell and Dots

Shell and Dots, made by the Jefferson Company in 1905, is nothing more than the well-known Beaded Fans pattern with a series of bubble-like dots on the base. This pattern can be found in white, green, and blue opalescent.

Shell and Wild Rose

This 1906 Northwood pattern is called Wild Rose by carnival glass collectors. The Wild Rose pattern is exterior, but the interior can be plain or have a stippled ray design of which there are two variations. Opalescent colors are white, blue, green, and the very rare vaseline shown. The open edged inverted heart border is a real piece of mould maker's art.

Shell Beaded

While this Dugan pattern is known as Shell in opalescent glass, collectors of carnival and other types of glass recognize it as the Beaded Shell pattern. It was made in 1905, in a host of shapes including water sets, berry sets, cruet, toothpick holder, salt shaker, mug, rare compotes, and cruet set. Colors are white, green, blue, canary, electric blue, and apple green plus carnival colors. It has been reproduced by Mosser.

Shoe

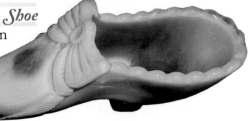

This English novelty shoe had an Rd. #65455 indicating it was made in 1887. It is a simple shoe design with a bow near the top of the opening. Blue is the only color I've had reported but expect other colors were made. Photo courtesy of the Petrasichs.

Silver Overlay Vase

Several companies made silver overlay treatments of glass, including Westmoreland, Cambridge, and Heisey. The vase shown here was made at the Dugan/Diamond factory and has an added treat of opalescent glass. The example here is about 7" tall and is really the Dugan's Junior JIP vase shown elsewhere with a silver overlay treatment!

Simple Simon

Carnival glass collectors know this pattern as Graceful. It was a product of the Northwood Company dating from 1908 to 1909. In carnival glass, it is made in most Northwood non-pastel colors, but in opalescent glass the colors are limited to green, white, and a scarce blue. While the design isn't too well planned, the compote's shape adds class, and the workmanship is quality.

Singing Birds

Singing Birds is one of Northwood's best-known patterns, especially in carnival glass. The mug is also found in rare opalescent pieces in white, blue, and vaseline (shown). In addition, tumblers have been reproduced and I show an example in section III.

Single Poinsettia

With the evidence of this bowl in amethyst opalescent glass, I can now declare the maker of this pattern Fenton. Bowls are found in ruffled or the squared shape shown. Thanks to John Loggie III for sharing this find with me.

Sir Lancelot

Sir Lancelot was advertised in a Butler Brothers ad in 1906 along with several well-known Northwood patterns, including Shell and Wild Rose, Diamond Point, and Hilltop Vines. The shapes are novelty bowls with a dome base in white, blue, and green opalescent glass. The design, three fleur-de-lis and three starburst figures on a stippled background, is very interesting and quite attractive. The dome base is rayed.

Six Petals

This Dugan Glass Company pattern, from before 1910, is well known to carnival glass collectors but this is the first example of opalescent glass I've heard about. It is a ruffled 7½" bowl with very heavy opalescence over most of the surface. I suspect green and blue were also made. Thanks to the Hollenbachs for sharing it.

Skirted Dots

I'm uncertain what the function of this piece is; some are calling it a salt dip, some an open sugar, and others a marmalade. I have no dimensions to make a call either way. The looks indicate it being English and this is only a guess. This vaseline piece is the only item reported to me but I feel others may turn up eventually.

Smooth Rib

Since I first showed this simple bowl pattern, I've seen it with a cranberry frit edge like the example shown, so I now suspect this was a Jefferson Glass pattern. The bowl, on a collar base, has 20 interior panels. The collar base (marie) measures 2½" across and the exterior is completely plain. There is also a bowl in a metal holder known. Colors are white, blue, vaseline, and green.

Snail Loop and Ball

I'm told that this supposedly English creamer (maker and origin is uncertain) is known by the name I've listed, but some collectors also know it as Porpoise. White is the only color I've seen and the creamer is the only reported shape at this time. Photo courtesy of the Petrasichs.

Snowball Royale

The owner of this rare Christmas ornament (vaseline opalescent only found to date) is likely correct in saying that this pattern is of British origin, due to the fact that the previous owner bought three examples at the Newark Antique Fair in England. As you can guess, these ornaments are able to be displayed in various ways, either on a table stand, a table wire hanger, or a tree by the attached wire loop. If you locate one of these be prepared to pay a hefty price as they don't sell cheap. Many thanks once again to Dave and Vickie Peterson for sharing another rarity from their fine collection.

Snowflake

This pattern is actually from Hobbs, Brockunier & Company, not Northwood, as I stated in a previous edition of this book. It is called Daisy or Clover Leaf in trade papers. Date of production was 1891, and shapes and sizes include flat and footed hand lamps, a sewing lamp, a night lamp with matching shade, and five styles of stand lamps. Colors are white, blue, and cranberry opalescent. Shown are a hand lamp in white and a table lamp in cranberry.

Snowflake Spatter

If you compare this vase and its treatment with other pieces of spatter ware, you will see this piece has a much finer allover opalescent look, rather like a snowstorm. This is a Dugan vase and sometimes this treatment is called granite. It is known in white, green, and blue as far as I know.

Snowstorm

This is not truly an opalescent treatment in the strict sense of the term. This pattern, made by Hobbs, Brockunier, is really a rubina overlay treatment with white craquelle added. It dates to the mid-1880s and is found in 7" bowls, a 6½" crimped rose bowl, and the 6½" smooth-top rose bowl shown. Thanks to Don and Jane Henson for the nice photo.

Solar Flare

I think this is a really good name for this pattern. The outer flames certainly appear to be activity coming off the surface of the sun. This vaseline plate is the only piece I've had reported as of this writing, but I'd be willing to bet there are other shapes and possibly other colors in this pattern that will show up by the next edition. Photo courtesy of the Sandemans.

Somerset

Somerset was made by Davidson in 1895 with an Rd. #254027. Shapes reported are an 8" bowl, two shapes of nappies, oval dish in five sizes, small pitcher, sugar bowl, 3" tumbler, underplate for the water set, and a waste bowl. Other shapes are shown in an 1896 catalog but are unreported to me at this time. Colors are blue and vaseline opalescent. The pattern is considered highly collectible and is quite expensive.

Sowerby Basket

This dainty little basket measures only 3½" by 2" and is a real treasure for any collection. The looped handles are ribbed and step up from bottom to top. This is a Sowerby product that has the diamond lozenge dating it to 1879. I like the tight shape between the handles and would love to see it in another color, however white opalescent is the only color I've seen at this time. Thanks again to the Petrasichs for sharing this beauty.

Spanish Lace

This pattern, introduced by the Northwood Company to American collectors in 1899, has also been known as Opaline Brocade. Shapes made are water sets (three pitcher styles), table sets, cruet, salt shaker, wine decanter (very rare), night lamp, water bottle, perfume bottle, rose bowl, a celery vase, and vases in several sizes. In addition several items are fitted with metal parts including a bride's basket and cracker jar. Colors are white, blue, and cranberry, with limited production of some shapes in green, and a few items in a canary that are likely of an English origin. A handled basket, a cruet, and a rose bowl have recently been made by Fenton in cranberry, but these are the only items that are not old.

Spatter

This treatment was used by both Northwood and Dugan/Diamond on water sets, bowls, and vases, but I feel from both the shape and top design, this piece is from Dugan/Diamond. It stands 9" tall, and the random opalescent swirling through the glass is quite attractive.

Spattered Coinspot

The shape of this very beautiful pitcher seems to be the same ball shape that Northwood used on the Daisy and Fern pitcher, but it may well belong to another maker. I'm confident it is old, dating from the late 1800s. As far as desirability is concerned, it would have to be quite high. The coloring is simply beautiful with spatters of cranberry mixed with flecks of white.

Speckled Celery Vase

Although very similar in appearance to Dugan's Venetian line, this is reported to be a product from the Northwood factory. This shape in the speckled treatment has been reported in blue, white, green, and cranberry.

137

Speckled Chrysanthemum Base (Northwood)

This pattern was first made at American, Buckeye, and then Northwood in their speckled treatment in berry sets, table sets, water sets, a finger bowl, cruet, syrup, toothpick holder, sugar shaker, mustard jar, celery vase, and a lidded straw holder.

Speckled Stripe

This pattern, from Model Flint Glass at Albany, Indiana, is distinguished by the stripe being broken and not solid. It was made in the pitcher shown, a barber bottle, finger bowl and underplate, sugar, and three sizes of vases. Colors are white (clear), blue, and canary opalescent glass.

Spiny Cactus Vase

The Hollenbachs named these vases and say a former owner of the small ones got them in England in the 1940s. I believe they are called thorn vases and are mould blown with applied feet. I've heard of them in canary as well as the white shown. The large vase is 5" tall and the small ones are 3¹⁄₈" tall.

Spiralex Vase

If you compare this vase and the Twisted Rib vase shown elsewhere in this edition, you will see it swirls to the right and the Spiralex swirls to the left. In addition, the latter has thinner ribs and less of a ball on the top of each rib. Both are from Dugan and then Diamond Glass.

Spiral Optic (Fenton)

Fenton's Spiral Optic was made with the same treatment as the Stripe pieces from other companies. This is the first example I've heard about in amethyst opalescent glass. I believe this piece dates from the 1915 production of this color but have no proof. Amethyst opalescent glass was first made in 1908 and continued until 1918 or 1919.

Spiral Web

This marmalade bowl was made in the Stourbridge region of England, circa 1900s. It has an interlocking spiral opalescent pattern reminiscent of a spider web. The maker is believed to be Thomas Webb, but I have no positive identification. The glass is vaseline, with a vaseline petticoat retaining skirt to hold it suspended in the frame. The top rim is cranberry, with opalescent highlights on the outside edge. The base has a polished pontil. Many thanks to Dave Peterson for the photo, name, and information provided.

Spokes and Wheels

This well-known 1906 Northwood Glass Company pattern is found primarily in bowls or plates. Opalescent colors are white, blue, green, and a rare aqua. Please compare this design to the Spokes and Wheels Variant below. This piece is a tri-cornered plate with ruffled edges.

Spokes and Wheels Variant

Just why this variant was made after the first version is a mystery. A close comparison of the two patterns shows the variant has the area between the top of each oval notched out, omitting the blossom and stem that were there. This variant, found mostly on the plates or ruffled plates, is known in white, blue, green, and the rare aqua shown.

Spool

Spool is very similar to Spool of Threads, but without the vertical ribs. The Spool piece surely came first and then the mould was retooled to produce the other design. Both patterns are credited to Northwood and both can be found in the usual white, blue, or green opalescent. In addition, Spool is found in custard glass and purple slag. Shapes of the top may be flared as shown or in a standing candy-ribbon ruffle.

Spool of Threads

This pattern was made by the Northwood Company, first in purple slag in 1902 and then in opalescent glass in 1905. Primarily a compote pattern, this stemmed piece can be shaped in several ways, sometimes ruffled and sometimes not. Opalescent colors are white, blue, canary, and green. The design is a simple one but easily recognized.

Square

This companion pattern to Sowerby's Triangle vase, shown elsewhere, has four sides and feet. The two patterns are exactly the same size but beyond that, I know little. Both blue and white examples are reported and these 4" tall pieces are considered spills or match holders.

Squirrel and Acorn

Here is one of the most appealing patterns in opalescent glass and in the whimsey section I show the vase. At this time, I do not know the maker of this pattern but can tell you it is quite rare, especially in blue and white. It was also made in a very scarce green. The footed bowl, the compote, and the vase are from the same mould showing six panels with alternating designs of a frisky squirrel, acorn, and leaves. The base has a raised scale-like pattern. I'm sure the pattern dates from the 1904 – 1910 era.

S-Repeat (National)

This pattern was first advertised in a Butler Brothers ad from the newly formed Dugan Glass Company. S-Repeat (or National as it was then called) seems to be a pattern designed while the plant was still operated by Northwood as a part of National Glass, but only released once Dugan had taken over. The ad dates from May 1903. In opalescent glass, the colors made were white, vaseline, blue, and green in limited amounts. Additional types of glass, including crystal, apple green, blue, vaseline, and amethyst, were decorated and made in a wide range of shapes. In opalescent glass, shapes known are table sets, water sets, and berry sets. In addition, the goblet has now been found in blue opalescent formed into a compote shape with the Constellation pattern added to the interior (shown elsewhere in this book).

Star Base

Thanks to Ron Teal's excellent book about Albany Glass, I now know this pattern was Albany's #21 or Plain Pattern. It is reported in both large and small square bowls, plate, cup and saucer, a square nappy, and a salt and pepper set, all in blue opalescent glass. The catalog cuts show round bowls too, as well as a spooner and a creamer. It was also made in crystal, according to shards found at the factory site.

Starflower

The 7¼" tall vase shown is quite similar to both the Daffodils and the Crocus patterns, but is definitely a different design. It is on canary glass and very thin. I suspect this piece may be from either England (maybe John Walsh Walsh) or Europe (possibly Czechoslovakia) but have no proof. The name is mine so this may be known by another name to some collectors.

Star in Diamond

This little 5⅜" by 3½" oval bowl is the only shape in this pattern (which I've named) that I've had reported to me to date. I'm confident that other shapes must exist, and possibly colors other than the blue opalescent shown. I have no information as to the maker but believe it to be English. Photo courtesy of the Petrasichs.

Starry Night

So far this bowl is the only shape reported to me and white opalescent is the only opal color reported, although I have owned examples in crystal. The maker hasn't been established yet but I do want to warn readers that it should not be confused with the 1902 Westmoreland pattern Star Berry. They are close in appearance, except the Westmoreland pattern has a rayed base and a deeply scalloped and serrated edge. I encourage anyone with information on this pattern to contact me. Photo courtesy of the Petrasichs.

Stars and Bars

Glass furniture knobs were the first pieces of pressed glass made in this country beginning in the 1820s, so it isn't surprising to see examples of opalescent knobs like the one shown. Today, these are scarce and finding a complete set is next to impossible. The example shown has a series of stars in prisms around the top and rows of bars on the sides. It is but one of many designs known and is found in at least two sizes. Most of these knobs are white but cranberry opalescent is also known.

Stars and Stripes

This pattern has been reproduced by the Fenton Company for the L.G. Wright Company, particularly in tumblers, a pitcher, and a small milk pitcher with reeded handle. This design originally came from Hobbs (1890) and later from Beaumont (1899). Original shapes were water sets, a barber bottle, cruet, finger bowl, and lamp shades. Colors were white, blue, and cranberry opalescent. The Wright reproduction cruets can be found with both ruffled and tri-cornered tops, and both have reeded handles. Some of the repro items, especially the new water pitchers in blue, are very poorly done and the matching tumblers have thick, splotchy coloring.

Stippled Ivy

Although the maker has not been firmly established on this nice basket, the handle almost certainly indicates it being a Greener & Co. product. The basket is 6⅜" long and 3" wide and has been reported in blue opalescent only. The leaf and vine pattern is accented by a stippled background and has a basketweave bottom. This is a great looking basket and I consider it one of my top 5 favorite baskets in opalescent glass. Thanks to the Petrasichs for sharing this beauty.

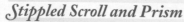

Stippled Scroll and Prism

After receiving a long letter from Seigmar Geiselberger, a glass researcher in Germany, I am now able to place this pattern as one made in either Saxonia or Bohemia. The date of production was around 1900, in a style the Germans call Second Rokoko. In addition more than one size in this piece is known (5¼", 7½", and 9"). The larger piece is also found with a lid. Colors are blue, vaseline, and clear, as well as the opalescent pieces in the same colors.

Stork and Rushes

Storks and Rushes is found mostly in carnival glass in several shapes. This quite scarce mug and a tumbler are the only known shapes in opalescent glass. Colors reported from Dugan Glass Company ads dating from 1909 are white and blue, but certainly green and vaseline may exist. There are two border bands on this pattern but as you can see, the opalescent pieces have the diamond file designed band at the top and bottom. The second banding, a series of dots, seems to appear only on carnival items.

Stork and Swan

This very attractive syrup seems most likely to be of English origin. It is white with heavy opalescence from top to bottom. The handle is applied and the piece measures 5½" tall with a base width of 2¾". The metal lid is marked Patd. Nov. 16th 1869. On one side is a very attractive swan design featuring cattails and the floating swan, and on the reverse side, a stork (or crane) stands among cattails with a blooming tree on the opposite area. The rest of the piece is filled with vertical ribbing.

Stourbridge

This pattern is thought to be from the Stourbridge region of England around 1890 and was named by the owner. Shapes are a 5¼" creamer and a 4¼" sugar. The only color reported to me so far is vaseline opalescent with green/vaseline crested edges around the tops of each piece. Thanks to the Petrasichs for sharing these pieces.

Strawberry

This pattern was made by the Fenton Art Glass Company with production in the 1915 – 1919 period. This pattern is better known in carnival glass. For some reason, only the two-handled bonbon shape is known in either carnival glass or opalescent glass (in the latter, only white opalescent is reported). In an earlier edition of this book I reported a bowl shape but that was a mistake, so I happily correct it here.

Strawberry and Dahlia Twist

This is somewhat of a mystery. This Strawberry design was made by Dugan and the Dahlia Twist Lily was originally a product of Jefferson. In fact the carnival version of this epergne has a different lily and was advertised in 1910 while the opal version came along in 1916 (after Dugan had purchased the Dahlia Twist Lily and mated it with their Strawberry base). Opalescent colors are white, blue, and green.

Stripe

Stripe, or Oval Stripe as it is also known, was made by many glass companies including Northwood, Nickel Plate, Jefferson, Buckeye, Beaumont, and even some English producers. It dates from 1886, and continued at one concern or another until 1905. Colors are white, blue, canary, cranberry, and even some rubina opalescent glass. Shapes include water sets with many shapes of pitchers, cruets, salt shakers of several shapes, syrups, finger bowls, sugar shakers, two caster sets, various oil lamps and miniature lamps, lamp shades, vases, celery vases, bowls, toothpick holder, barber bottle, wine decanter, several sizes in tumblers, and shot glasses. Reproductions are well known in the barber bottle, small 5" – 7" pitchers, and perhaps other shapes. I believe the example shown is Nickel Plate glass.

Stripe Bracket Lamp

This seldom found bracket lamp is a beautiful example of just how many uses the makers of glass could find. It rested in this metal holder or bracket that was attached to the wall. It is shown in cranberry but was also made in white, blue, and canary. I have seen these with new burners and in new metal wall brackets which look a bit suspicious, so beware as they are possibly being reproduced, although this has not been confirmed to date. Thanks to Kelvin Russell and Debra Jennings for sharing it.

Stripe Condiment Set

First advertised in an 1889 Butler Brothers ad, this very fine condiment set was made by the Belmont Glass Company, not Hobbs or Northwood as previously stated. This set is very collectible, consisting of a white opalescent base or server, a white mustard pot, a cranberry vinegar bottle (stopper is not original), and a pair of shakers, one in blue and one in white.

Striped Lemonescent

This color was made by Thomas Webb, circa 1900s. The color combination is similar to rubina verde opalescent by Hobbs, Brockunier & Co. Lemonescent was Webb's trade name. A small gather of cranberry, followed by a larger gather of vaseline opalescent glass, then the opalescent is obtained by returning the piece to the glory hole. These are three shapes, but an epergne horn has also been seen. Although the primary color the eyes see is cranberry, the entire outside layer is covered with a thin layer of vaseline opalescent glass and glows green under a UV light. Thanks to Dave Peterson for sharing this information and photo.

143

Stripe with Fan

This interesting bowl-shaped piece in cranberry opalescent shows a fan near the top of every other point and these points are twisted in a very eye-catching fashion. The yellow enameled decoration is very similar to some pieces listed as being made by Consolidated Glass, although recent information has been given to me which may indicate that Harrach Glass in the Czech Republic may in fact be the maker of many of these type pieces, but further research and time will be the deciding factor. Thanks to Ruth Harvey for sharing the photo.

Stripe with Fly

This frame was obviously made for this vaseline creamer (as well as a cranberry opalescent Polka Dot example), as the silver-plated holder is marked Western Silverplate, which would indicate a U. S. manufacturer. Just why a fly was incorporated into the holder design is uncertain. I'd be interested in hearing from readers who may have this creamer in another color, pattern, or with a different variation in the holder design. Thanks to Dave Peterson for the photo and information.

Sunburst-on-Shield

This fine Northwood pattern was made in crystal in 1905 and in opalescent glass the following year. It was originally called Diadem (a superior name as far as I are concerned). Shapes include a table set, berry set, water set, a nappy, novelty bowls, a cruet, two-piece breakfast set, as well as a very scarce celery tray. Opalescent colors are mostly canary or blue, but white exists in some shapes.

Sunderland

This Greener and Co. pattern, Rd. #138051 from 1889, has been reported to me in a basket and tumbler shape in blue opalescent as well as the compote shape shown in vaseline. Anyone having additional shapes and colors should feel free to contact me.

Sunk Honeycomb

This novelty bowl is a bit of a mystery. It is reputed to be from McKee Glass but they aren't known for producing opalescent glass. The only color reported is vaseline opalescent. The bowl is considered a rarity. Thanks to the Hollenbachs for sharing it.

Sunset

I am told by the owner of this piece it is from Duncan-Miller and the color is called Sunset. I do know this firm began making opalescent glass in the 1920s and continued with this treatment for more than a decade. The bowl shown is 9" across at the widest point and the color ranges from orange to pink to clear.

Surf Spray

This Jefferson Glass Company pattern (#253 pickle dish), which is similar to their Sea Spray pattern, is found only in the pickle dish shown. It was first advertised in 1906 and can be found in white, blue, and green opalescent glass.

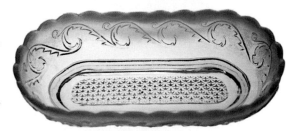

Sussex

To the best of my knowledge, this English pattern hasn't been previously listed anywhere. It has no RD number. I feel sure it had a matching open sugar and possibly other matching shapes. I've given it a name but if readers know any contradictory information, I'd certainly like to hear from them.

Swag with Brackets

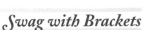

Swag with Brackets by Jefferson Glass Company dates from 1904. It can be found in white, blue, green, and canary opalescent glass, as well as crystal, amethyst, blue, and green, that is often decorated. Shapes are table sets, water sets, berry sets, toothpick holders, salt shakers, cruets, jelly compotes, and many novelties.

Swastika

Shown on the Diamonds and Clubs mould, this Dugan/Diamond opalescent pattern can also be found on a ball-type pitcher mould, as well as on tumblers and a syrup. Colors are white, green, blue, and cranberry. The syrups can be found in both paneled and ball shapes. All pieces date from 1907 production and are currently demanding a high price. It is a shame more shapes weren't developed in this pattern. Thanks to Frank and Melissa Keathley for sharing this rare item.

Swirl

Virtually every glass company who made opalescent glass had a Swirl design, and it is quite difficult to distinguish one maker's examples from the others except by shapes known to have been favored by some companies. It is for this reason I believe this pitcher and tumbler shown came from the Jefferson Glass Company, since it matches the shape of pitchers they made in both Swirling Maze and Lattice. Colors are blue, white, and cranberry, with green and canary strong possibilities. Notice that the handle is not reeded as on the Lattice pitcher in this shape. (The Swirling Maze also has no reeding.)

Swirl (Northwood Ball Shape)

Here's another look at one of the many Swirl patterns. This one is on Northwood's ball shape in the water set. This shape was also made by the Dugan Company and dates from 1890 (Hobb production). The Northwood version is sometimes called a variant. Colors are primarily white, blue, and cranberry, although rare examples of canary are known.

Swirled Interior Flute

Like the Interior Flute vase I show elsewhere in this edition, this vase has the interior pattern swirled. The color on the vase shown is a very deep blue with good opalescence and I've heard of no other colors at this time. I thank Ruth Harvey for sharing this and many other items with me.

Swirling Maze

Apparently the questions about this pattern still persist and I am no closer to all the answers than before. I do know that Jefferson Glass showed this pattern in ads as early as 1903 and into 1904, but just who advertised the water sets after that is still a mystery. There are three distinct pitcher shapes as well as the 6" milk pitcher. In addition, salad bowls are known. Colors are white, blue, green, canary, and cranberry opalescent glass. I was recently told that Fenton made this pattern after 1910 so that would dispel some of the mystery, if true. Thanks to Tim Cantrell for the photo.

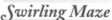

Target

This Dugan/Diamond vase pattern is best known to carnival glass collectors, but it was also made in crystal and opalescent glass where it is very scarce. Opalescent colors are white, blue, and green. Sizes range from 7" tall to 14", depending on how much the vase was swung or slung out, once it was taken from the mould.

Target Swirl

I believe this pattern may be British but have no confirmation at this time. Shapes known are a tumbler, a bottle, a tall vase, a hard-to-find salt in metal holder, and the squat vase shown. Colors reported are cranberry and white opalescent, but it was made in blue opalescent as well.

Tazza

This very attractive English compote shows a very intricate pattern and a lovely flowered style foot. The interesting part of this compote, which happens to be the stem, can't be seen but it comes off the base and makes a pigtail loop before it attaches to the top portion. Vaseline is the only color reported to me. The stem suggests Thomas Webb as the maker since some items have the same looped stems, but this is pure speculation. Thanks to the Sandemans for sharing it.

Thin and Wide Rib

This very nice Northwood vase is found primarily in carnival glass but is also known in custard glass, crystal, and opalescent glass. The design is one of a wide or thick rib with thinner ribs on either side. Opalescent colors are white, blue, green, and vaseline.

Thistle and Wreath

The owner believes this 3½" diameter cup plate may well be English. It is very much like Thistle and Clover shown in Mollie McCain's *Field Guide to Pattern Glass*. I certainly welcome any information on this pattern and its maker. I thank the Petrasichs for sharing it.

Thistle Lily Vase

The silver holder, with its thistle and leaf pattern, is just as impressive as this rubina verde glass lily. I thank Ruth Harvey for sharing this fine vase. I believe the entire piece is English.

Thistle Patch

This was first a 1906 Northwood pattern called Poppy Wreath (used as an exterior pattern with Amaryllis on carnival glass), then it was produced by Dugan/Diamond as Intaglio Poppy. Unfortunately, Heacock didn't look for these previous titles and tacked on a third title of Thistle Patch. Opalescent colors are white, blue, and vaseline, all scarce colors in this pattern.

Thistles

Like the beautiful Primrose shade shown elsewhere, this one has the rubina verde treatment. The design of thistles runs up and down the shade. The base coloring is a good vaseline and the opalescent treatment is just superb. The maker of this fine item is unknown to me at this time.

Thomas Webb Crocodile

What a neat little English novelty piece this is, and I love the detail. (Some examples will have tails that are pulled longer than others.) This 1890s Richardson piece would certainly be cause for conversation in any collection. Vaseline is the only reported color so far but I would love to see a set in various colors, if they in fact existed. Many thanks to Dave Peterson for sharing this super little gem with me.

Thorn Lily Epergne

This 21" tall epergne, with three side lilies and a tall center one, is probably from Europe or Britain. It has metal fittings, much like those found on British pieces. The design of pulled thorn-like projections along the lilies and the peachy interiors of their throats add appeal to this piece. I suspect both blue and white pieces were made as well as the vaseline opalescent one shown.

Thorn Vase

This pattern is credited to Thomas Webb & Sons of Stourbridge, England. In the last edition I showed this vase with a twisted stem, running leaf foot, and thorns on the body, but here I'm happy to show a flat based example in blue opalescent. It is known in both vaseline and white opalescent. It is a blown item and very collectible. Thanks to Ruth Harvey for sharing it.

Thousand Eye

Thousand Eye was first made in 1888 by Richards and Hartley and later by U.S. Glass once they had absorbed the factory in 1892. It can be found in white opalescent, crystal, and several colors in plain crystal. Shapes are numerous and include table sets, berry sets, water sets, compotes, a celery vase, a cruet, shakers, a toothpick holder, bottles of various sizes, novelty bowls, and various compotes.

Thread and Rib

Harry Northwood patented Thread and Rib in 1906, Wide Rib in 1909, and the universal receiving tube in 1916. This is his #305 Flower Stand. However this epergne has been reproduced by L.G. Wright in the 1940s, so be sure of what you are buying. The originals came in blue, white, and canary opalescent glass. Wright's reproductions are found in these treatments as well as white, pink, and blue opaque, all with casing on the lily openings!

Threaded Grape

This smaller than average fruit compote is a real beauty, as is the harder to find banana boat shape. It was made in 1909 by the Dugan Glass Company. So far it is reported only in opalescent glass in white, blue, and green. The pattern is all exterior with the grape and leaf clusters fanning out from the center of the bowl, and the base has a teardrop and beading design. A band of eight threads circle the outer rim of the bowl.

Threaded Melon Basket

This basket with a twisted handle and candy-ribbon edge is a real beauty. The glass is a beautiful blue opalescent treatment with a cranberry handle and edge casing. I believe this piece to be English but have no proof. Thanks to Ruth Harvey for sharing it with me.

Threaded Optic

While I've named this pattern Threaded Optic, it could be called Inside Ribbing with Threading as well. It may be a spin-off pattern from the well-known Inside Ribbing pattern made by the Beaumont Glass Company of Martins Ferry, Ohio, but it has the look and coloring of a Dugan product. I've only seen the rose bowl in blue opalescent, but it was made in other colors and shapes from the same mould such as three sizes of bowls, plates, and vases. The ribbing or optic is all interior and the threading or horizontal rings are on the outside. The marie is plain and slightly raised. It is also called Band and Rib.

Threaded Stripe

The name of this pattern comes from the band of threading that runs around the body of the bowl. The color is a very strong amber. I believe this piece is English, possibly from Greener & Company who made a fair amount of amber opalescent glass. I welcome any information on this pattern.

Three Fruits

This 1907 Northwood pattern is mostly known in carnival glass, but it was also made in limited amounts of opalescent glass in white and blue. The exterior pattern is called Thin Rib, and the interior pattern of cherries, pears, and apples with leaves is an attractive one.

Three Fruits with Meander

In carnival glass this pattern is known as Three Fruits Medallion because of the leaf medallion in the interior's center. The Meander pattern is on the exterior and shows through nicely with the pattern of fruits and leaves on the inside. This Northwood pattern is found on both white and blue opalescent glass and many colors of carnival.

Three Lily Waterfall Epergne

These multi-lily epergnes are found in opalescent glass and carnival glass and made in America and England (the one shown here is English). They are known with three, four, five, or six lilies. The example shown has vaseline lilies (or trumpets). Thanks to Ruth Harvey for sharing it.

Tines

Since I haven't been able to find another name for this (I suspect it may be British in origin), I named it Tines after the fork-like ridges that run vertically on the exterior from top to bottom. It also has a nice interior optic or ribbing. The opalescence is around the neck where the glass color is actually blue instead of the green found on the rest of the vase! This beauty stands 9½" tall and is very graceful indeed. The quality of the glass is very fine.

Tiny Rib

This pattern comes as a real surprise to me and I can't be sure of the maker (Northwood or Jefferson? Dugan, perhaps?). The bowl sits on three scroll feet and the only pattern is the interior ribbing. It measures about 6" across. I'd welcome any information on this piece.

Tiny Tears

Very little information seems to be available for this vase although it appears to have the same coloring as so many vase patterns from either Northwood or Dugan/Diamond. The example shown stands 14" tall, has a marie with 28 rays, and an extended ridge above the base with fine ribbing on the inside all around the base. I'm sure this was made in the usual opalescent colors and must have come from the 1903 – 1910 era.

Tokyo

Jefferson Glass's Tokyo is a very distinctive pattern found in table sets, water sets, berry sets, salt shakers, cruet, jelly compote, toothpick holder, vase, and a footed plate. Colors are white, blue, and green in opalescent glass and plain crystal, decorated blue, and apple green glass. A few years ago Tokyo was reproduced in several shapes including the compote, so buy with caution.

Trafalgar Fountain Epergne

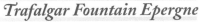

Smaller than some of the epergnes previously shown, this one has no large under-bowl but sits on a wide, slightly ruffled base. The lily holders are also glass, rather than metal, but I still think this is from England and have named it accordingly. Colors seen are vaseline, white, and amber opalescent, but I'm confident blue was made too.

Trailing Vines

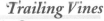

Trailing Vines was made by the Coudersport Tile & Ornamental Glass Company in crystal, amber, pink, custard, opaque blue, opaque white, and blue and canary opalescent glass. Shapes included table sets and berry sets, but opalescent colors are found only on novelty bowl shapes. In addition white opalescent pieces are known in these same novelty pieces. All pieces, though heavily produced, are considered somewhat rare today.

Tree Form

This posy from Thomas Webb reminds me of a harp and you can also see a resemblance to the Thorn vase from Thomas Webb shown elsewhere. This piece has branch or root like feet commonly seen on many English pieces. Colors reported to me are vaseline opalescent (shown) and blue opalescent. Photo courtesy of the Sandemans.

Tree of Life

I am now reasonably sure this pattern is from the Dugan Glass Company. It is known in the vase shape shown in blue opalescent and white opalescent. Wall pocket vases and baskets are known in this pattern in other glass treatments.

Tree of Love

Siegmar Geiselberger, a glass researcher in Germany, has traced this pattern to the Fenne Glassworks of Saarland, Germany. So if some pieces are marked Sabino as reported, the moulds must have traveled from Germany to France before 1920. Shapes include a compote, plate, basket, bowl, a bowl with metal center handle, cup, covered cheese dish, and covered butter dish (not all shapes are known with opalescence, however).

Tree Stump

While this very interesting mug shape is usually called just Stump, the formal name is Tree Stump. The mould work is very good as are the color and the opalescence. Most collectors feel this item is from the Northwood Company, and I agree it certainly has all the attributes of Harry Northwood's quality. In size it is shorter than most mugs and the very realistic tree branch handle and the knots on the bark add real interest. Colors are green, white, and blue opalescent, and all are rather scarce.

Tree Trunk

This well-known Northwood vase is sometimes marked and was made in several sizes in carnival glass, including a huge example with an 8" base diameter called an elephant vase. In opalescent glass, I know of only the standard size (3¼" base) that can be stretched from 7" to 14" in height. Opalescent colors are white, green, and blue, and date from 1907 to 1908. Besides carnival glass and opalescent glass, Tree Trunk can be found in Northwood's Opal (milk glass), Ivory (custard glass), or a rare color called Sorbini, a blue marbled opaque glass with a marigold iridized spray coating.

Trellis

This stemmed tumbler stands 4½" tall. Aside from that, I can offer very little information. The opalescence forms a diamond quilting and there is an optic effect, but the difference from the Diamond pattern is evident. Origin may be English, but I can't be sure. I base this opinion on the heavy opalizing and the general shape.

Triangle

There may well be another name for this 4" tall match holder, but I haven't heard it. The sides measure 3" across. The pattern relies on the three-corner columns and the bands at the top and bottom; the rest of the glass is plain. The entire piece stands on ball feet. Colors are primarily white and blue, but green and vaseline may well exist. It was made by Sowerby of England.

Trident

This pitcher was named by the owner. I really love the design and overall look. The bottom has a smooth polished pontil and the height is 9½" tall. I'm going to assume a tumbler exists although I have not seen one. The only color to date is a nice amber opalescent. It is suspected that this may be Bohemian. Many thanks to the Petrasichs for sharing this nice item.

Tulip

This cylinder shade in rubina verde is almost certainly English, although I have no confirmation as to the maker at this time. The design consists of four tulips within a shield, all linked together with a scroll like design near the bottom. This is the only shape and color reported to me to date and I'd love to hear of others if anyone has them. Thanks to the Sandemans for sharing it with me.

Tulip Vase

Made by Richardson's of England in the 1890s, this 6" tall vase is a masterwork of design. It stands on a vaseline stem and leaf-work base, but the bowl is wide-striped in opal and has an amethyst tint to the glass. I thank the Sandemans (Steve and Radka) for this exciting piece of glass. Tops can be ruffled or flared as well.

Tut

While these very plain stemmed pieces may have another name, this is the one I've heard them called. The maker hasn't been confirmed as far as I know, but Northwood and Jefferson seem likely candidates. They can be found in various shapes. Colors reported are white, blue, green, and canary.

Twigs

First advertised in 1898 as a Northwood product in opalescent glass, the Twigs pattern was another of those patterns later produced by Dugan/Diamond once Northwood left the Indiana, Pennsylvania, plant. In opalescent glass, Twigs is found in two sizes (the smaller 5" size and a slightly larger 6½" example). The smaller size can be found in various shapes and colors are blue, white, green, and canary. In carnival glass, Dugan later made the same twig footed vase and a sister vase without twig feet called Beauty Bud Vase. These Dugan vases can be found in marigold, amethyst, and peach opalescent, and I recently saw a strange tortoise-shell-over-marigold example that must have been an experimental item.

Twigs and Leaves

This basket with twig handles was made by Greener & Co., England, and was registered on March 27, 1888. The piece is unmarked, but was issued the Registration number 96775 for the unique twig handles. It was never named by Greener & Co. It is found in both vaseline opalescent and blue opalescent. The mold was manipulated into various twig basket shapes, all having the distinctive twig handles. Thanks go to Dave Peterson for this photo and information.

Twist

As a part of the National Glass Company, Model Flint Glass of Albany, Indiana, produced this very collectible miniature table set consisting of the covered butter, sugar, creamer, and spooner. Colors known are white, blue, and vaseline opalescent and crystal (plain, frosted, or decorated). A secondary name for this pattern is Ribbed Swirl. The examples shown are a spooner in white and a butter base and sugar base in vaseline.

Twisted Rib

This well-known 1906 Dugan/Diamond vase pattern is a spin-off of the Wide Rib pattern that has simply been worked with a twist. Made in crystal, colored glass, carnival glass, and opalescent glass where the colors are the usual white, blue, and green opalescent (green is the hardest to find). Vases measure 9" to 14" depending on the swinging of each example.

Twisted Rope

Shown are two examples of this very rare vase. These vases are 8" tall and have a 3" base with only a flattened ball stem. To date there are two vaseline, three blue opalescent, two white, one green, and I'm told there is one pink example without opalescence on the edge. Thanks to Dave Peterson for sharing these vases and the information.

Twisted Trumpet

What joy epergnes were and this is one of the most imaginative examples. The stem has been twisted while the glass was still hot and then pulled into the graceful lily shape. I suspect it is English and must have been made in blue opalescent glass as well as the canary example shown. Please note that the top of the lily goes from opal to clear vaseline again in the twisting.

Twister

Twister was shown in a 1908 Jefferson Glass Company ad in Butler Brothers. It is found in bowls, plates, and whimsey vases, all from the same mould. Colors are white, blue, and green opalescent. Plates are scarce in this pattern, even more so than the whimsey vase shape.

Universal Epergne

These are available in such a wide variety of single lily epergnes, I decided to lump them all into one category. They can be found with many different bases and a host of lilies from various makers as well as a variety of base designs; Single Spool Lily (plain lily), Cherub base (Dahlia Twist lily) Epergne, Elephant base (Thorn lily) Epergne, and this list goes on and on. It would be interesting to know just how many variations exist. Colors found to date are blue, green, white, and vaseline.

Universal Northwood Tumbler

When the Northwood Company produced Alaska and Klondyke (Fluted Scrolls or Jackson), the same tumbler mould was used for both patterns. By adding an enameled design (forget-me-nots for Alaska, daisies for Fluted Scrolls), the company not only saved money but also produced similar but distinctive patterns. I am showing one of these tumblers without the enameling to show the design as it came from the mould. Naturally it came in all colors of each pattern and was made in opalescent glass, custard, crystal, and emerald green. In addition to the tumbler, a similar universal salt shaker was produced for these patterns.

Venetian Beauty Night Lamp

This 3¼" miniature lamp is now felt to have been a product of the Buckeye Glass Company. It was shown in an 1890 Butler Brothers ad. Colors are white, blue, and vaseline opalescent with a rare cranberry opalescent known. The shade on the example shown is not original, but a matching chimney was advertised in opalescent glass.

Venetian Drape

Here is a pattern that is appropriately named for the glass is from Venice. It is blown Italian opalescent glass with a hand-applied gold decoration of drapery and a rim of beading. I thank Ruth Harvey for sharing it with me.

Venice

This very beautiful table lamp, shown in the 1888 American Potter and Illuminator, had a matching shade and is said to have been made with either a blue or white opalescent stripe on the fonts. They came in 8", 9", and 10" sizes.

Victoria and Albert

Victoria and Albert was made by Davidson of England as Rd. #303519 in 1897. This pattern is found in both blue and canary opalescent glass. Shapes include a biscuit jar, a creamer, an open sugar, a crimped plate (6½" x 9"), a water set with a matching platter, a 4" plate, and a compote. Davidson was one of three major English glass factories that produced opalescent wares. The others were Sowerby & Company and Greener & Company.

Victorian Hamper

This very pretty little novelty basket was listed in an 1882 Sowerby pattern book as #1187½. It measures 5" long and 2½" tall. It has two rope-like handles and a woven pattern that goes from the rope edging to the ground base. The coloring is very soft like so much glass from England and it has good opalescence. It was probably made in canary as well as the advertised crystal (flint), opal, turquoise, Patent Queen's Ware, and Blanc de Lait treatments. Queen's Ware is an opaque glass with a yellow tint, similar to custard glass, and Blanc de Lait is milk glass. The hamper was also made in malachite or slag glass.

Victorian Stripe with Flowers

While this is certainly pure art glass like so many items of the 1890s, I felt one piece of decorated glass with applied floral sprays might be in order to set a bit of perspective as to where the opalescent glass craze started before it progressed into the mostly pressed items I show elsewhere. This beautiful 10" vase is likely British and is tissue-paper thin, with stems of applied clear glass and flowers that have a cranberry beading. Notice the flaring base, much like many Northwood tankard pitchers that came later.

Victorian Swirl with Flowers

Although very much like the Victorian Stripe with Flowers vase shown above, this one has the swirl pattern and is shaped differently. Both are blown vases and both have applied glass flowers and leaves. Thanks to Ruth Harvey for this piece.

Viking

This beautiful 8½" boat-shaped piece is obviously from England. I am told by the owners, the Petrasichs, that they believe it is from Greener & Company and may have been made in amber as well as the blue. The design is very strong with leaves and roping covering much of the piece. I welcome any information about this piece.

Vintage (Fenton)

Seen mostly in carnival glass, this very distinct Fenton pattern dates from 1909 – 1910 and can be recognized by its large leaf center as well as the five bunches of grapes that are grouped around the bowl. The exterior is plain, as is the marie. Colors reported are white, blue, and a rare amethyst opalescent. All colors are hard to find and well worth the search.

Vintage (Jefferson/Northwood)

This was an opalescent pattern from Jefferson Glass found on the exterior of dome-based bowls that was later used by Northwood as a carnival glass pattern exterior. Jefferson called this their #245 pattern and opalescent colors are white, blue, and green. Occasionally the white pieces were trimmed with goofus decoration. Jefferson pieces date to before 1907 and Northwood used this pattern after that time.

Waffle

I know very little about the origin of this attractive epergne except it originally came from Germany, carried by hand aboard a commercial airline a few years ago. It stands some 20" tall on an ornate metal base and the lily fits into a metal cup. The beautiful waffle design is olive green, shading to an attractive pink just before the opalescent edging starts. The glass is very fine and thin and is mould blown.

War of the Roses

War of the Roses, made by George Davidson & Company in England, has Rd. #212684, dates to 1893, and can be found in blue and vaseline opalescent glass. Shapes include the boat shape (7½" and 9½"), novelty bowls, three-pointed and four-pointed star dish, and a two-handled posy trough. Be aware, however, that the canoe shape was reproduced by L.G. Wright in all sorts of glass treatments in the 1940s, but not in opalescent glass that I'm aware of.

Waterlily and Cattails (Fenton)

The Fenton version of this pattern in opalescent glass is known in several shapes including table sets, water sets, berry sets, a tri-cornered bonbon, a square bonbon, a rose bowl, handled relish, bowl novelties, plates, vase, and a breakfast set consisting of an individual creamer and sugar. Colors are white, green, blue, and amethyst as well as carnival glass items.

Waterlily and Cattails (Northwood)

In carnival glass, Northwood made this pattern in only a water set, so it isn't surprising to also find it showing up in opalescent glass. The example shown is marked with the Northwood mark. Blue is the only color I've heard about and this pattern in opalescent glass dates from 1905. Shown is the rare pitcher (first one reported to me) in blue. Thanks to Dennis Crouse for the nice photo.

Waves

This shape came as a complete surprise to me and it reminded me so much of the Diamond Wave pattern that I gave it this name. The color is a soft vaseline (blue is reported as well as a cranberry pitcher, and I suppose a cranberry tumbler was made too). I'm told that John Walsh is the maker. The shade is mould blown and is very thin glass. It can also be found in a water set, decanter, and a guest set (tumble-up). Anyone with additional information about this pattern is urged to contact me.

Webb Centerpiece

Reportedly from Thomas Webb in 1900, this centerpiece, with three lilies, is a beauty. The feet and stem are rough worked while the lilies are white opalescent glass. I certainly thank Ruth Harvey for sharing it.

West Virginia Stripe

I am listing this pattern under this title as iffy. The shape is the same as the West Virginia Glass Company's Polka Dot and Fern pitchers, so I feel confident it was from that short-lived company and was made between 1893 and 1895. This example shown has an enameled decoration and may have been available in blue, white, and cranberry opalescent glass. I'd appreciate any information about this pattern.

Wheat

This short stem oil lamp, complete with chimney and shade resting on what is referred to as the spider, has an English look but no maker has been established. The only color reported to me at this time is vaseline opalescent. Additional information would be appreciated. Photo courtesy of the Sandemans.

Wheel and Block

Wheel and Block was shown as early as 1905 in ads with other Dugan Glass patterns. It has been seen in deep bowls, a vase whimsey, and a square plate, all from the same mould. Colors are blue, green, and white with the latter sometimes having a goofus treatment as on the square plate shown.

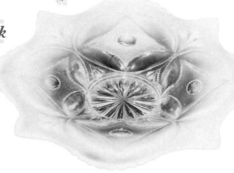

Wide Panel

Here is the second Northwood epergne design, called Wide Panel or Colonial by some collectors. It is well known in carnival glass and is equally respected in opalescent colors of green, white, and blue. Notice that the four lily receiving tubes have been moulded into the glass and the whole design sweeps in a wide paneling from lily to the base. It is less formal than the first epergne design, Thread and Rib, and has no metal in the fittings at all! The fall Butler Brothers catalog of 1909 lists this in opalescent colors at $1.25 each, and the 1913 April catalog from the same concern has the carnival glass at $1.50 a piece! How times have changed.

Wide Rib Vase

The carnival version of this vase was made by the Northwood Company and is so marked, but I strongly suspect the opalescent vase with the frit top was a product of Jefferson Glass. It is 13½" tall and has the heaviest frit I've ever found. Perhaps this is another of those moulds Northwood obtained from Jefferson and then marked with the Northwood trademark. I feel certain this opalescent vase was made in other colors that may include blue, white, and cranberry.

Wide Stripe

I believe this shade was made by the Nickel Plate Glass Company about 1890. Colors known are cranberry, blue, white, and green opalescent. While both Fenton and Imperial made similar versions of these shades in the late 1930s, the shaping was different. Wide Stripe is known in water sets, cruets, syrups, sugar shakers, toothpick holders, salt shakers, and lamp shades.

Wild Bouquet

Apparently Northwood first made the opalescent pieces in this pattern while a part of National, and the design was then continued by Dugan/Diamond. Shapes made are table sets, berry sets, water sets, a cruet, a toothpick holder, salt shakers, and a cruet set on a tray (the same tray as with Chrysanthemum Sprig). Colors in opalescent glass are white, blue, green, and rarely canary; other treatments are custard and possibly Dugan colored glass in blue and green.

Wild Daffodils

Although similar to the Wild Rose pattern by Fenton, this one has a different flower altogether. The shape of the mug and its handle are exactly like the Fenton Orange Tree mug. Colors known are amethyst, white (often with gold trim), and a strange custard-like opalescence with gilding. Production probably dates from 1909 or thereabouts.

Wild Grape

Prior to seeing this compote, I found only a marigold carnival glass bowl with a dome base. The compote is 4½" tall, has a 3¼" base, and is 4¾" across the top. I believe other colors in opalescent glass were made but haven't confirmed them, and other shapes may exist.

Wild Rose (Fenton's)

Wild Rose was made at the same time as the Wild Daffodils mug from the Fenton Company and with the same technique. This bowl can be found in white, green, and deep blue opalescent glass (amethyst is certainly possible too). The bowls may be ruffled, pulled into a banana bowl shape, or flattened into a plate shape. The pattern consists of four groups of roses and leaves sections, very realistically done, with buds and thorned stems.

Wild Rose Shade

This shade is found in both the electric style and the gas shade as shown. It is called this name by carnival glass collectors. This is the first I've seen in opalescent glass and I thank Ruth Harvey for sharing it with me. This design is not the same Wild Rose pattern as the oil lamp attributed to first Riverside and then Millersburg.

William and Mary

This Davidson Company of England pattern was first made in 1903 and has a registration number of 413701. It is found in several shapes that include a table set, compote, biscuit jar, celery vase, handled nappy, oval salt dish, round salt dish, 9" cake plate, and oval or round bowls in several sizes. Colors are blue and vaseline opalescent.

Willow Reed Basket

I believe this handled basket is English, possibly Greener, but I have no proof. The design is a good one with a natural reed, binding, and ribbing. Canary probably exists but I haven't seen it. Thanks to Ruth Harvey for sharing it with me.

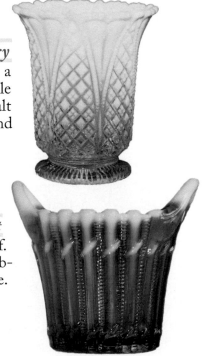

161

Wilted Flowers

This Dugan/Diamond pattern is called Single Flower by carnival glass collectors. It was part of their 1909 Intaglio line. Besides bowl shapes, there are handled baskets, tri-cornered bowls, banana bowls, rose bowls, and whimsied nut bowl shapes. Treatments are goofus, white opalescent, and blue opalescent glass, as well as plain crystal and carnival treatments. The flower design is a weak one and looks best with the goofus treatment as shown.

Windflower

Windflower is a Diamond Glass Company product that is better known in carnival glass than in opalescent, where it is considered rather rare. It was first advertised in 1907. The opalescent pieces are known in white and blue. In a 1914 Butler Brothers ad they can be seen along with equally rare opalescent patterns like the Mary Ann vase, the Constellation compote (pulled from the S-Repeat or National goblet shape with an added interior pattern), a Fish-scales and Beads bowl, and Stork and Rushes mug and tumbler. A green opalescent Windflower bowl would be a great rarity, but I have no knowledge that one even exists.

Windflower Nappy

This nappy by the Diamond Company, seldom found in carnival glass, is a real rarity in opalescent glass and to date I've seen only two in white. The bowl in this pattern, shown above, is part of a very small production run, so to find this nappy is a real surprise. I would surely like to hear from anyone knowing of additional opalescent colors in this piece if they exist.

Windows (Plain)

Originally a Hobbs, Brockunier pattern, Windows was later produced by Beaumont Glass and dates from 1889. Shapes known are water sets, finger bowls, bitters bottles, a crimped bowl, oil lamps in several shapes, and two sizes of miniature lamps. Colors known are white, blue, and cranberry. Notice on the tumbler shown that the windows continue onto the bottom of the piece, where on the late piece they stop at the bottom edge.

Windows (Swirled)

This Hobbs, Brockunier pattern is sometimes called Hobbs Swirl. The swirl is in the moulding of the glass. It can be found in white, blue, and cranberry opalescent. Shapes reported are water sets, cruets, salt shakers, a syrup, table sets, a finger bowl, berry sets, a sugar shaker, a mustard pot, a toothpick holder, and a celery vase. Strangely, the shapes in this pattern all seem to have an oval shape. Production started in 1889.

Windows on Stripes

I have no information on this Windows pattern oil lamp other than to say the only reported color is vaseline opalescent. It has some resemblance to the other Windows patterns, however I don't think it is a product of Hobbs, Brockunier or Beaumont, though I could be wrong. I urge anyone with additional information to contact me. Photo courtesy of the Sandemans.

Windsor Stripe

I feel sure this stripe pattern is English, and I've added the Windsor to establish this. The vase is cranberry with a great amount of opalescence. It stands 4¾" tall, and has a six-scallop top and a pontil mark. I would expect other colors and shapes to exist and would be happy to hear from anyone about these.

Winged Scroll

This A.H. Heisey Company pattern from 1888 can normally found in crystal or custard glass and is sometimes found in milk glass. Here though is the very rare 4" berry bowl in vaseline opalescent glass. A creamer is also known. I want to thank Douglas S. Sandeman for sharing this find with me through his son, Steve.

Winter Cabbage

This Dugan pattern very closely resembles another Dugan pattern called Cabbage Leaf. Both patterns date from 1906. The difference is the number of leaves, with Winter Cabbage having only three and Cabbage Leaves having overlapping leaves. Winter Cabbage is known in bowls that rest on three vine-like feet that bend back and join the drooping marie of the bowl. Colors are white, green, and blue in opalescent glass.

Winterlily

This very pretty vase was first made in 1906 and was shown in Dugan ads in 1908. It was apparently one of those items made in small amounts for the blue is very hard to find, the green is scarce, and the white seldom found. The mould work is superior with twig feet turning into rows of vertical beading and a leaf vining around the vase. The lily shape has a glass twist at the top, much like the Cleopatra Fan vase.

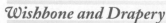

Wishbone and Drapery

Jefferson Glass's Wishbone and Drapery, from 1903, is found on bowls and plates in white, green, and blue opalescent. While the design is a pleasant one, it didn't take much imagination and could not be called exciting. However, the coloring is nice, especially on the blue pieces.

Wood Vine Lamp (Gaiety Base)

It has been speculated that this smaller size oil lamp is a Northwood product but I have no information to confirm such. This ribbed lamp has a variety of opalescent designs running throughout the font with no particular theme in mind. White is the only color reported at this time and the small/medium size is the only size I've heard about. Thanks to the Petrasichs for sharing it.

Woven Wonder

Northwood's Woven Wonder is actually the same pattern as the exterior of the Rose Show bowl and even the same as Frosted Leaf and Basketweave without the leaf. Perhaps the latter's sugar base was flared for these exterior patterns, but I can't prove it. At any rate, Woven Wonder can be found in novelty bowls like the tri-cornered one shown, as well as rose bowls, and I suspect even a vase is within the realm of possibility. Colors reported are white and blue, but green and canary may well have been made.

Wreath and Scroll

This oil lamp's very busy pattern has almost total coverage consisting of an alternating wreath and scroll, two each around the font. The design seems to be English but I have no proof of such at this time. The color is vaseline and this lamp would certainly grace any opalescent or oil lamp collection. Thanks to the Sandemans for sharing it.

Wreath and Shell

This pattern was originally named Manila by Model Flint Glass (their #905). It was made in 1900 in crystal (rare), colored glass, and opalescent glass (sometimes decorated). Shapes include a water set, table set, berry set, celery vase, toothpick holder, rose bowl, lady's spittoon, cracker jar, salt dip, bonbon, a footed tumbler, and various whimsey type pieces. Colors in opalescent glass include white, blue, green, and vaseline.

Wreathed Grape and Cable

This was Fenton's #920, made in 1911. It was named for the wreath of leaves around the collar, It can be found on opalescent or crystal glass (the leaves were removed before carnival glass production) and is rare in either treatment. I am greatly indebted to both the late Jack Beckwith as well as Kathryn McIntyre for sharing this fine item. The footed fruit bowl shown measures 5" tall and has a diameter of 10".

X-Hatch

I love this name and expect it may very well be the only pattern listed in the "X" area of the alphabet for some time. A series of interlinking Xs with a background of vertical bars, although simple, make for a pleasing pattern indeed. The color is rubina verde and this is the only reported shape to date, although I'm certain there are others. Thanks to the Sandemans for the photo and name.

Zinfandel

This is a really lovely water set, which I believe may be from Consolidated Glass, although I have no solid evidence yet. The enameled pattern consists of a grape and leaf design on the pitcher with an added circle of beads around the hip section of the tumblers. I've heard this color referred to as rose opalescent and will stick with that color designation unless I hear different. Many thanks to John and Mary Petrasich for sharing this wonderful set.

Zipper and Loops

Apparently this vase was the only shape made in this pattern by the Jefferson Glass Company in 1908. It may have been intended as a celery holder, but if so, there should have been other table pieces. At any rate, it is found in opalescent colors of white, blue, and green. If anyone knows of additional shapes or colors in this pattern, I'd like to hear about them. Sizes are 7" or 11½".

Zippered Flute

Not only does this vase have an interesting shape with three corners pulled into flames but the design of flutes that have an edging of zipper-like cuts is one I haven't seen before. The color is dark green and I welcome any information from readers about this pattern.

Part II: Whimsey Pieces

Webster's Dictionary defines a whimsey as an odd fancy and that definition certainly fits the glass items in this section.

Generally speaking, the glassmakers were very skilled artisans and liked nothing better than to show off these skills. Often, when they grew bored or tired of the same shapes being turned out, they produced one of these odd fancies that was not a part of regular production but could nevertheless be sold as either a novelty or sometimes given to a friend or loved one a special gift. Many whimsies were made to be slipped out of the factory by the glassmaker at the end of the day, to be taken home and presented to a wife or family member.

For these reasons, whimsies have become a much loved part of glass collecting and it is a pleasure to show a few examples here, so that the collector of today may understand just what whimsies are and how attractive they may be.

And perhaps I should also say that some whimsies were so popular they did go into limited production from pattern to following pattern. Such examples of lady's spittoons as I show here became very popular and were produced over the years on many types of glass, especially in the years of carnival glass production, until they were no longer considered whimsies.

Many whimsies, however, are a bit grotesque in their shaping and seem strange indeed. Just remember, every one of these odd fancies was the product of a master craftsman in the days when glassmaking was an art.

*As I mentioned at the beginning of this book, you will note that a good deal of the whimsies shown in previous editions have been removed, as they were not true whimsies, but rather production pieces. This was also done to allow for the growth of this edition as well as future editions.

Astro Hat

This hat whimsey, made from the common bowl shape, is actually much prettier than the original shape and could have even been pulled into a vase. It just shows what a little imagination and a good bit of skill can do in adding to the design.

Barbells Vase Whimsey

This vase whimsey stands 5½" tall and is pulled from the regular Barbells bowl, made by Jefferson Glass in 1905. I've called the bowl undistinguished, and it certainly is when compared to this very beautiful vase shape. It was probably made in white, green, and canary opalescent as well as the blue shown. Thanks to Richard Petersen for sharing this whimsey.

Blooms and Blossoms Proof Nappy

Occasionally, you will find a piece of old glass that has only part of the design finished. These are called "proofs" and are very collectible. On the nappy shown here, the outline of the blossoms and the leaves are there, but the detail of the design is missing. Since only a few of these pieces were produced before the finished design was completed, these proof pieces are always scarcer than the normal pattern.

Cashews Whimsey Bowl

It is hard to imagine a bowl more whimsied than this one. The rim is pulled into three extreme peaks and the rest is rolled into a low flowing sweep that gives the piece an almost unusable shape. It does have a strange appeal however and certainly would be a conversation piece.

Cherry Panel (Dugan)

Here is the Dugan Cherry Panel three-footed bowl with the edges ruffled into a JIP shape that is tri-cornered. It is found in carnival glass as well as the opalescent treatment, but the green color shown is a scarce color. Please notice the ruffling is a variety called candy-ribbon edge. The same pattern is also found in white, blue, and vaseline opalescent glass.

Cherry Panel Nut Bowl Whimsey

This piece is one of the nicer shapes in this Dugan pattern. It was pulled from the stemmed bowl and is deep, with straight sides, making a nut bowl shape. Colors are white, blue, canary, and goofus.

Cherry Panel Vase Whimsey

This Dugan pattern, pulled from the large footed bowl shape, is usually found in a ruffled bowl. It is also found in carnival and goofus glass. Here I show a rare vase whimsey, pulled up to a three-sided vase with the top edges in an arc-and-point edge. And since the bowls are found in blue and canary opalescent glass, perhaps this vase whimsey was also made in those colors. Thanks to Arthur Van Curen Jr. for sharing this fine item.

Compass Whimsey Rose Bowl

This Dugan/Diamond pattern, also known as Dragon Lady (a terrible name!), is mostly found in bowls, but here I show one pulled up and crimped into a nice rose bowl shape in a rich green. This same shape is known in white opalescent glass as well.

Concave Columns JIP Whimsey

This was originally the #617 design in National Glass ads (later continued at Dugan Glass). In carnival glass it is called Pressed Coinspot and is found in compote, goblet, and vase shapes. Here I show a vase that has been pulled into a JIP top shape but with the front not turned down.

Daffodils Whimsey Bowl

What a beautiful whimsey this piece is. The top has been pulled out into v-folds, giving it a flower-like shape. The color is vaseline but white and blue must have been made also.

Daisy and Plume Basket Whimsey

This is the first of these I've seen and it has to be a scarce item. It was made by Dugan, from the footed rose bowl mould and simply turned out on two sides, turned up on the other two, and a handle was added to form a basket.

Daisy and Plume Whimsey

This Dugan version of the pattern has holes in the legs. It had been whimsied with the top flared out into a bowl shape that could almost be called a nut bowl. Thanks to the Petrasichs for sharing it.

Davidson Shell Ruffled Whimsey

While I've showed this piece previously as Davidson Shell, it is really a whimsey with the top ruffled. The original shape is shown in the first section and as you can see, it has no ruffling and the top is straight, making it a true spill vase.

Diamond and Daisy Rose Bowl Whimsey

This Dugan pattern, called Caroline by carnival glass collectors, was made in 1909 and is usually found in ruffled bowls where the exterior design is unimpressive. Here is a rose bowl whimsey and the design actually shows. Thanks to the Petrasichs for letting me show it.

Diamond Stem Vase Whimsey

Shown is one of three whimscy shapes in this Northwood and Model Flint Glass vase. On this one the front three edges are pulled down and the rear three are turned up, giving the vase a JIP shape as well as a square look. This vase was made in 6½", 8½", and 10½" in white, canary, blue, and green opalescent glass as well as the same colors in opaque glass.

Feathers Bowl Whimsey

Since the second edition of this book, this bowl whimsey has shown up in all colors (white, blue, and green), so it was less rare than I thought. It was made from the same mould as the well-known Northwood Feathers vase, so other whimsey shapes probably exist. The bowls may be deep or shallow, but all I've seen are ruffled.

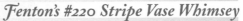

Fenton's #220 Stripe Vase Whimsey

This 8" Fenton Stripe vase whimsey was made from the same mold as the water pitcher and can be found in the same colors (blue, green, white, and vaseline). Thanks to Phil Barber for sharing this piece.

Finecut and Roses Bowl Whimsey

Shown in a 1908 Butler Brothers ad, this Jefferson Glass whimsey is really a production item, flattened and rolled out and up on four sides. Colors are blue, white, and green opalescent glass. This pattern later became part of Northwood's patterns purchased from Jefferson, then made in carnival and custard glass.

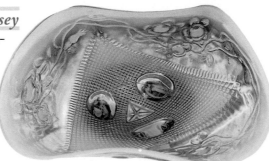

Frosted Leaf and Basketweave Whimsey Vase

This pattern is now known to have been produced by the Chicago Flint Glass Company of Chesterton, Indiana. These vase whimsies are pulled from the spooner shape and are very hard to find. Most measure from 9½" to 11" and can be found in white, blue, and vaseline opalescent glass.

Interior Panel Rolled Rim Whimsey

Here's the Fenton vase I've previously shown in a fan shape. This example too, is in a cameo opalescent treatment, but with a rolled rim. There are other whimsey shapes made from the same mould. Courtesy of John and Mary Petrasich.

Inverted Fan and Feather Large Whimsey Rose Bowl

This true delight is a rose bowl whimsey shaped from the large berry bowl. It was made by Dugan/Diamond probably in the usual colors of white, blue, canary, and green, which is a scarce color in this pattern. The piece shown measures 4" tall and 5½" across the top.

Inverted Fan and Feather Spittoon

Here is one of the very attractive spittoon whimsey pieces pulled from the spooner shape. In carnival glass, these pieces are called ladies' spittoons, for rumor has it that women actually were the users. I can't verify this, but the possibility certainly does exist.

Inverted Fan and Feather Vase

Shown in a 1908 Butler Brothers ad, this very scarce Dugan/Diamond vase was a carry-over at the factory and was made in limited amounts in blue, green, and white opalescent glass.

Iris with Meander Whimsey Vase

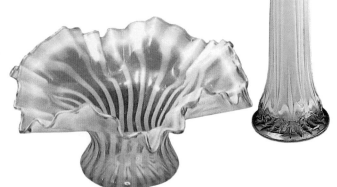

The vase shown is 13½" tall and has a base diameter of 3" to 3¾". I believe this vase was either pulled from the spooner mould or the master bowl mould. I've seen these vase whimsies in blue, green, white, and vaseline opalescent glass, so they aren't rarities but they are very collectible, especially the three stronger colors.

Jefferson Stripe Whimsey Bowl

Jefferson Stripe is normally found in bowl or vase shapes. This whimsey has been pulled from a vase and is almost a ruffled compote whimsey. It has the typical cranberry frit decoration.

Jewels and Drapery Bowl Whimsey

This whimsey, like the Feathers bowl shown elsewhere, was made from the vase mould. Both patterns are from the Northwood Company so it isn't surprising to find these pieces. Colors in opalescent glass are blue, green, and white. Needless to say, these whimsies are rather scarce.

Keyhole Rose Bowl Whimsey

To date, three of these whimsey pieces have been reported, and all were in blue opalescent. This is a Dugan/Diamond pattern made in opalescent glass in 1905. It was later used as an exterior pattern with the carnival glass production of the Raindrop pattern. Opalescent pieces sometimes have a goofus treatment.

Lady Caroline Whimsey Piece

This Davidson novelty or whimsey shape has three handles and has been pulled up and crimped into an almost unusable shape. Other novelty shapes include a two-handled basket with the tops crimped in and a vase shape.

171

Lattice Medallions Nut Bowl

What a pretty whimsey this nut bowl shape is. And while Northwood was not known for items whimsied into this shape, a few examples are known, especially in carnival glass. Please note the unusual knobby feet on this pattern. They seem to go unnoticed with the usual bowl shape but show to an advantage here.

Lattice Medallions Rose Bowl Whimsey

Like the nut bowl I show, this Northwood pattern is much prettier on these whimsey shapes, and this rose bowl whimsey is the top of the line. Colors are white, blue, and green opalescent glass.

Leaf and Beads (Flame)

Shaped much like the regular tri-cornered bowl in this pattern, this example has the flames on the edging pulled to much exaggerated points, making this an attractive and unusual piece.

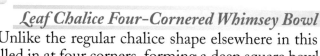

Leaf Chalice Four-Cornered Whimsey Bowl

Unlike the regular chalice shape elsewhere in this book, this piece is pulled in at four corners, forming a deep square bowl shape that is quite attractive. It can be found in all opalescent colors, including blue, white, green, vaseline, and cobalt blue.

Lorna Vase Whimsey

Actually, both this shape and the one shown elsewhere in this book could be called whimsies since the tops are often fashioned into these odd shapes. Here I show a vase with the tops tightly ruffled and then flared. Lorna is from Model Flint Glass.

Meander Nut Bowl Whimsey

While this pattern was produced first by Jefferson (their #233) and later by Northwood, the nut bowl shown is most likely from Jefferson. Without question, it shows the design to a far better advantage than the bowl shapes. Colors are white, green, and blue opalescent glass, and all are collectible.

Ocean Shell

Not as obvious as some whimsey pieces, this Ocean Shell relies on the one edge being pulled out to form a tail-like section while the opposite side has been scooped into a small spout. It is almost as if the glassmaker wanted to form a gravy boat without the handle.

Open O's Rose Bowl Whimsey

What a pleasant surprise this pretty rose bowl was when I first saw it. I debated whether to call it a rose bowl whimsey or a spittoon whimsey, but since the top is turned in, it must be a rose bowl. It is Northwood, of course, and may well have been made in other colors like the other shapes.

Palm and Scroll Rose Bowl Whimsey

Again, here is a whimsey shape that is much nicer than the original bowl shape. Dugan/Diamond is the maker, and they certainly made the right move when they made this piece. The feather-like palms seem to be made just for this shape. Colors are blue, white, and green.

Palm Beach Card Tray Whimsey

What a wonderful and rare item this is! Pulled from the rare jelly compote shape and flattened into a card tray on a stem, it has to be near the top of this pattern's desirability. Palm Beach was a U.S. Glass pattern (their #15119), found in both carnival glass and opalescent glass. It was also made in clear and stained crystal and is a popular pattern with collectors.

Piasa Bird Spittoon

Probably no other pattern in opalescent glass can be found in more whimsey shapes than this one. This one is the spittoon shape and while it became an in-line item, it is nevertheless a whimsey shape as are all spittoons. All Piasa Bird whimsey pieces were created from the bowl shape.

Piasa Bird Vase

Although much like the regular vase in this pattern, this whimsey has one top flame pulled into a grotesque spike and it is for this reason it has to be called a whimsey. Just what the glassmaker had in mind is hard to imagine. Surely he didn't just have a bad day, for several of these vase whimsey pieces are known.

Pompeian

These were made by Dugan and shown in old Butler Brothers ads from the 1905 – 1906 period. The Pompeian line is very similar to Dugan's Venetian and Japanese lines. Various colors, shapes, and sizes were made. Shown here is a whimsey jack-in-the-pulpit shape with a candy ribbon edge in white opalescent. Thanks to Casy Rich for the nice photo.

Popsicle Sticks Nut Bowl Whimsey

This novelty shape in this Jefferson pattern is called a nut bowl. Colors are white, green, and blue opalescent.

Pressed Coinspot Rose Bowl Whimsey

Here is the white rose bowl whimsey pulled from the compote shape shown elsewhere. This pattern is also known as Concave Columns in the vase shape and was made in 1901, first by National (Northwood) and then by Dugan as their #617 pattern. It is also found in carnival glass.

Reflecting Diamonds

The ice cream bowl isn't an ordinary shape in this Dugan pattern, and in fact, few bowls from this company are found in this shape. For novices, ice cream bowls are round without ruffling and have a slightly turned-in edge.

Reverse Drapery Whimsey Vase

If you compare the Boggy Bayou vase shown elsewhere in this edition and the Reverse Drapery bowl (also shown in this edition), you will see just how this whimsey vase, shaped from the bowl, has been widely confused with the Boggy Bayou vase. The design on the marie is quite different however and starts higher above the marie. In addition, the top flaming is very different and usually has little flare.

Ribbon Swirl

Ribbon Swirl is found on vases, bowls, and rose bowls, but here I show a spittoon shape in vaseline. (Some may not consider this a whimsey, but I'll leave it for now.) This pattern is also found with cranberry decoration, so I feel there is a strong possibility it was made by Jefferson. Colors are white, blue, green, and vaseline opalescent.

Squirrel and Acorn Rose Bowl Whimsey

This rose bowl whimsey is from the same mould as the other shapes in this pattern: a stemmed bowl, compote, vase, and vase whimsey. The maker hasn't been determined at this time but production seems to be in the 1904 – 1910 era. Colors are white, blue, and green opalescent glass, and all pieces are scarce.

Squirrel and Acorn Vase

If you will compare this with the standard compote in this pattern shown elsewhere, you will see just how much of a whimsey this piece has become, especially with the three flattened flames that are almost comical. But despite this odd shaping, this piece is quite attractive and would add much to any collection, especially since the pattern is very rare.

Stripe Spittoon Whimsey

This beautiful piece of glass is 3" tall, 4" wide, and has a top opening of less than 1". It is blown glass and may well be of English origin although the shape seems to indicate it isn't. Many American companies made a Stripe product, and it could be from any of these, especially Northwood, but I can't be sure. Any information on this piece would be greatly appreciated.

Swirl (Handled Novelty Whimsey)

I suppose this 3½" tall piece started out as a creamer but somewhere along the way the top was ruffled and the spout was left out so it has become a novelty or whimsey piece. Thanks to Ruth Harvey for sharing it with me.

Tree of Life Vase Whimsey

If you will examine the Tree of Life vase shown in the first section of the book, you will see just why I call this vase a whimsey. It has been pulled in like a corset in the middle and the top has been flared and ruffled. I've now seen this Dugan product in blue, green, and white opalescent glass. There is also another ruffled vase without the pinched in middle section.

Tulip Compote Whimsey

This 1880s Richardson (England) vase form was pulled into a ruffled compote. The coloring is the same as the vase I show with wide stripes of opalescent glass and amethyst, while the stem and base are vaseline glass.

Twister Vase Whimsey

This vase, pulled from the bowl (or plate) shape, is a scarce item. It was shown as a bowl in a 1908 Butler Brothers ad for the Jefferson Company. Vase colors are the same as bowl or plate colors, white, blue, and green opalescent.

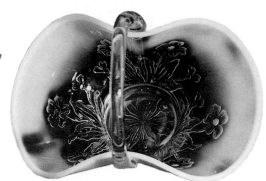

Wilted Flowers Basket Whimsey

This Dugan pattern is called Single Flower in carnival glass and the original design was part of Dugan's Intaglio line. Here I show the handled basket, made from a standard bowl with an added handle. It is known in white opalescent glass also with added goofus, blue opalescent, crystal, and carnival glass.

Wreath and Shell Spittoon

This pattern was made by Model Flint Glass of Albany, Indiana, in several shapes and treatments. The spittoon whimsey is a very collectible item, especially for advanced collectors who recognize its rarity. Colors are the usual white opalescent, blue opalescent, and canary opalescent as well as a very rare example with pink opalescence around the rim.

Wreath and Shell Whimsey Ivy Ball

Shaped from the flat tumbler (tumblers in this pattern can be flat based or footed), this whimsey is called an ivy ball and is one of my very favorite pieces in this pattern. It is rare and very collectible, and I wish I owned one!

Wreathed Grape and Cable Centerpiece Whimsey

Named for the wreath of leaves around the collar, this was Fenton's #920, made in 1911. It can be found on opalescent or crystal glass (the leaves were removed before carnival glass production) and is rare in either treatment. This somewhat whimsey piece is shaped from the same mould as the regular orange or fruit bowl in this pattern. This has been flared to become what collectors call a centerpiece bowl. I sincerely thank Ruth Harvey for sharing this bowl and many other fine items with me.

Part III: Opalescent Glass, 1930 – 1970

Wherever I've gone to photograph items for this book, I've found examples of glass made after the time frame generally accepted as old opalescent glass. Some of this newer glass is very attractive in its own right, and some is an obvious attempt to copy old patterns.

For the sake of identification, I've decided to show a limited selection of these items so that the collector will be aware of them. I have set a cut off date of 1970, which will eliminate pieces made when Fenton began using their popular logo. Also, certain patterns, such as Fenton's Hobnail, Coinspot, and others have been condensed in the price guide because of the vast number of shapes.

Actually an entire book could be filled with new items and many more are being produced every year. When collecting, be alert, handle as much glass and you can, and study it (both old and new). You will soon be able to tell a difference and in most cases will not find yourself paying huge prices for new glass or reproductions.

Remember, the majority of the patterns (approximately 90 percent) have not been reproduced. Of course, I do not have to tell you that patterns like Hobnail, Coinspot, Swirl, and Stripe have many copies and should only be purchased as old once you are comfortable with your knowledge. Buy only from a reputable dealer who will stand behind the sale if you do suspect your purchase to be questionable.

Beyond that, all I can say is happy hunting!

Adam's Rib

This Diamond Glass Company pattern (#900), first advertised in 1925, was primarily a colored glass or carnival pattern. So it was a real puzzle when this opalescent candlestick (there are a pair) turned up. I have to conclude that it is a repro, but just who is making them is a mystery.

Apple Tree Whimsey Vase

This was first made in carnival glass in 1912 as Fenton's #1561 pattern. It is found in milk glass, black glass, crystal, and this rare topaz opalescent vase shape (shaped from the water pitcher mould without a handle). I suspect this item was made in 1933 or 1934.

Butterfly Atomizer

This piece does not have a fitting on the top but I do suspect with the flattened rim and small opening it was possibly an atomizer at one time. Both Fenton and Duncan Miller come to mind as possible makers but I have no proof of such at this time. The design is a grouping of butterflies circling the entire piece as if flocking to a spring flower. The only color reported so far is blue. Thanks to the Petrasichs for sharing it.

Cactus

Cactus was originally a Greentown pattern. It was made again by Fenton in 1959 in milk glass, topaz (vaseline) opalescent, and blue opalescent. Later production included several treatments such as dusty rose and even chocolate glass for Levay. Fenton shapes include bowls, plates, an epergne, cruet, basket, vases, covered candy, cream and sugar, stick butter dish, compote, and a handled nappy. Shown is a 9" vase shape.

Canterbury

Canterbury was made by Duncan Miller and shown in their 1943 catalog. This pattern can be found in a wide variety of shapes, baskets, bowls, and vases to mention a few. Colors are blue, white, and pink opalescent glass. Thanks to the Sandemans for the photo.

Checkerboard (Westmoreland)

Carnival glass collectors will be familiar with the Westmoreland pattern, their #500, first produced in crystal in 1915. It was briefly made in carnival glass in the water set, but all other pieces (including this celery tray shown) are new. The water set has been greatly reproduced in iridized glass.

Coin Dot (Fenton)

Here are two Fenton items in cranberry Coin Dot. The vase was their #194 and was made first in 1948, while the 8½" barber bottle was made in the 1950s. Both pieces, despite being recent glass, are quality all the way as Fenton products are.

Corn Vase Reproduction

If you compare this new vase with the originals shown earlier, you can see the top isn't pulled like the old ones and in addition, the husks are solid glass from outer edge to the vase itself, not open like those Dugan/Diamond originally made. The repros have been seen in blue, amber, vaseline, and a strange pale blue that had no opalescence. These repros are credited to L. G. Wright from the 1950s to the 1960s, so be sure of what you have before you buy.

Cosmos Flowers Atomizer

This pretty atomizer bottle was made by the Fenton Company for DeVilbiss in 1932. It is found in white, blue, or green opalescent glass. This pattern is also called Floating Snowflake.

Cubist Rose

In the 1930s when the Art Deco craze swept America, glass products were radically changed. The bowl shown is certainly no exception. It is called Cubist Rose and is typical of glass in the mid-1930s. It was made by Jobling (Rd. #780719) in 1933.

Daisy and Button (Fenton)

This Daisy and Button pattern was made by Fenton in the 1950s and again in the 1980s and 1990s. It has panels of vertical bars. The rose bowl on a metal stand dates to the 1980s but various shapes are known including bowls, rose bowls, a hat shape, vases, shoes, slippers, and baskets of various sizes. The rose bowl shown was their #1927 pattern, according to a catalog.

Daisy and Button with Thumbprint

This 1950 – 1960 L.G. Wright goblet was part of a huge Daisy and Button line. Shapes were made in many treatments that included opalescent glass in both vaseline and some blue.

Dancing Ladies

Dancing Ladies was made by the Fenton Glass Company for about five years, beginning in 1931. This very collectible pattern is also called Dance of the Veils by carnival glass collectors. The pattern was Fenton's #900 and #901 and can be found in opalescent, carnival, opaque, satin, crystal, colored crystal, and even moonstone glass. Some pieces have lids and handles, and sizes range from 5¼" to 9¼". Vases, pitchers, bonbons, and compotes are known.

Deco Daisy

This Jobling plate has a registration number 777134, indicating it was made in 1932. The design is interesting with typical deco parts. It was named by the Petrasichs.

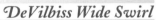

DeVilbiss Wide Swirl

This perfume bottle with matching stopper was made for the DeVilbiss Company in the 1930s and 1940s in a wide swirl pattern. It has a DeVilbiss paper label still intact as well as the original ribbon.

Diamond Optic Water Carafe

This Fenton Art Glass Company version of the Lattice (Bubble Lattice) pattern is found in many shapes. Production of this pattern began in the 1950s and continued for more than three decades. Shown is a water bottle or carafe in cranberry opalescent glass.

Dogwood

In 1910, Earnest Jobling Purser took over the Greener & Company plant in England. He began to produce a treatment he called Opalique, in an attempt to capitalize on the popularity of France's Rene Lalique. He called this glass Jobling's Opalique and produced it from 1910 to 1932. Many pieces were signed but some were not. The Dogwood bowl with the butterfly I suspect is Opalique but it isn't signed. Any information on this pattern would be appreciated.

Duncan and Miller

This well-known firm was organized in 1874 and over the years has made many types of glass. It is their opalescent items made in the 1920s and 1930s that most impress collectors today. For this reason I'm showing two examples of their work. First is an ashtray in vaseline opalescent glass from a line known as Sanibel. It has a very modern look, came in many colors, and certainly would not be confused with old glass. Next is a pale blue opalescent vase called Cogs et Plume. Its artistic quality is obvious and compares with items from Lalique glass.

Easter Chick (with Leaf & Scroll Border)

Plates like this, mostly in decorated milk glass, were very popular in the early 1900s. The one shown here was made by Westmoreland for the Levay Company in the 1960s or 1970s. Other patterns made at the same time in blue opalescent glass were Contrary Mule and Cupid & Psyche. All are 7½" plates with decorative borders.

Ellen

Since I first showed this vase pattern, I've learned it is a bit newer than I thought and now falls near the 1930 time frame. It is 5" tall and has a scalloped base with six wide panels that run all the way to the top. Colors include green, white, and pink opalescent glass. It has also been seen flared out to a bowl shape.

Eye Dot

This beautiful reproduction oil lamp from L. G. Wright is a quality item and would be an asset to any collector. Just don't pay old prices for it and you'll be fine.

Fenton Coin Dot Basket

This basket shape was first made about 1947. It has a lot of quality, as do nearly all Fenton products. The giveaway as to age is two-fold: the shape is not found in old American opalescent glass and the sectioned handle so looks like bamboo. Remember, unless you are confident about age, always avoid reeded or sectioned handles!

Fenton Coin Dot Pitcher

Fenton called this pattern their Dot Optic pattern and it dates to the 1940s in most shapes. Here I show the #1353 water pitcher in cranberry. Note that it has the reeded handle and the lip is pulled in to form an ice cube trap, a dead-giveaway of its age.

Fenton Hand Vase

This 3½" tall miniature vase was made by the Fenton Glass Company in 1942 or 1943. It is their #38, and can be found in both blue and white opalescent glass as well as other treatments. It is still being made and recently I saw a Burmese glass example. And even though it isn't old glass, this is one of the very collectible items from Fenton.

Fenton Hobnail

This has been one of Fenton's most commonly recognized patterns. Production began in the mid 30s and continued into 2007. It has been a long standing favorite with collectors. The amount of shapes is staggering, including lamps, bowls, shoes, vases, hats, baskets, candy jars, compotes, bonbons, and bells. Some of the popular colors are blue, white, green, vaseline, cranberry, orchid, and cameo opalescent, to mention a few. Since this pattern is covered extensively in other works, the list here as well as in the price guide will be condensed.

Fenton Rib

This 1951 Fenton square ashtray was copied from the old Beatty Rib pattern. It was shown in their ads of the time as part of a four-piece smoking set. It can be found in both white and blue opalescent glass and the quality of the piece is very good. The boxed set was listed as their #1728 pattern.

Fenton's #37 Miniature Creamer

This 1942 Fenton piece was made from the same mould as the vase shape shown elsewhere. It can be found in blue, vaseline, and white opalescent glass. A handle was added to make the creamer shape.

Fenton's #37 Miniature Vase

This often seen miniature was made by the Fenton Company from 1942 to 1944 in blue, vaseline (topaz), and white opalescent glass. It was fashioned as a creamer, a handled basket, as the vase shown, and a toothpick holder. Tops can be straight or ruffled, and some examples have a gilded rim.

Fenton's Beatty Honeycomb

This copy of Beatty's Honeycomb was made by the Fenton Art Glass Company about 1959. Fenton made these pieces in vases and rose bowls primarily, in blue and dark green opalescent. Here I show the reproduction vase in blue.

Fenton Spanish Lace

This very pretty Fenton reproduction is so well done it compares favorably with old pieces. Aside from being marked, this piece has a reeded handle that has to be a warning. Just remember, the Fenton Company has made many patterns and pieces over the years in opalescent glass and most have been well cataloged in several Fenton books, so there is little reason to mistake these pieces. Add to that the fact that Fenton began marking all their glass in 1970, and the task becomes simple.

Fenton Swirl

Swirl was made by the Fenton Art Glass Company from the 1930s through to modern day. It was made in many shapes including vases, bowls, hats, basket, and the list goes on. Colors are blue, white, green, topaz and cranberry to mention a few. As with the Hobnail pattern, this one is shown in other works in its entirety and the list here and in the price guide will be condensed.

Fishbone Scroll

Imperial's #721 pattern was made beginning in the late 1920s and continuing into the late 1930s. Opalescent colors are blue, green, and vaseline. Shapes reported are a creamer, two-handled open sugar, a two-handled celery tray, and the rose bowl shown. One rare rose bowl has been found in a marigold carnival treatment. This pattern is also known as Scroll Fluted.

Fostoria Heirloom

Here are three shapes that were all grouped in Fostoria's Heirloom line, made between 1959 and 1970. The bowl was listed as #2183, the star-shaped plate as #2570, and the rolled novelty bowl that I called Rolled Rib as #2727. This latter piece had several shapes, including a deep bowl, and the other two items were also available in more shapes. I've seen these items in green, white, cranberry (light), vaseline, and two shades of blue, the one shown and a very light airy one. The quality of all these items is outstanding and should be collected with the best of glass items of the 1960s and 1970s.

Frisco (Fostoria)

This original pattern was called Frisco when it was made by Fostoria in 1904 (their #1229), but I don't believe Frisco was ever made in old opalescent glass. Here is a small rose bowl shape. I would love to hear more about this pattern from readers. The owner calls it Beaded Jewel.

Gibson Spittoon

This dark green opalescent spittoon was made by Gibson Glass and is clearly marked on the base. It is, of course, late glass. Still the coloring is good, the opalescence outstanding, and the design better than average. There are narrow ribs on the exterior that cover the piece and are swirled above the neck. I am uncertain as to the age of this pattern. Any information would be appreciated.

Grape and Vine

The latest information on this pattern tells me it was made by the Fenton Glass Company in 1990. Nevertheless, it is a pretty piece of glass that may be part of the Paneled Grape pattern after all. However, the jack-in-the-pulpit shape does make it better than average.

185

Hobnail (Czechoslovakian)

Made in the 1950s, these two pieces, a cranberry puff box with cover and a vaseline tumbler, are very pretty examples of the world famous Hobnail pattern, this time made in Czechoslovakia. Note that the hobs go all the way over the bottom of these pieces. I've seen several items, including small dishes, a small vase, and perfume bottles that match the puff box. Colors I know about are cranberry, vaseline, a very dark blue, and a dark green.

Hobnail Variant

I've called this Hobnail pattern a variant because of the odd seam-like sections that are on opposite sides of the piece. I've named this a zipper mould because it looks just like a zipper's fittings to me. It looks to have been made in the late 1940s and early 1950s. Quality-wise, it isn't top-notch. The maker is uncertain at this time.

Hobnail (Westmoreland)

I'm told this is a Westmoreland pattern made around 1970. I will stick with this attribution unless I find out different. The color is a deep rich blue and shapes reported to me are the creamer and sugar as well as a goblet. Photo courtesy of the Petrasichs.

Honeycomb with Flower Rim

This pattern has been widely reproduced, so I am placing this previously unreported toothpick holder here with the glass after 1930. It is also known as Inverted Thumbprint with Daisy Band and Vermont Honeycomb. I'd appreciate any information about this piece and thank the Petrasichs for sharing it.

Jersey Swirl (L.G. Wright)

This goblet shape, made for L.G. Wright and advertised as Jersey Swirl, was made in opalescent treatment in 1950. Other pieces were a covered compote, low covered compote, 6" plate, 10" plate, salt dip, master salt dip, 4" footed sauce, and a wine.

Lace-Edged Basketweave

This Fenton pattern (their #992) was mislabeled in previous editions as being Imperial and I do apologize. This one has a strong basketweave as the exterior design. Here is a beautiful green opalescent example and it is known in white and blue opalescent too. Date of production is from the early 30s to the early 50s.

Lace-Edged Buttons

This Imperial pattern, also known as Sugar Cane, dates from 1937 and was still being made in 1942. I've seen more than one shape but all had the open-edged treatment. Colors are blue, green, and white, but there may well be others. While attractive, the value isn't much more than it was when these items were made.

Lace-Edged Diamonds

Like its close companion Lace-Edged Buttons, this is another Imperial pattern made in the late 1930s and early 1940s. It is a very nice design, made in white, green, and blue, but again, the value is small and only slightly more than when manufactured.

Moon and Stars

This reproduction was made for the L.G. Wright Company, starting in the 1950s and continuing off and on until 1970. It was never made in old opalescent glass, It is found in several glass treatments as well as blue and vaseline opalescent glass. Shapes include stemmed bowls, compote, lamp, a goblet, wine, covered compote, covered candy dish, and a jelly compote (from the goblet).

Nautilus

The anchor stem gives this rare beauty its name. A product of Duncan Miller from 1935, this piece is seldom found and when it does show up it brings top dollar. The color is a strong vaseline. Thanks to the Sandemans for sharing it.

Needlepoint

This is a Fostoria pattern and is signed on the bottom in script. These tumblers were made in three sizes and at least three colors including green (shown), blue, and orange. They first appear in Fostoria ads in 1951 and have no other shapes listed.

Opalberry

Like the Dogwood bowl shown earlier, I believe this is an example of Jobling's Opalique ware, made at the Greener plant in England, between 1910 and 1935 by Ernest Jobling Purser. The plate shown has three clusters of leaves and berries that cover much of the surface with overlapping leaves in the center. It is a beautifully designed piece of glass. Further information about this pattern would be appreciated.

Open-Edge Basketweave

While Fenton made this very pattern in opalescent glass in 1911 – 1913, it wasn't made in this royal blue color until 1932, so I can be sure this is a newer piece. Old colors are blue (regular), green, and white, as well as a pastel vaseline.

Panache

This 1940s Fenton atomizer was likely done for DeVilbiss. The pattern, also called Style, consists of six plumed panels and a scalloped base. The color is blue but I feel certain other colors were made. Thanks to Samantha Price for sharing it.

Peacock Garden Vase

This very beautiful 10" vase in French opalescent glass was a product of the Fenton Company (their #791) and was made in 4", 6", 8", and 10" sizes in 1934. The 8" and 10" moulds originally came from the old Northwood Company, it is believed, where a carnival version was made. It is thought that the 4" and 6" moulds were made at the Fenton Factory. Since the early 1930s, Fenton has made this vase (in the 8" size mostly) in several dozen treatments. The 4", 6", and 10" examples are considered quite rare and are very collectible. The 8" ones, although considered very scarce, can be found on occasion.

Petticoats

This very attractive perfume, which was also called Flounces, was made by the Fenton Art Glass Company for DeVilbiss in 1933. It can be found in white, blue, and canary (topaz) opalescent glass.

Pinecone and Leaves

This pattern was first made at Greener and Company in jet glass (black) bearing Rd. #777133. It was later made in Jobling Opalique opalescent glass in the beautiful bowl shown. Opalique was a glass made by Ernest Jobling Purser at the Greener Factory between 1910 and 1935 in the manner of Rene Lalique's famous French opalescent ware.

Pinecone Spray

This piece is similar to the Pinecone and Leaves pattern by Jobling I show elsewhere, but has fewer sprays and a more deco look. I believe this piece may also be from Jobling or even from Sabino, but have no proof and welcome any information from readers.

Plume Twist Atomizer

This 1940s DeVilbiss atomizer can be found in white opalescent, as shown, or in vaseline. It stands nearly 4" tall and has a series of feathers that wind around the bottle.

Plymouth

In 1935 Fenton made a large line of this pattern, all very useful items including plates, wines, high-balls, old-fashioned glasses, a rare mug, and this pilsner shown. These were all done in their French opalescent glass and are quality all the way. Additional shapes were added, including a cocktail glass and a goblet.

Queen's Petticoat

Only after the first edition of this book came out did I learn this pretty little vase was made by Fostoria in 1959 as part of their Heirloom collection. It was listed as their #5056 and can be found in opalescent colors of yellow, blue, pink, green, ruby, and bittersweet (orange). I am sorry that I may have misled some collectors into thinking this was an old piece, but it is just that good!

Quilted Pinecone

This atomizer was made by Fenton for DeVilbiss. It can be found in blue and I'm certain other colors are available as well. Thanks to Wayne and Joan Joliffe for sharing it.

Ring

This 1933 Fenton Ring pitcher is actually very scarce and highly collectible. It stands 7" tall. I'm sure Fenton made this in their usual colors of the time, so green, blue, and vaseline are possibilities.

Seaweed and Shell

This small shallow bowl consists of six shells, three of which are surrounded by seaweed. The bowl measures 5 ¾" in diameter and is in blue opalescent. I'm told it is French and possible makers are Etling and Ezell. Any information is appreciated. Thanks to the Petrasichs for the photo.

Spiral Optic (Fenton)

This Fenton pattern was called Spiral Optic and was made primarily from the 30s to the 50s (and into the 70s). It can be found in white, blue, and cranberry opalescent. A variety of shapes can be found, vases of various shapes and dimensions, hat shapes, candy boxes, and the list goes on. Since this pattern is covered extensively in other works, the list of shapes and the list in the price guide have been condensed.

Spiral Waves

I have no information on this pattern other than it was possibly made by Ezell or Etling of France. This large plate measures 15" in diameter and is found so far in only white opalescent. Thanks to Samantha Prince for sharing it.

Stamm House Dewdrop (#1886/642)

This a fine piece of new glasswork was made by the Imperial Glass Company in 1966 in 10" and 5" bowls in a beautiful canary opalescent glass. It has the look of old English opalescent glass and since Imperial made very little opalescent glass at any time, this is a collectible item indeed and one of the collectibles of the future.

Stars and Stripes

Stars and Stripes was originally from Hobbs, Brockunier and then Beaumont. It was revisited in the 1940s by Fenton for L.G. Wright in tumblers, a creamer, barber bottle, cruet, basket, finger bowl, syrup, and other novelties in blue and cranberry opalescent glass. Shown are the cruet and barber bottle.

Swan Bowl

Apparently this bowl and its companion pieces (smaller bowls and candlesticks) were first made at the Diamond plant from 1926 to 1927 and later at the Fenton Art Glass factory from 1934 to 1939. The Dugan/Diamond version is known in pink, green, and black glass, and the Fenton pieces are advertised in opalescent colors; so it appears the master bowl shown is a Fenton item despite its color matching so many of Dugan's blue opalescent items. At any rate, these blue pieces are considered rare, as are the green opalescent items. Other treatments at the Fenton factory are satinized crystal (1939), amber (1938), amethyst (1938), and the large bowl is currently being made in a pretty misty green.

Swirl

This well done Fenton pattern was made for the L.G. Wright Glass Company in cranberry in 1973 (other opalescent colors were made earlier). Shapes known are the pitcher, tumblers (tall or standard), a sugar shaker, vases (large and small), lamps, barber bottles, syrup, finger bowl, a pickle caster in metal stand, and a small pitcher. Note that the handle is reeded.

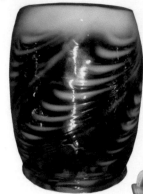

Swirled Feather

This 1953 Fenton pattern can be found in a fairy lamp, candy dish, vase, cruet, hurricane lamp, a vanity set, and a water set (tumbler shown). It was an attempt to reproduce the Blown Twist pattern and can be found in white, green, blue, and cranberry.

Sylvan

This pattern, like Canterbury, was shown in a 1943 catalog from Duncan Miller. It is found in a variety of shapes including, but not limited to, bowls, relish trays, candy dishes, and vases. The colors are blue, white, and pink opalescent. Photo courtesy of the Petrasichs.

Tokyo Reproduction

If you look closely at the compote shown, you can see the color is light and the opalescence thin. The original pattern was made by Jefferson Glass in 1905, but this piece when held and examined is obviously not of that quality. I do not know of other shapes having been reproduced but it is possible.

Trout

When I first showed this pretty bowl, I speculated it might be French. It is, in fact, Verlys, made by the Holophane Company of France in 1931, so I've moved it from the old glass section. Fenton bought the mould in 1966 and has reproduced this piece. New treatments include an acid finish with opalescence. The bowl has an 8½" diameter and stands 3½" tall.

Twigs Reproduction

On close examination, you will see some differences from the regular Twigs vase. First, the lip has a cased edge, a clear applied edging. On some, not all however, the area between the legs and the body of the vase is filled solid with glass. Beware of these and always know the dealer before you buy this pattern. Colors of the reproductions are vaseline, blue, and white opalescent (so far). The white opal ones are also being iridized to create copies in peach opal. The old vase was never made in this treatment.

Water Ballet

I'm told this low bowl or plate is from France and have no information to dispute it. The only color reported to me to date is a nice white opalescent, but others may exist. I have assigned what I consider to be an appropriate name, but if anyone knows it by a previously established named I'd certainly like to hear from them. Thanks to Samantha Prince for the nice photo.

Wildflower

This reproduction of the old U.S. Glass pattern was first sold by L. G. Wright in the 1940s and then in an expanded line in the 1959 – 1960 era. It can be found in several treatments, including crystal, amber, blue, and green, as well as vaseline and blue opalescent glass. Reproduced shapes include covered compotes, a table set, goblets, square plates, salt dips (two styles), footed sauce, covered candy jar, and a 7½" footed vase. No old opalescent pieces exist!

Windows (L.G. Wright)

This was made in the 1950s by the Fenton Art Glass Company for L.G. Wright. Fenton called this Window Pane. Shapes reproduced include an epergne, lamps, fairy light, water set, syrup, vase, creamer, cruet, and a finger bowl. Colors were cranberry and blue, often satin finished.

Wreathed Cherry

Apparently all the opalescent items in this Dugan/Diamond pattern are new, made for and distributed by the L. G. Wright Company starting in 1963 and continuing for several years. Colors are blue and vaseline in opalescent glass, as well as some non-opalescent runs that include amber, red, emerald green, and blue.

Wright's Thread and Rib Epergne

In 1940 L. G. Wright reproduced the Northwood #305 (Thread and Rib) epergne from moulds from Island Mould and Machine Company. Fenton was the maker of the epergnes in several crest or cased edge treatments as well as plain blue and vaseline opalescent ones. These epergnes continued in production into the 1950s and were sold through a New York import dealer, Kosherak Brothers. Beware of all cased examples or ones with the flames pulled. They are all reproductions.

Price Guide

As in my past price guides, I've attempted to include in a complete and up-to-date manner American and English opalescent glass production from 1890 to 1930, a natural time frame for such glass, one that separates antique production from contemporary. Prices followed by an asterisk (*) are speculative. The same mark (*) after a pattern name indicates this pattern has been reproduced in some shape(s). In a few instances, prices have been averaged where several variations of a shape exist, but I've tried to list prices as completely as possible.

Values in this guide were determined from dealers' lists, shop taggings, antique guide listings, and personal observation. Auction prices played only minor roles due to their often inflated bidding value. All items are priced as in mint condition and with average opalescence; flaws or poor coloring reduces value. Please remember this is only a guide and prices herein are not set in stone. As with all my price guides, this one is meant to advise the buyer rather than set prices.

Most pattern names conform to those most frequently encountered but where more than one name is commonly in use, I've included both names in the interest of clarity.

Of course, I welcome all constructive comments from readers and ask anyone with more information to contact me. Please include a self-addressed, stamped envelope with your correspondence. I am always looking for information or photos of patterns I haven't covered in this edition. That's how I learn and how I improve these books with each new edition. Items with goofus treatment should be priced 10 percent higher than listed prices.

Pattern Name	Blue	Green	White	Vaseline/ Canary	Cranberry	Other
ABALONE						
Bowl	45.00	35.00	25.00	50.00		60.00 Emerald
ACORN BURRS (NORTHWOOD)						
Bowl, sauce, very rare	175.00		100.00			
ACORNS						
Jar with lid	200.00		150.00			
ADONIS PINEAPPLE						
Claret bottle	400.00					400.00 Amber
ALA-BOCK						
Bowl whimsey, ruffled	115.00			130.00		
Candy dish	95.00			100.00		
Rose bowl	130.00			140.00		
Pitcher	235.00			250.00		
Tumbler	25.00			35.00		
ALASKA						
Banana boat	235.00		200.00	265.00		270.00 Emerald
Bowl, master	175.00		125.00	165.00		165.00 Emerald
Bowl, sauce	65.00		30.00	60.00		60.00 Emerald
Bride's basket	300.00		135.00	375.00		350.00 Emerald
Butter	415.00		300.00	450.00		375.00 Emerald
Celery tray	195.00		140.00	225.00		175.00 Emerald
Creamer	90.00		70.00	85.00		80.00 Emerald
Cruet	325.00		280.00	300.00		325.00 Emerald
Pitcher	425.00		350.00	450.00		500.00 Emerald
Tumbler	80.00		60.00	80.00		90.00 Emerald
Shakers, pair	170.00		90.00	185.00		125.00 Emerald
Spooner	100.00		70.00	90.00		90.00 Emerald
Sugar with lid	165.00		150.00	175.00		175.00 Emerald
ALBANY REVERSE SWIRL						
Bowl, 9"	65.00		45.00	70.00		
Butter	135.00		100.00	145.00		
Celery vase	70.00		55.00	75.00		
Creamer or spooner	60.00		50.00	65.00		
Pitcher	290.00		225.00	325.00		
Tumbler	50.00		35.00	60.00		
Rose bowl	85.00		60.00	90.00		
Sugar	75.00		60.00	85.00		
Sugar shaker	125.00		90.00	135.00		
Syrup	200.00		125.00	235.00		
Toothpick holder	80.00		55.00	90.00		
Water bottle	165.00		115.00	185.00		
ALBANY STRIPE (ALBANY)						
Barber bottle	275.00		200.00	300.00		
Pitcher	425.00		325.00	500.00		600.00 Decorated
Sugar bowl	200.00		175.00	225.00		
Vase, 4¾"	250.00		225.00	250.00		
ALHAMBRA						
Rose bowl	150.00		120.00	160.00	275.00	
Syrup	375.00		300.00	400.00	590.00	

Pattern Name	Blue	Green	White	Vaseline/ Canary	Cranberry	Other
Tumbler	75.00		55.00	70.00	120.00	
ALVA						
Oil lamp	250.00		220.00			
ARABIAN NIGHTS						
Pitcher	400.00		285.00	400.00	1,100.00	
Tumbler	65.00		50.00	75.00	125.00	
Syrup	225.00		185.00	275.00		
ARCHED PANEL						
Bowl, master	110.00	120.00	70.00	100.00		
Bowl, sauce	40.00	45.00	25.00	30.00		
ARGONAUT SHELL *(NAUTILUS)						
Bowl, master	150.00		125.00			
Bowl, sauce	65.00		50.00			
Butter	325.00		275.00			
Creamer	200.00		150.00			
Cruet	500.00		350.00			
Jelly compote	125.00		75.00	90.00		
Novelty bowls, tray, etc.	65.00		50.00	100.00		
Pitcher	500.00		375.00			
Tumbler	125.00		100.00	100.00		
Shakers, pair	110.00		85.00	100.00		
Spooner	200.00		150.00			
Sugar	265.00		225.00			
Whimsey banana boat	65.00		50.00	75.00		
Add 15% for script signed pieces						
ARGUS (THUMBPRINT)						
Compote	90.00	95.00	50.00	80.00		
ARROWHEAD						
Lidded jar				165.00		
Shade				125.00		
ASCOT						
Biscuit jar	175.00			160.00		
Bowl	55.00			75.00		
Creamer	85.00			90.00		
Open sugar	85.00			85.00		
ASTRO						
Bowl	55.00	50.00	40.00	50.00		60.00 Emerald
Hat whimsey	75.00	70.00	65.00	75.00		
AURORA BOREALIS						
Novelty vase	90.00	80.00	65.00			
AUTUMN LEAVES						
Banana bowl	50.00	70.00	40.00			75.00 Emerald
Bowl	75.00	95.00	50.00			
Nappy			125.00			
AZZURO VERDE						
Vase	150.00*			200.00*		
BABY COINSPOT*						
Syrup			140.00			
Vase		100.00	60.00	90.00		
BALL FOOT HOBNAIL						
Bowl			75.00			
BAND & RIB (THREADED OPTIC)						
Bowl, 7"-9"	60.00		45.00			
Rose bowl	40.00		30.00			
BANDED HOBNAIL						
Dresser bottle	75.00		50.00			
BANDED LILY EPERGNE						
Single lily epergne				375.00		
BANDED NECK SCALE OPTIC						
Vase			55.00			
BARBED WIRE						
Shade				225.00		
Vase				175.00		
BARBELLS						
Bowl	40.00	50.00	30.00	45.00		
Vase, rare	100.00	120.00				
BEADED BASE VASE						
Vase	75.00		45.00			
BEADED BASKET (DUGAN)						
Basket, handled, very scarce			150.00			
BEADED BLOCK						
Bowl	65.00	60.00	35.00			
Celery vase	85.00	75.00	45.00			
Creamer			65.00			
Milk pitcher, rare				700.00.*		
Nappy, handled			40.00			

Pattern Name	Blue	Green	White	Vaseline/Canary	Cranberry	Other
Rose bowl, scarce	65.00	70.00	55.00	85.00		
Sugar			75.00			
BEADED BUTTON ARCHES						
Compote				210.00		235.00 Blue pearline
Creamer				75.00		90.00 Blue pearline
Sugar				95.00		110.00 Blue pearline
BEADED CABLE						
Bowl, footed	50.00	45.00	35.00	45.00		
Rose bowl, footed	65.00	60.00	45.00	60.00		
*Add 10% for interior pattern						
BEADED DRAPES						
Banana bowl, footed	50.00	50.00	45.00	40.00		
Bowl, footed	45.00	40.00	30.00	50.00		
Rose bowl, footed	55.00	55.00	40.00			
*Add 10% for frit						
BEADED FANS						
Bowl, footed	40.00	45.00	35.00			
Rose bowl, footed	50.00	50.00	40.00			
BEADED FLEUR DE LIS						
Bowl, novelty	55.00	55.00	45.00			
Bowl, whimsey	90.00	95.00	75.00			
Compote	50.00	50.00	45.00			
Rose bowl	60.00	60.00	50.00			
BEADED MOON & STARS						
Banana bowl, stemmed	85.00	90.00	65.00			
Bowl	70.00	90.00	50.00			
Compote	80.00	95.00	60.00			
BEADED OVALS IN SAND						
Bowl, master	75.00	70.00	50.00			
Bowl, sauce	35.00	30.00	20.00			
Butter	300.00	250.00	185.00			
Creamer	90.00	80.00	45.00			
Cruet	250.00	225.00	175.00			
Nappy	55.00	45.00	25.00			
Pitcher	425.00	375.00	300.00			
Tumbler	100.00	85.00	60.00			
Shakers, pair	100.00	85.00	75.00			
Spooner	100.00	85.00	65.00			
Sugar	250.00	225.00	165.00			
Toothpick holder	200.00	175.00	125.00			
BEADED OVALS WITH HOLLY						
Spooner, rare			150.00			
BEADED STAR MEDALLION						
Shade	70.00	55.00	40.00			
BEADED STARS						
Advertising bowl, rare	350.00	400.00	275.00			
Advertising plate, rare	450.00	500.00	400.00			
Bowl	45.00	55.00	35.00			
Plate	100.00		60.00			
Rose bowl	60.00	60.00	40.00			75.00 Lime opal
BEADED V'S AND BUTTONS						
Creamer	80.00					
BEADS & BARK						
Vase, footed	135.00	100.00	70.00	125.00		
BEADS & CURLYCUES						
Novelty bowls, footed	50.00	50.00	40.00			
BEATTY HONEYCOMB*						
Bowl, master	50.00		40.00			
Bowl, sauce	25.00		20.00			
Butter	225.00		175.00			
Celery vase	80.00		70.00			
Creamer	90.00		50.00			
Cruet	200.00		175.00			
Individual cream/sugar set	150.00		125.00			
Mug	55.00		40.00			
Mustard pot	100.00		75.00			
Pitcher	200.00		150.00			
Tumbler	50.00		35.00			
Shakers, pair	80.00		60.00			
Spooner	90.00		50.00			
Sugar	125.00		100.00			
Toothpick holder	200.00		150.00			250.00 Violet opal
BEATTY RIB						
Bowl, master	55.00		35.00			
Bowl, novelty	75.00		65.00			
Bowl, sauce	30.00		20.00			

196

Pattern Name	Blue	Green	White	Vaseline/ Canary	Cranberry	Other
Butter	200.00		125.00			
Celery vase	75.00		65.00			
Cracker jar	125.00		100.00			
Creamer	60.00		40.00			
Finger bowl	30.00		20.00			
Match holder	50.00		35.00			
Mug	55.00		40.00			
Mustard jar	150.00		125.00			
Nappy, various	40.00		25.00			
Pitcher	200.00		150.00			
Tumbler	50.00		30.00			
Shakers, pair	75.00		60.00			
Salt dip	60.00		45.00			
Spooner	60.00		40.00			
Sugar	145.00		100.00			
Sugar shaker	125.00		100.00			
Toothpick	65.00		55.00			
BEATTY SWIRL						
Bowl, master	55.00		40.00			
Bowl, sauce	30.00		20.00			
Butter	175.00		150.00			
Celery vase	75.00		60.00			
Creamer	75.00		60.00			
Mug	65.00		35.00	85.00		
Pitcher	185.00		125.00	225.00		
Tumbler	40.00		30.00	50.00		
Spooner	75.00		60.00			
Sugar	125.00		100.00			
Syrup	250.00		200.00	275.00		
Water tray	100.00		65.00	110.00		
BEAUMONT STRIPE						
Pitcher	325.00		285.00	350.00		
Tumbler	65.00		50.00	70.00		
BEAUMONT SWIRL						
Pitcher	350.00	325.00	300.00			
Tumbler	80.00	70.00	55.00			
BERRY PATCH						
Bowl, square	55.00		40.00			
Novelty bowl, square	50.00	45.00	30.00			
Plate	75.00	75.00	50.00			
BIG WINDOWS SWIRLED						
Barber bottle	175.00		135.00		200.00	
Bowl, two sizes	60.00-125.00		40.00-95.00		75.00-145.00	
Butter	225.00		165.00		245.00	
Creamer	65.00		50.00		80.00	
Oil lamp	425.00		300.00		500.00	
Shaker	125.00		95.00		135.00	
Spooner	65.00		50.00		75.00	
Sugar	95.00		75.00		95.00	
Syrup	165.00		125.00		175.00	
BIRD IN A TREE						
Novelty bowl						250.00 Rose opal
BLACKBERRY						
Bon-bon			50.00			80.00 Amethyst
Bowl			30.00			70.00 Amethyst
Nappy	40.00	45.00	30.00			60.00 Amethyst
Plate, 6"			30.00			85.00 Amethyst
BLACKBERRY SPRAY						
Hat	55.00		25.00			85.00 Amethyst
BLOCK						
Celery vase	60.00	60.00	40.00	55.00	80.00	
Novelty bowl	50.00	45.00	30.00	45.00	65.00	
BLOCK (ENGLISH)						
Pitcher	175.00					225.00 Amber
Platter	75.00					95.00 Amber
Tumbler, two sizes	60.00-85.00					75.00-95.00 Amber
BLOCKED THUMBPRINT & BEADS						
Bowl	50.00	55.00	40.00			
Nappy	40.00	40.00	30.00			
Plate						75.00 Emerald
BLOOMS & BLOSSOMS						
Nappy, handled	50.00	50.00	40.00			
Proof whimsey, scarce	100.00	65.00				
BLOSSOMS & PALMS						
Bowl	70.00	65.00	45.00	95.00		

Pattern Name	Blue	Green	White	Vaseline/Canary	Cranberry	Other
BLOSSOMS & WEB						
Bowl, rare	225.00	175.00	150.00			
BLOSSOM TOP CASTER SET						
Caster set	275.00		200.00	350.00		
BLOWN DIAMONDS						
Pitcher, scarce				300.00		
BLOWN DRAPERY						
Pitcher	550.00	500.00	350.00		900.00	
Tumbler	175.00	150.00	165.00		300.00	
Sugar shaker	500.00	450.00	300.00			
Vase	225.00	200.00	175.00			
BLOWN ROPE						
Whimsey vase				200.00*		
BLOWN TWIST						
Celery vase	400.00		350.00	450.00		
Pitcher	550.00	500.00	350.00	525.00	900.00	
Tumbler	200.00	175.00	150.00	175.00	325.00	
Sugar shaker	200.00	185.00	175.00	200.00	600.00	
Syrup	250.00		200.00		400.00	
BOAT WITH WHEELS						
Boat shape				235.00		
BOGGY BAYOU						
Vase	40.00	35.00	25.00			85.00 Amethyst
BOHEMIAN STRIPE						
Vase, decorated	150.00					
BOUGH & BLOSSOM						
Rose bowl						175.00 Lavender
BRASS NAILHEAD						
Mug			75.00			
BRICK						
Novelty match holder			100.00			
BRIDESHEAD (DAVIDSON)						
Basket, handled	90.00					
Butter	100.00					
Celery vase	60.00					
Compote	70.00					
Creamer	65.00					
Novelty bowl	55.00					
Oval tray	125.00		100.00	120.00		
Pitcher, two sizes	145.00-165.00					
Tumbler	100.00					
Sugar	75.00					
BRIDESMAID (GREENER & CO.)						
Bowls, various sizes, rare	65.00-100.00					80.00-140.00 Amber
Bowl, large, oval, rare	125.00					165.00 Amber
Pitcher, rare	200.00					400.00 Amber
Tumbler, rare	70.00					100.00 Amber
Tray, rare	100.00					175.00 Amber
BRILYNACEE LACE (ALBANY)						
Pitcher	425.00*		300.00*			
BRITISH FLUTE						
Vase				140.00		
BROKEN PILLAR						
Card tray (from compote shape)	170.00		135.00	165.00		
Compote	160.00		125.00	155.00		
BUBBLE LATTICE						
Bowl, master	70.00	50.00	45.00	65.00	80.00	
Bowl, sauce	30.00	25.00	20.00	30.00	35.00	
Bride's basket	125.00	100.00	75.00	130.00	225.00	
Butter	225.00	200.00	150.00	200.00	725.00	
Celery vase					125.00	
Creamer	60.00	50.00	50.00	55.00	150.00	
Cruet, average pricing	175.00	160.00	135.00	170.00	400.00	
Finger bowl	45.00	40.00	25.00	45.00	125.00	
Pitcher, various	300.00	275.00	225.00	275.00	750.00	
Tumbler, various	50.00	50.00	40.00	45.00	125.00	
Rose bowl	75.00					
Shakers, various	150.00	125.00	100.00	175.00	150.00-300.00	
Spooner	60.00	50.00	50.00	55.00	200.00	
Sugar	125.00	100.00	75.00	100.00	425.00	
Sugar shaker	235.00	225.00	185.00	225.00	300.00	
Syrup, various	225.00	200.00	175.00	200.00	750.00	
Toothpick holder	300.00	275.00	200.00	350.00	300.00-550.00	
BUBBLE LATTICE LAMP (NORTHWOOD'S PANELED MOULD)						
Lamp			250.00			

Pattern Name	Blue	Green	White	Vaseline/ Canary	Cranberry	Other
BUCKEYE BUBBLE LATTICE						
Cylinder shade	125.00		85.00	175.00	200.00	
Pitcher	225.00		150.00	325.00	375.00	
Salt shaker	100.00		75.00	150.00	200.00	
Tumbler	65.00		45.00	90.00	110.00	
BULBOUS BASE COINSPOT						
Sugar shaker	125.00		90.00		175.00	
Syrup	160.00		110.00		225.00	
BULL'S EYE						
Bowl	50.00				65.00	
Shade	60.00		40.00			
Water bottle			175.00		265.00	
BULL'S EYE & FAN VARIANT						
Bowl		90.00				
BULL'S EYE & LEAVES						
Bowl, with goofus trim			100.00			
BUSHEL BASKET						
One shape, scarce	150.00	250.00	150.00	550.00		
BUTTERFLY (FENTON)						
Compote, either shape			50.00			
BUTTON PANELS						
Bowl	45.00		35.00	50.00		
Rose bowl	45.00		40.00	55.00		
BUTTONS & BRAIDS						
Bowl	50.00	55.00	30.00		85.00	
Pitcher	350.00	400.00	175.00	900.00	700.00	
Tumbler	60.00	70.00	50.00	110.00	100.00	
CABBAGE LEAF						
Novelty bowl, footed	80.00	65.00	50.00			
CACTUS (NORTHWOOD)						
Shakers, each	85.00			100.00	135.00	
CALYX						
Vase, scarce	85.00		60.00	90.00		
CANARY/BLUE J.I.P.						
Vase, 6½"						450.00
CANE & DIAMOND SWIRL						
Stemmed tray	75.00			70.00		
CANE RINGS						
Bowl, 8½"	75.00			85.00		
Celery vase	55.00			65.00		
Creamer	60.00			65.00		
Sugar	65.00			70.00		
CAROUSEL						
Bowl	55.00	50.00	35.00			
CASBAH						
Bowl			120.00			
Compote			140.00			
CASHEWS						
Bowl	50.00	45.00	30.00			
Bowl, tricornered	65.00	60.00	45.00			
Rose bowl, rare	90.00	85.00	60.00			
Whimsey bowl	55.00	50.00	35.00			
CENTIPEDE						
Bowl, scarce	125.00			160.00		
CHERRY						
Bowl, master	70.00					
Bowl, small	25.00					
Covered butter	225.00					
Creamer	110.00					
Sugar	125.00					
Spooner	115.00					
Goblet	75.00					
Wine	80.00					
Plate, rare	160.00					
Open compote	90.00					
Covered compote	125.00					
Novelty bowls	60.00					
CHERRY PANEL						
Novelty bowl	70.00		55.00	70.00		
Nut bowl whimsey	90.00		75.00	100.00		
Vase whimsey			150.00			
CHIPPENDALE						
Bowl, 9½"	85.00			115.00		
Basket	60.00			80.00		
Compote	75.00			95.00		
Creamer	50.00			65.00		

Pattern Name	Blue	Green	White	Vaseline/Canary	Cranberry	Other
Sugar, open	45.00			60.00		
Plate, 6¼"	75.00			95.00		
Pitcher	150.00			165.00		
Salt dip	40.00			50.00		
Tumbler	40.00			45.00		
Vase whimsey			175.00			
CHRISTMAS PEARLS						
Cruet	300.00	280.00	350.00			
Shakers, pair	165.00	140.00	175.00			
CHRISTMAS SNOWFLAKE*						
Pitcher, either	675.00		525.00		950.00	
Tumbler, average	110.00		100.00		125.00	
CHRYSANTHEMUM						
Bowl, footed, 11"	275.00		200.00			400.00 Amethyst
CHRYSANTHEMUM BASE SWIRL						
Bowl, master	55.00		45.00		120.00	
Bowl, sauce	35.00		25.00		50.00	
Butter	325.00		300.00		500.00	
Celery vase	140.00		115.00		225.00	
Creamer	100.00		75.00		400.00	
Cruet	225.00		200.00		500.00	
Custard cup	75.00		50.00		110.00	
Finger bowl	45.00		30.00		140.00	
Mustard pot	150.00		120.00		240.00	
Pitcher	400.00		350.00		900.00	
Tumbler	100.00		75.00		125.00	
Shakers, pair	125.00		100.00		300.00	
Spooner	100.00		75.00		215.00	
Straw holder with lid	500.00		400.00		1,200.00	
Sugar	200.00		175.00		350.00	
Sugar shaker	200.00		175.00		275.00	
Syrup	200.00		175.00		500.00	
Toothpick holder	100.00		75.00		300.00	
CHRYSANTHEMUM SWIRL VARIANT						
Pitcher, rare	400.00		275.00		925.00	375.00 Teal
Tumbler, rare	100.00		65.00		110.00	
CIRCLED SCROLL						
Bowl, master	175.00	150.00	125.00			
Bowl, sauce	55.00	50.00	35.00			
Butter	475.00	350.00	300.00			
Creamer	175.00	170.00	125.00			
Cruet	700.00	675.00	465.00			
Jelly compote	150.00	140.00	125.00			
Pitcher	475.00	425.00	400.00			
Tumbler	100.00	85.00	75.00			
Shakers, pair	325.00	300.00	250.00			
Spooner	175.00	170.00	125.00			
Sugar	250.00	225.00	200.00			
CLEOPATRA'S FAN						
Vase, novelty, rare	100.00	90.00	75.00			
COIN DOT CHEVRON BASE						
Oil lamp	300.00		200.00			
COIN DOT LAMP						
Lamp, three sizes	225.00-325.00		175.00-250.00			
Finger lamp	250.00		185.00	450.00		
COINSPOT*						
(Includes variants, prices averaged. All makers, not all shapes; made by all companies.)						
Barber bottle	175.00	170.00	125.00		300.00	
Bowl, master	50.00	40.00	30.00		70.00	
Bowl, sauce	30.00	25.00	15.00		40.00	
Celery vase	125.00	110.00	100.00	125.00	185.00	
Compote	65.00	45.00	35.00			
Cruet, various	250.00	225.00	125.00	250.00	400.00	375.00 Rubina
Lamp (from syrup)	300.00		250.00		900.00	
Novelty bowls	60.00	55.00	35.00			
Perfume	65.00	75.00	55.00			
Pickle castor	300.00		225.00		750.00	
Pitcher	275.00	250.00	175.00	200.00	400.00	225.00 Rubina
Tumbler	40.00	35.00	25.00	35.00	100.00	100.00 Rubina
Shakers, each	150.00	100.00	75.00	100.00	200.00	
Sugar shaker	125.00	100.00	80.00	110.00	390.00	250.00 Rubina
Syrup	175.00	155.00	150.00		400.00	325.00 Rubina
Toothpick holder	275.00	250.00	150.00	240.00	275.00	300.00 Rubina
Tumble-up	155.00	150.00	125.00		300.00	
Water bottle			150.00		350.00	

Pattern Name	Blue	Green	White	Vaseline/Canary	Cranberry	Other
COINSPOT & SWIRL						
Cruet, rare	150.00		100.00		200.00	235.00 Amber
Syrup, rare	175.00		125.00		235.00	250.00 Amber
COLONIAL STAIRSTEPS						
Creamer	100.00					
Sugar	100.00					
Toothpick holder	200.00					
COMMONWEALTH						
Tumbler			20.00			
COMPASS (DUGAN/DIAMOND)						
Bowl, scarce	150.00	150.00	80.00			
Plate, rare	250.00	225.00				
Rose bowl whimsey	160.00	160.00	90.00			
CONCAVE COLUMNS (#617)						
Vase	100.00		75.00	100.00		
Vase whimsey	125.00		100.00	125.00		
CONCH & TWIG						
Wall-pocket vase	250.00			250.00		
CONSOLIDATED CRISS-CROSS						
Bowl, master			125.00		200.00	
Bowl, sauce			50.00		75.00	
Butter			450.00		900.00	
Celery vase			150.00		175.00	
Creamer			250.00		375.00	
Cruet			275.00		800.00	
Finger bowl			100.00		125.00	
Ivy ball			300.00		700.00	
Mustard pot			150.00		275.00	
Pitcher			750.00		3,000.00	
Tumbler			100.00		125.00	
Shakers, each			100.00		100.00	185.00 Rubina
Spooner			225.00		300.00	
Sugar			350.00		400.00	
Sugar shaker			325.00		600.00	600.00 Rubina
Syrup			325.00		825.00	725.00 Rubina
Toothpick holder			200.00		500.00	
CONSOLIDATED SHELL						
Rose bowl	175.00		125.00	250.00		265.00 Rubina
CONSTELLATION (SEAFOAM)						
Compote	225.00		150.00			
CONTESSA						
Basket, handled	60.00			75.00		250.00 Amber
Breakfast set, footed, two pieces	155.00					350.00 Amber
Pitcher	125.00					325.00 Amber
CONVEX RIB						
Vase	80.00	65.00	50.00			
CORAL						
Bowl	50.00	40.00	25.00	45.00		
CORAL & SHELL						
Bowl 9½"	130.00					
CORAL REEF						
Bitters bottle	200.00		125.00		300.00	
Barber bottle	200.00		125.00		300.00	
Finger bowl	175.00		110.00		225.00	
Mini nightlamp	500.00		400.00		1,900.00	
Oil lamp, stemmed	450.00		335.00		1,800.00	
Finger lamp, footed	425.00		325.00		1,700.00	
Finger lamp, stemmed	500.00		400.00		2,100.00	
Rose bowl, rare	400.00			750.00		
CORINTH						
Vase, 8"-13"	40.00		30.00			
CORNUCOPIA (NORTHWOOD)						
Handled vase	75.00		60.00			
CORNUCOPIA VASE						
Vase on stand				165.00		
CORN VASE *						
Fancy vase, scarce	235.00	280.00	125.00	230.00		
COROLLA						
Vase	225.00		175.00	200.00		
CORONATION						
Cake stand	100.00			70.00		
Creamer	45.00			40.00		
Sugar	45.00			40.00		
Pitcher	225.00			165.00		
Platter, oval	70.00			50.00		
Tumbler	40.00			40.00		

Pattern Name	Blue	Green	White	Vaseline/Canary	Cranberry	Other
COUNTER SWIRL						
Vase	80.00			110.00		
COUNTRY KITCHEN & VARIANT						
Bowl, small, flared			200.00			
Bowl, small, square			250.00			
Bowl, large, 8", deep round			275.00			
Bowl, medium, 7½", square,			300.00			
Bowl, large, ruffled			300.00			
CROCUS						
Vase, rare	325.00	300.00	225.00	375.00		
CROWN JEWELS						
Creamer	80.00					
Pitcher	200.00					
Tumbler	60.00					
Plate	100.00					
Platter	110.00					
Sugar	95.00					
CURTAIN CALL						
Castor set, rare						550.00 Cobalt
CURTAIN OPTIC						
Guest set, two pieces	125.00	100.00	80.00	125.00		
Pitcher, various	225.00	210.00	150.00	200.00		
Tumbler, various	50.00	45.00	35.00	45.00		
CURVY						
Epergne				165.00		
CYCLONE						
Vase, very rare	1,000.00		650.00	900.00		
DAFFODILS						
Bowl whimsey	165.00		125.00	235.00		
Hand lamp	325.00	300.00	225.00	300.00	525.00	
Oil lamp	350.00	325.00	300.00	350.00	675.00	
Pitcher	900.00	950.00	600.00	1,500.00	7,500.00	
Tumbler, rare	400.00	350.00	300.00	400.00	550.00	
Vase	300.00			265.00		
Vase, with "thorn" feet				350.00		
Add 25% for goofus						
DAFFODILS SHADE (ENGLISH)						
Shade				325.00		
DAHLIA (DUGAN)						
Pitcher, gold trim	250.00					
Tumbler, gold trim	40.00					
DAHLIA TWIST						
Epergne, scarce	350.00	325.00	300.00			
Epergne, cherub with one lily	150.00		125.00	170.00		
Vase, scarce	90.00	70.00	55.00			
DAISIES LAMP						
Oil lamp				725.00		
DAISIES IN PENTAGON						
Oil lamp				875.00		
DAISY & BUTTON						
Bowl, novelty	65.00			65.00		
Bun tray	150.00			150.00		
Lifeboat	85.00			85.00		
DAISY & BUTTON WITH DIAMONDS						
Bowl, 4½"				85.00		
DAISY & DRAPE						
Vase, very rare				1,900.00		
DAISY & FERN (NORTHWOOD)						
(All moulds)						
Barber bottle					500.00	
Bowl, master	80.00	100.00	55.00		250.00	
Bowl, sauce	40.00	45.00	25.00		150.00	
Butter	225.00	250.00	175.00		300.00	
Creamer	75.00	90.00	60.00		425.00	
Cruet	200.00	175.00	150.00		525.00	
Finger bowl	200.00	150.00	175.00		450.00	
Mustard pot	100.00	125.00	75.00		150.00	
Night lamp	225.00	250.00	175.00		325.00	
Perfume	175.00	200.00	125.00		250.00	
Pitcher, three shapes	300.00	300.00	200.00		300.00–750.00	
Tumbler	50.00	50.00	25.00		100.00	
Rose bowl					125.00	
Shakers, pair	300.00	275.00	175.00		300.00	
Spooner	75.00	100.00	55.00		425.00	
Sugar	100.00	125.00	75.00		250.00	
Sugar shaker	200.00	225.00	175.00		275.00	

Pattern Name	Blue	Green	White	Vaseline/Canary	Cranberry	Other
Syrup, various	250.00	225.00	200.00		400.00	
Toothpick holder	160.00	175.00	125.00		225.00	
Vase	150.00	150.00	100.00		200.00	
Prices for either mould used and also for Dugan pieces found.						
DAISY & GREEK KEY						
Sauce, footed	75.00	60.00	35.00			
DAISY & PLUME						
Basket, rare			150.00			
Bowl footed	50.00	45.00	30.00			
Rose bowl, footed	60.00	55.00	35.00			
Whimsey, flared bowl	95.00					
DAISY BLOCK						
Rowboat, 10", 12" and 15"		275.00	165.00	250.00		
DAISY DEAR						
Bowl, rare	65.00	55.00	35.00			
DAISY DRAPE						
Creamer				90.00		
DAISY IN CRISS-CROSS						
Barber bottle	1,700.00					
Pitcher	300.00				450.00	
Tumbler	60.00				100.00	
Syrup	275.00				475.00	
DAISY MAY (LEAF RAYS)						
Nappy or bon-bon	55.00	45.00	35.00			
Whimsey on metal stand		95.00				
DAISY SWIRL						
Bowl	85.00			90.00		
Bowl whimsey	75.00	65.00	45.00			
Whimsey on metal stand	80.00		60.00			
DAISY WITH PANELS						
Bowl, footed	95.00					
DAISY WREATH						
Bowl, rare	165.00					
DANDELION						
Mug, very rare	850.00			1,200.00		
DAVIDSON DRAPE						
Vase, squat	150.00			150.00		
DAVIDSON GERMANY SOUVENIR						
Plate, 5½				125.00		
DAVIDSON OPEN SALTS						
Salt dip, various shapes and sizes				50.00-90.00		
*Add 25% with metal holder						
DAVIDSON PEARLINE						
Epergne, 14"	300.00			300.00		
DAVIDSON SHELL						
Spill vase	125.00			125.00		
Whimsey, ruffled	200.00					
DAVIDSON SPILL						
Vase	250.00			250.00		
DECO LILY						
Vase, 7¾"		100.00				
DECORATED ENGLISH SWIRL						
Rose bowl					250.00	
DESERT GARDEN						
Bowl	45.00	40.00	25.00			
DIAGONAL WAVE						
Tumbler			25.00	65.00		
Vase	95.00			150.00		
DIAMOND & DAISY						
Basket, handled	100.00	110.00	55.00			
Bowl novelty	60.00	70.00	35.00			
Rose bowl, whimsey		90.00				
DIAMOND & OVAL THUMBPRINT						
Vase	40.00	45.00	25.00			
DIAMOND DOT						
Compote				100.00		
Shade				135.00		
DIAMOND-IN-DIAMOND						
Vase	250.00		200.00			
DIAMOND MAPLE LEAF						
Bowl, handled	75.00	70.00	45.00			
Novelty, handled	40.00	50.00	25.00	50.00		
Add 10% for signed pieces						
DIAMOND OPTIC						
Compote	50.00		40.00			
Stemmed cardtray	60.00		50.00			

Pattern Name	Blue	Green	White	Vaseline/Canary	Cranberry	Other
DIAMOND POINT						
Vase	40.00	50.00	30.00			
DIAMOND POINT & FLEUR DE LIS						
Bowl, novelty	50.00	55.00	40.00			
Nut bowl		65.00				
DIAMOND POINT COLUMNS						
Vase, scarce	200.00	175.00	75.00			
DIAMOND PYRAMID						
Bowl	250.00				200.00	
DIAMOND RINGS						
Bowl, rectangular				95.00		
DIAMONDS						
Bowl, various	65.00-100.00		50.00-75.00		90.00-165.00	80.00-155.00 Rubina
Bowl, handgrip	75.00		50.00		100.00	85.00 Rubina
Cruet	95.00		75.00		350.00	250.00 Rubina
Pitcher, two shapes	300.00		225.00		400.00	275.00 Rubina
Sugar shaker	130.00		100.00		165.00	145.00 Rubina
Tumbler	60.00		45.00		70.00	65.00 Rubina
DIAMONDS AND SWAGS						
Bowl				85.00		
DIAMOND SPEARHEAD						
Bowl, master	180.00	185.00	125.00	180.00		140.00*
Bowl, sauce	55.00	60.00	35.00	45.00		40.00*
Butter	500.00	575.00	400.00	500.00		475.00*
Celery vase	250.00	250.00	150.00	250.00		250.00*
Creamer	200.00	225.00	150.00	200.00		200.00*
Cup and saucer set				250.00		
Goblet	175.00	150.00	100.00	150.00		135.00*
Jelly compote	200.00	150.00	125.00	175.00		200.00*
Mini creamer	200.00	200.00	125.00	200.00		225.00 Sapphire
Mug	180.00	200.00	100.00	150.00		175.00*
Oil bottle	125.00			100.00		100.00
Pitcher	725.00	625.00	400.00	500.00		625.00*
Tumbler	125.00	100.00	60.00	90.00		100.00*
Shakers, pair	150.00	175.00	130.00	175.00		175.00*
Spittoon whimsey		55.00		500.00		
Spooner	175.00	200.00	150.00	175.00		175.00*
Sugar	250.00	225.00	175.00	250.00		250.00*
Syrup	650.00	700.00	550.00	625.00		750.00*
Tall creamer	200.00			200.00		275.00
Tall compote	400.00	400.00	300.00	400.00		425.00
Toothpick holder	150.00	125.00	100.00	125.00		145.00
Water carafe	200.00		175.00	225.00		
*Emerald or sapphire						
DIAMOND STEM						
Vase, three sizes, rare	150.00	175.00	80.00	150.00		125.00 Aqua
Vase, J.I.P whimsey	175.00	200.00	100.00	175.00		
DIAMOND TREE						
Bowl, scarce				140.00		
DIAMOND WAVE						
Demitasse cup and saucer, pair				110.00		
Pitcher with lid				350.00	175.00	250.00 Amethyst
Tumbler				65.00	50.00	
Vase, 5"				80.00	85.00	
DIAMOND WIDE STRIPE						
Finger bowl					175.00	
Pitcher					450.00	
Rose bowl					200.00	
Tumbler					125.00	
DIMPLE						
Vase	140.00		110.00	185.00		
DOGWOOD DRAPE (PALM ROSETTE)						
Compote	150.00		120.00			
Plate, rare	125.00		90.00			
DOLLY MADISON						
Bowl, ruffled, 8"	50.00	40.00	35.00			
Bowl, master	60.00	70.00	50.00			
Bowl, sauce	30.00	35.00	20.00			
Butter	325.00	350.00	250.00			
Creamer	90.00	100.00	70.00			
Pitcher	400.00	425.00	300.00			
Tumbler	80.00	95.00	50.00			
Spooner	80.00	90.00	50.00			
Sugar	150.00	160.00	100.00			
Plate, 6", scarce	110.00	110.00	65.00			
Bowl, novelty	60.00	70.00	45.00			

Pattern Name	Blue	Green	White	Vaseline/Canary	Cranberry	Other
DOLPHIN*						
Compote, scarce	85.00		50.00	75.00		
DOLPHIN & HERONS						
Compote, footed, novelty	495.00		280.00	425.00		
Tray, footed, novelty	490.00		275.00		800.00	
DOLPHIN & SHELL						
Spill vase			75.00			
DOLPHIN PETTICOAT						
Candlesticks, pair	175.00		125.00	165.00		
DORSET (ENGLISH)						
Bowls, various sizes	50.00-110.00			75.00-225.00		
DOT OPTIC						
Bowls, various	35.00-90.00	40.00-95.00	25.00-70.00	45.00-100.00		
Pitchers, two styles	135.00-160.00	140.00-170.00	85.00-120.00	150.00-225.00		
Tumblers, two styles	30.00-45.00	35.00-45.00	25.00-40.00	40.00-55.00		
Vases, various	45.00-75.00	50.00-80.00	40.00-60.00	50.00-95.00		
DOTTED SPIRAL						
Bowl in metal holder				145.00		
Vases, various				65.00-90.00		
DOUBLE DIAMONDS						
Bowl				90.00		
DOUBLE DOLPHIN (1533)						
Compote, rare	150.00		100.00			
DOUBLE GREEK KEY						
Bowl, master	75.00		60.00			
Bowl, sauce	40.00		25.00			
Butter	325.00		250.00			
Celery vase	175.00		125.00			
Creamer	100.00		75.00			
Mustard pot	200.00		150.00			
Pickle tray	150.00		90.00			
Pitcher	400.00		325.00			
Tumbler	90.00		60.00			
Shakers, pair	250.00		175.00			
Spooner	110.00		70.00			
Sugar	200.00		125.00			
Toothpick holder	250.00		200.00			
DOUBLE PANEL (ENGLISH)						
Bowls, engraved				65.00-135.00		
DOUBLE RIB & BLOCK						
Bowl, 5½" with souvenir label				200.00		
Nappy				80.00		
Salt dip				70.00		
DOUBLE STEMMED ROSE						
Bowl, very scarce			150.00			
DOVER DIAMOND						
Bowl	35.00			35.00		
Creamer	30.00			30.00		
Sugar, open, stemmed	35.00			35.00		
DRAGON & LOTUS						
Bowl, rare						325.00 Amethyst
DRAGONFLY LAMP						
Oil lamp with chimney			1,400.00			
DRAPERY (FENTON)						
Pitcher	450.00	425.00	275.00			
Tumbler	75.00	65.00	40.00			
DRAPERY (NORTHWOOD)						
Bowl, master	110.00		75.00			
Bowl, sauce	40.00		25.00			
Butter	200.00		175.00			
Creamer	10.00		80.00			
Pitcher	250.00		225.00			
Tumbler	75.00		50.00			
Rose bowl	100.00		75.00			
Spooner	85.00		70.00			
Sugar	145.00		125.00			
Vase	175.00	200.00	155.00	175.00		
DUCHESS						
Bowl, master	100.00		65.00	85.00		
Bowl, sauce	35.00		25.00	35.00		
Butter	200.00		150.00	175.00		
Creamer	65.00		45.00	65.00		
Cruet	225.00		175.00	200.00		
Lampshade	100.00		75.00			
Pitcher	200.00		165.00	185.00		
Tumbler	40.00		25.00	35.00		

Pattern Name	Blue	Green	White	Vaseline/Canary	Cranberry	Other
Spooner	70.00		50.00	70.00		
Sugar	110.00		75.00	110.00		
Toothpick holder	165.00		125.00	150.00		
DUGAN'S #1013 (WIDE RIB)						
Vase	65.00	75.00	50.00			
Bowl, whimsey	50.00	55.00	40.00			
Plate	70.00	80.00	60.00			
DUGAN'S DIAMOND COMPASS (DRAGON LADY)						
Rose bowl	160.00	150.00	90.00			
Novelty bowl	140.00	130.00	90.00			
Vase	100.00	100.00	60.00			
DUGAN'S HEXAGON BASE						
Vase, two sizes		25.00-45.00	20.00-40.00			
DUGAN'S HONEYCOMB						
Bowl, various shapes, rare	175.00	175.00	150.00	200.00		
DUGAN'S INTAGLIO ACORN						
Bowl, 10"	115.00					
DUGAN'S INTAGLIO CHERRY						
Bowl			80.00			
DUGAN'S INTAGLIO DAISY						
Basket	130.00	150.00	100.00			
Bowl	90.00	100.00	75.00			
Plate	110.00	125.00	90.00			
DUGAN'S INTAGLIO GRAPE						
Plate, 12½", rare			250.00			
Bowl			125.00			
Compote			85.00			
DUGAN'S INTAGLIO HOLLY						
Bowl			75.00			
Compote			85.00			
Plate			95.00			
DUGAN'S INTAGLIO MORNING GLORY						
Bowls, two sizes			40.00-85.00			
Compote			110.00			
DUGAN'S INTAGLIO PEACH						
Bowl			90.00			
Compote			100.00			
Plate, 13"			175.00			
DUGAN'S INTAGLIO PEAR & PLUM						
Bowl, 10"			135.00			
DUGAN'S INTAGLIO ROSE						
Bowl, small			35.00			
Bowl, large			80.00			
Plate, 10"			145.00			
DUGAN'S INTAGLIO STRAWBERRY						
Bowl, 9"			65.00			
Fruit bowl, stemmed			85.00			
DUGAN'S JUNIOR						
Vase, 4½"	50.00	50.00	35.00			
Vase, with silver filigree	70.00	75.00	55.00			
Floral etched add 15%						
DUGAN'S OLIVE NAPPY						
One shape	45.00	40.00	25.00			
DUGAN'S PLAIN PANELS						
Vase	55.00	55.00	35.00			
EIGHT RAYED NAPPY						
Nappy with handle						15.00 Purple opalescent
ELLIPSE & DIAMOND						
Pitcher					500.00	
Tumbler					115.00	
ELSON DEWDROP						
Berry bowl, small			15.00			
Berry bowl, large			45.00			
Butter, covered			115.00			
Creamer or spooner			35.00			
Sugar with lid			60.00			
Mug			65.00			
Breakfast set, two pieces			95.00			
Celery vase			65.00			
ELSON DEWDROP #2						
Bowl, sauce			15.00			
Cruet			90.00			
Punch cup			35.00			
Shakers, pair			110.00			
Spooner			35.00			

Pattern Name	Blue	Green	White	Vaseline/Canary	Cranberry	Other
EMBOSSED SPANISH LACE						
Vase, 4¼"				100.00		
ENGLISH BEADED PANELS						
Creamer	65.00					
ENGLISH CENTIPEDE						
Bowl	150.00		170.00			
ENGLISH DRAPE						
Vase				135.00		
ENGLISH DUCK						
Novelty dish	150.00			150.00		
ENGLISH FERN						
Vase		70.00				
ENGLISH LILY VASE						
Vase				175.00	165.00	
ENGLISH OAK LEAF						
Boat shape	100.00			75.00		
Bowl	150.00			200.00		
Rectangular posy	125.00			165.00		
ENGLISH OPTIC EPERGNE						
Epergne						500.00 Rubina verde
ENGLISH RIPPLE						
Tumbler	80.00			80.00		
ENGLISH SALT DIP						
One shape				75.00		
ENGLISH SPOOL						
Vase	75.00			70.00		
ENGLISH SWAN						
Novelty dish, two sizes				150.00-200.00	175.00-225.00	
ENGLISH SWIRL						
Pitcher						200.00 White/cran-cased
Tumbler						50.00 White/cran-cased
ENGLISH WIDE STRIPE						
Pitcher					350.00	
ENTANGLED BRANCHES						
Oil lamp				350.00		
ESTATE						
Vase, scarce	95.00	85.00	65.00			
EUROPEAN LILY EPERGNES						
Single lily epergne, two sizes	145.00		125.00	175.00		
EVERGLADES						
Bowl, oval, master	200.00		125.00	200.00		
Bowl, oval, sauce	45.00		25.00	50.00		
Butter	325.00		250.00	375.00		
Creamer	150.00		95.00	150.00		
Cruet	425.00		325.00	475.00		
Jelly compote	125.00		95.00	150.00		
Pitcher	475.00		375.00	500.00		
Tumbler	85.00		60.00	100.00		
Shakers, pair	275.00		225.00	300.00		
Spooner	125.00		95.00	150.00		
Sugar	185.00		120.00	225.00		
EVERGLADES (CAMBRIDGE)						
Compote			75.00			
EXTERIOR THUMBPRINT						
Vase				275.00		
FAN						
Bowl, master	75.00	70.00	65.00			
Bowl, sauce	30.00	30.00	20.00			
Butter	400.00	400.00	200.00			
Card tray whimsey	125.00	110.00	90.00			
Creamer	125.00	120.00	75.00			
Gravy boat	50.00	50.00	35.00			
Novelty bowls	40.00	40.00	25.00			
Pitcher	300.00	300.00	200.00			
Tumbler	40.00	30.00	20.00			
Spooner	125.00	110.00	85.00			
Sugar	200.00	200.00	150.00			
Whimsey bowls	55.00	55.00	35.00			
FAN & SHELL (ENGLISH)						
Vase, stemmed				250.00		
FANCY FANTAILS						
Bowl	40.00	45.00	25.00	40.00		
Rose bowl	45.00	50.00	30.00	45.00		
FEATHERED HEARTS						
Shade					150.00	

Pattern Name	Blue	Green	White	Vaseline/Canary	Cranberry	Other
FEATHERS						
Vase	35.00	30.00	25.00			
Whimsey bowl, rare			125.00			
Whimsey nut bowl, rare	150.00	150.00				
FENTON'S #100						
Bowl				50.00		65.00 Amethyst
FENTON'S #220 STRIPE						
Creamer or sugar	75.00	80.00	65.00	95.00		
Pitcher with lid	250.00	250.00	175.00	225.00		
Tumbler, handled	45.00	50.00	35.00	60.00		
Tumble-up, complete	150.00	150.00	100.00	145.00		
Vase whimsey, 8", from pitcher	125.00	125.00	75.00	120.00		
FENTON'S #260						
Compote, tall	50.00		35.00	50.00		
FENTON'S #370						
Bowl						45.00 Amber
Vase						50.00 Amber
Nappy						55.00 Amber
Bon-bon						50.00 Amber
Whimsey, ruffled, from candy jar						95.00 Cameo opal
FENTON'S #950						
Cornucopia candlestick, each						100.00 Amethyst
FENTON'S PLAIN JANE						
Hat whimsey			30.00			65.00 Amethyst
Pitcher			110.00			190.00 Amethyst
Tumbler			25.00			55.00 Amethyst
FERN						
Barber bottle	150.00		100.00		300.00	
Bowl, master	100.00		80.00		125.00	
Bowl, sauce	50.00		40.00		55.00	
Butter	275.00		225.00		400.00	
Celery vase	125.00		100.00	600.00	150.00	
Creamer	125.00		100.00		150.00	
Cruet	225.00		225.00		500.00	
Finger bowl	75.00		50.00		100.00	
Mustard pot	150.00		125.00		175.00	
Pitcher, various	275.00		200.00		750.00	
Tumbler	50.00		50.00		110.00	
Shakers, pair	175.00		100.00		165.00	
Spooner	125.00		100.00		150.00	
Sugar	200.00		175.00		250.00	
Sugar shaker, various	125.00		100.00		550.00	
Syrup	275.00		220.00		600.00	
Toothpick holder, rare	350.00		200.00		475.00	
FERN PANELS						
Hat						150.00 Amethyst
FESTIVE FLOWERS						
Vase, decorated			100.00			
FIELD FLOWERS						
Bowl, 7¾"	110.00		90.00			
Compote, two sizes	200.00		150.00	250.00		
FIELD OF FLOWERS						
Compote	125.00					
FILE & FAN						
Bowl	90.00					
FINECUT & ROSES						
Novelty bowls	45.00	50.00	40.00			
Rose bowl, rare	65.00	75.00	50.00			
FINE RIB (FENTON)						
Vase, very rare			500.00			
FINE RIB (NORTHWOOD)						
Vase	70.00	65.00	50.00	65.00		
FINE RIB EPERGNE						
Epergne				250.00		
FISH IN THE SEA						
Vase, scarce	375.00	425.00	275.00	550.00		
Vase whimsey, scarce	295.00	390.00	270.00			
FISHNET						
Epergne (one shape, two pieces)	175.00		145.00			
FISHSCALE & BEADS						
Bowl	50.00		30.00			
FLEUR-DE-LIS						
Pitcher			150.00			
FLEUR-DE-LIS IN PANELS						
Marmalade dish				150.00		

Pattern Name	Blue	Green	White	Vaseline/ Canary	Cranberry	Other
FLORA						
Banana bowl whimsey	120.00		100.00	150.00		
Bowl, master	100.00		80.00	100.00		
Bowl, sauce	50.00		30.00	40.00		
Butter	300.00		200.00	265.00		
Celery vase	130.00		100.00	110.00		
Creamer	100.00		80.00	100.00		
Cruet	750.00		450.00	600.00		
Jelly compote	150.00		110.00	150.00		
Novelty bowl	70.00		45.00	60.00		
Pitcher	500.00		410.00	480.00		
Tumbler	90.00		65.00	85.00		
Shakers, pair	400.00		300.00	400.00		
Spooner	110.00		300.00	375.00		
Sugar	145.00		100.00	125.00		
Syrup	410.00		300.00	400.00		
Toothpick holder	480.00		300.00	400.00		
FLORADINE						
Bowl, 8"						350.00-750.00
Butter						1,100.00
Creamer						400.00-800.00
Cruet						600.00-1,200.00
Pitcher						1,100.00-1,400.00
Sauce, 4"						250.00-350.00
Shakers, each						450.00-700.00
Spooner						350.00-600.00
Sugar						450.00-850.00
Sugar shaker						550.00
Syrup						1,600.00
Toothpick holder						700.00
Tumbler						450.00-1,400.00
FLORAL AND VINES						
Shade				110.00		
FLORAL EYELET						
Pitcher	525.00		400.00		850.00	
Tumbler	100.00		100.00		250.00	
FLORAL FREEZE						
Creamer	85.00					
Sugar, open	70.00					
FLOWER FORM						
Bulbous single lily epergne				165.00		
Toothpick				90.00		
FLOWERING VINE						
Butter	240.00					
Creamer	100.00					
Spooner	90.00					
Sugar	100.00					
FLOWER STARBURST						
Oil lamp				475.00		
FLUTED BARS & BEADS						
Novelty bowl	60.00	55.00	50.00	70.00		
Rose bowl	70.00	65.00	60.00	75.00		
Vase whimsey	65.00	60.00	55.00	75.00		65.00 Emerald
FLUTED SCROLLS						
Bowl, master	85.00	90.00	60.00	95.00		
Bowl, sauce	35.00	45.00	30.00	45.00		
Butter	185.00		165.00	175.00		
Creamer	80.00		55.00	70.00		
Cruet	200.00		175.00	185.00		
Epergne, small	125.00	165.00	100.00	175.00		
Novelty bowl or whimsey	55.00		40.00	55.00		
Puff box (aka: baby butter dish)	80.00	90.00	60.00	95.00		
Pitcher	250.00		175.00	200.00		
Tumbler	100.00		50.00	75.00		
Rose bowl	150.00		100.00	125.00		
Shakers, pair	100.00		75.00	85.00		
Spooner	80.00		55.00	60.00		
Sugar	140.00		100.00	110.00		
Note: fluted scroll with flower band is priced the same as above.						
FLUTED SCROLL WITH VINE						
Vase, footed	100.00		50.00	110.00		
FOOTED STRIPE						
Bowl, footed				95.00		
FORKED STRIPE						
Barber bottle			275.00			

Pattern Name	Blue	Green	White	Vaseline/ Canary	Cranberry	Other
FOUNTAIN						
Vase					250.00	
FOUNTAIN WITH BOWS						
Shade				200.00	250.00	
Vase, various shapes				125.00	150.00	
FOUR-FOOTED HOBNAIL						
Butter			155.00	175.00		225.00 Cobalt
Creamer			70.00	90.00		100.00 Cobalt
Spooner			70.00	85.00		100.00 Cobalt
Sugar			80.00	125.00		150.00 Cobalt
FOUR PILLARS						
Vase	75.00	70.00	40.00	75.00		
FROSTED LEAF & BASKETWEAVE						
Butter	275.00		200.00	250.00		
Creamer	150.00		130.00	135.00		
Spooner	150.00		125.00	135.00		
Sugar	175.00		150.00	165.00		
Vase whimsey	150.00		125.00	140.00		
GARLAND OF ROSES						
Stemmed tray, rare	175.00		100.00			
GONTERMAN (ADONIS) HOB						
Cruet						425.00 Amber
GONTERMAN (ADONIS) SWIRL						
Bowl, master	100.00					100.00 Amber
Bowl, sauce	50.00					50.00 Amber
Butter	400.00					350.00 Amber
Celery vase	225.00					200.00 Amber
Creamer	175.00					125.00 Amber
Cruet	400.00					385.00 Amber
Pitcher	400.00					400.00 Amber
Tumbler	100.00					90.00 Amber
Shade	125.00					100.00 Amber
Spooner	150.00					125.00 Amber
Sugar	250.00					225.00 Amber
Syrup	400.00					375.00 Amber
Toothpick holder	300.00					200.00 Amber
GRACE DARLING						
Boat, 11¼" and 13"				400.00-450.00		
GRAPE & CABLE (NORTHWOOD & FENTON)						
Bon-bon				450.00		
Centerpiece bowl	300.00	300.00	225.00	325.00		
Fruit bowl, large	325.00	300.00	245.00	325.00		
GRAPE & CABLE WITH THUMBPRINT						
Bowl, scarce		175.00				
GRAPE & CHERRY						
Bowl	90.00	80.00	65.00	100.00		
GRAPE CLUSTER						
Bowl, 5⅜", square						100.00 Light blue opal
GRAPEVINE CLUSTER						
Vase, footed	175.00		125.00	165.00		200.00 Aqua
GRECIAN URN						
Vase, 4½"	65.00					
GREEK KEY & RIBS						
Bowl	65.00	55.00	35.00			
GREEK KEY & SCALES						
Novelty bowl	90.00	80.00	50.00			
GREELEY (HOBBS)						
Cruet	750.00					
Cup	265.00					
Finger bowl	225.00					
GREENER BOAT						
Boat shape, 5"	95.00					
Boat shape, 7"	125.00					
Pitcher	1,200.00					
GREENER DEWDROP						
Bowl, 5"						95.00 Amber
Platter, stemmed						175.00 Amber
GREENER DIAMOND COLUMN						
Epergne, 13"						350.00 Amber
HARLEQUIN						
Rose bowl	250.00			275.00		325.00 Cran/vaseline
Ewer, decorated				325.00		
Vase whimsey				350.00		350.00 Cran/vaseline
Vase, decorated				325.00	350.00	375.00 Cran/vaseline
HARROW						
Creamer	75.00					

Pattern Name	Blue	Green	White	Vaseline/Canary	Cranberry	Other
Sugar, open	70.00					
Wine, stemmed	40.00					
Cordial, stemmed	35.00					
HEART-HANDLE OPEN O'S						
Ring tray	85.00	75.00	60.00			
HEARTS & CLUBS						
Bowl, footed	60.00	55.00	35.00			
HEARTS & FLOWERS						
Bowl	185.00		150.00			
Compote	300.00		265.00			
HEATHERBLOOM						
Vase	40.00	30.00	20.00			
HEAVENLY STARS						
Bowl	185.00		125.00	250.00		
HELEN LOUISE						
Creamer	65.00			90.00		
Open sugar	60.00			80.00		
HERON & PEACOCK*						
Mug	75.00		65.00			
HERRINGBONE (PLAIN OR RIBBED)						
Bowl whimsey	250.00		200.00		400.00	
Cruet	350.00		225.00		850.00	
Pitcher	700.00		475.00		2,000.00	
Tumbler	90.00		65.00		150.00	
HERRINGBONE & CROCUS						
Vase		85.00				
HIDDEN HEARTS						
Hat shape, in metal holder					125.00	
HILLTOP VINES						
Novelty chalice	65.00	60.00	40.00			
HILLTOP VINES VARIANT						
Compote			65.00			
HOBBS POLKA DOT						
Bar bottle						175.00 Green/sapphire
Bowl						125.00 Green/sapphire
Celery						100.00 Green/sapphire
Cheesedish, covered						235.00 Green/ sapphire
Creamer						125.00 Green/sapphire
Cruet						225.00 Green/sapphire
Custard cup						100.00 Green/sapphire
Finger bowl						125.00 Green/sapphire
Lemonade mug						150.00 Green/sapphire
Pitcher						475.00 Green/sapphire
Shakers, each						145.00 Green/sapphire
Sugar						135.00 Green/sapphire
Sugar shaker						250.00 Green/sapphire
Syrup						225.00 Green/sapphire
Tumbler						100.00 Green/sapphire
HOBNAIL (HOBBS)						
Barber bottle	150.00		125.00	145.00		
Bowl, master, square	100.00		80.00	100.00		
Bowl, sauce, square	40.00		30.00	50.00		
Bride's basket	450.00			425.00	525.00	500.00 Rubina
Butter	300.00		200.00	225.00		
Celery vase	175.00		125.00	145.00		225.00 Rubina
Creamer	100.00		100.00	125.00		
Cruet	200.00		200.00	190.00		
Finger bowl	65.00		50.00	55.00		
Lemonade set, complete	600.00				700.00	
Pitcher, five sizes	200.00-400.00		150.00-250.00	175.00-325.00	300.00-600.00	250.00-450.00 Rubina
Tumbler	75.00		50.00	75.00		125.00 Rubina
Shakers, each			200.00		400.00	
Spooner	10.00		100.00	125.00		
Sugar	200.00		135.00	175.00		
Syrup	225.00		200.00	200.00		
HOBNAIL & PANELED THUMBPRINT						
Pitcher	300.00		150.00	300.00		
Tumbler	75.00		45.00	75.00		
Butter	200.00		145.00	175.00		
Sugar	125.00		100.00	90.00		
Creamer	85.00		60.00	75.00		
Spooner	85.00		65.00	75.00		
Bowl, master	75.00		60.00	65.00		
Bowl, sauce	35.00		25.00	30.00		
Sugar, open	70.00			65.00		
Wine, stemmed	40.00			40.00		

Pattern Name	Blue	Green	White	Vaseline/ Canary	Cranberry	Other
Cordial, stemmed	35.00			35.00		
HOBNAIL IN SQUARE* (VESTA)						
Barber bottle			120.00			
Bowl, master			75.00			
Bowl, sauce			25.00			
Bowl with stand	150.00					
Butter			200.00			
Celery vase			145.00			
Compote, various			100.00			
Creamer			100.00			
Pitcher			245.00			
Tumbler			50.00			
Shakers, pair			100.00			
Spooner			100.00			
Sugar			150.00			
HOBNAIL TOY MUG						
Mug, 2"				90.00		
HOBNAIL TWIST						
Vase, or lily in metal holder						140.00 Rubina verde
HOBNAIL WITH BARS						
Berry bowl, small			35.00			
Berry bowl, large			75.00			
Butter			165.00			
Creamer			65.00			
Cruet			90.00			
Spooner			55.00			
Sugar			70.00			
HOLLY (FENTON)						
Bowl, rare			150.00			
HOLLY & BERRY						
Nappy, very scarce			95.00			
HOLLY BERRY LAMP						
Oil lamp, rare			1,400.00			
HONEYCOMB						
Vase	75.00	100.00	45.00			
HONEYCOMB (BLOWN)						
Barber bottle	175.00		125.00		175.00	200.00 Amber
Bowl	95.00	70.00	55.00			
Cracker jar	325.00		250.00		400.00	425.00 Amber
Pitcher	325.00		225.00		500.00	450.00 Amber
Tumbler	80.00		50.00		100.00	75.00 Amber
Syrup	300.00		275.00		425.00	450.00 Amber
HONEYCOMB & CLOVER						
Bowl, master	100.00	75.00	50.00			
Bowl, sauce	50.00	35.00	25.00			
Bowl, novelty	75.00	75.00	50.00			
Butter	400.00	350.00	250.00			
Creamer	150.00	140.00	125.00			
Pitcher	400.00	350.00	285.00			
Tumbler	100.00	80.00	55.00			
Spooner	150.00	150.00	100.00			
Sugar	300.00	275.00	150.00			
HORSE CHESTNUT						
Blown vase				100.00		
Compote				250.00		
IDYLL						
Bowl, master	60.00	60.00	45.00			
Bowl, sauce	30.00	30.00	25.00			
Bowl, 6"-7"	40.00	45.00	30.00			
Butter	350.00	375.00	300.00			
Creamer	150.00	125.00	75.00			
Cruet	225.00	200.00	175.00			
Pitcher	375.00	375.00	300.00			
Tumbler	100.00	90.00	70.00			
Shakers, pair	125.00	115.00	100.00			
Spooner	150.00	125.00	75.00			
Sugar	175.00	200.00	150.00			
Toothpick holder	400.00	325.00	275.00			
Tray	125.00	110.00	100.00			
IMITATION CUT #1						
Basket	130.00					
IMITATION CUT #2						
Basket			100.00			
INFINITY						
Bowl, oval	80.00					

Pattern Name	Blue	Green	White	Vaseline/Canary	Cranberry	Other
INSIDE RIBBING						
Bowl, master	70.00		40.00	75.00		
Bowl, sauce	30.00		20.00	35.00		
Butter	225.00		150.00	250.00		
Celery vase	60.00		35.00	60.00		
Creamer	75.00		55.00	80.00		
Cruet	150.00		100.00	150.00		
Jelly compote	75.00		30.00	65.00		
Pitcher	300.00		160.00	300.00		
Tumbler	65.00		30.00	70.00		
Rose bowl	80.00					
Shakers, pair	125.00		75.00	100.00		
Spooner	75.00		60.00	80.00		
Sugar	125.00		100.00	125.00		
Syrup	155.00		100.00	150.00		
Toothpick holder	200.00		175.00	200.00		
Tray	55.00		30.00	50.00		
INTAGLIO (NORTHWOOD)						
Bowl, master, footed	225.00		100.00	250.00		
Bowl, sauce, std.	35.00		25.00	50.00		
Butter	500.00		275.00			
Creamer	100.00		50.00			
Cruet	200.00		150.00	300.00		
Jelly compote	60.00		45.00	80.00		
Novelty bowl	50.00		30.00	65.00		
Pitcher	250.00		150.00			
Tumbler	110.00		65.00			
Shakers, pair	100.00		75.00			
Spooner	100.00		60.00			
Sugar	175.00		100.00			
INTAGLIO HOLLY (DUGAN'S)						
See Dugan's Intaglio Holly						
INTAGLIO LATTICE						
Bowl			100.00			
INTAGLIO MORNING GLORY						
See Dugan's Intaglio Morning Glory						
INTAGLIO PANELS						
Bowl, 4¾"			45.00			
Celery vase			55.00			
INTERIOR FLUTE						
Vase	40.00	35.00	25.00			50.00 Lavender
INTERIOR PANEL						
Fan vase	55.00	50.00	30.00	55.00		100.00 Amethyst
Rolled rim whimsey						125.00 Cameo opal
Ruffled vase whimsey						100.00 Cameo opal
Trumpet vase whimsey						115.00 Cameo opal
INTERIOR POINSETTIA						
Tumbler	50.00	65.00	40.00			
INTERIOR SWIRL						
Rose bowl	100.00		60.00	100.00		
INTERIOR WIDE STRIPE						
Pitcher			140.00		200.00	
Tumbler			45.00		65.00	
INVERTED CHEVRON						
Vase	75.00	65.00	45.00			
INVERTED COINDOT						
Rose bowl			55.00	100.00		
Tumbler		60.00	35.00			
INVERTED FAN & FEATHER*						
Bowl, master	300.00		375.00		200.00	
Bowl, sauce	100.00	100.00		40.00		
Butter	450.00		365.00			
Card tray whimsey	225.00	250.00	175.00	250.00		
Creamer	225.00		175.00			
Cruet, rare	500.00					
Jelly compote, rare	250.00		175.00			
Novelty bowl, very rare		250.00		300.00		
Pitcher	725.00		475.00			
Tumbler	100.00		75.00			
Plate, very rare				500.00		
Punch bowl, rare	900.00					
Punch cup, rare	50.00					
Rose bowl	225.00	250.00		250.00		
Rose bowl whimsey	225.00	250.00	190.00	265.00		
Shakers, pair	350.00					
Spittoon whimsey	325.00		225.00	325.00		

213

Pattern Name	Blue	Green	White	Vaseline/Canary	Cranberry	Other
Spooner	200.00		150.00			
Sugar	275.00		225.00			
Toothpick, rare	450.00	550.00				
Vase whimsey, rare	200.00	175.00	150.00			
IRIS (ENGLISH)						
Hand lamp	225.00	250.00	145.00	325.00		
Pitcher	165.00	175.00	145.00	285.00		
Tumbler	50.00	60.00	40.00	75.00		
Vase	75.00	90.00	70.00	100.00		
IRIS (NORTHWOOD)						
Lamp	250.00	225.00	165.00	325.00		
Pitcher	275.00	225.00	175.00	275.00		
Tumbler	70.00	65.00	55.00	85.00		
Vase	75.00	70.00	60.00	95.00		
IRIS WITH MEANDER						
Bowl, master	200.00	150.00	75.00	155.00		
Bowl, sauce, two sizes	50.00	35.00	20.00	40.00		
Butter	300.00	275.00	225.00	275.00		
Creamer	100.00	80.00	60.00	75.00		
Cruet	500.00	400.00	275.00	400.00		
Jelly compote	55.00	50.00	35.00	45.00		
Pitcher	400.00	375.00	275.00	325.00		
Tumbler	80.00	75.00	55.00	75.00		
Relish/pickle dish	85.00	75.00	55.00			
Plate	100.00	85.00	60.00	80.00		
Shakers, each	225.00	200.00	125.00	350.00		
Spooner	100.00	80.00	55.00	75.00		
Sugar	175.00	150.00	100.00	175.00		
Toothpick holder	150.00	125.00	75.00	125.00		
Vase, tall	60.00	55.00	35.00	60.00		
IVY BALL						
Swirled ball in metal holder			50.00			
JACKSON						
Bowl, master	100.00	90.00	75.00	80.00		
Bowl, sauce	35.00	30.00	20.00	35.00		
Butter	200.00		125.00	225.00		
Candy dish	55.00		35.00	55.00		
Creamer	80.00		60.00	75.00		
Cruet	200.00		175.00	200.00		
Epergne, small	175.00		100.00	150.00		
Powder jar	90.00	80.00	45.00	95.00		
Pitcher	475.00		385.00	450.00		
Tumbler	80.00		65.00	85.00		
Spooner	80.00		65.00	75.00		
Sugar	125.00		100.00	125.00		
JAZZ						
Vase	50.00	55.00	30.00			
JEFFERSON #270						
Master bowl	100.00	85.00	55.00			
Sauce	45.00	45.00	25.00			
JEFFERSON SHIELD						
Bowl, rare	300.00	350.00	200.00			
JEFFERSON SPATTER						
Vase				75.00		
JEFFERSON SPOOL						
Vase	75.00	60.00	45.00	85.00		
Vase, variant	95.00	80.00	55.00	100.00		
Vase whimsey	85.00	70.00	60.00			
JEFFERSON STRIPE						
Bowl whimsey	85.00	90.00	65.00		125.00	
Vase, J.I.P.	60.00	65.00	40.00			
JEFFERSON WHEEL						
Bowl	50.00	45.00	35.00			
JEWEL & FAN						
Banana bowl	125.00	145.00	100.00	140.00		135.00 Emerald green
Bowl	60.00	55.00	40.00	75.00		
JEWEL & FLOWER						
Bowl, master	75.00		50.00	75.00		
Bowl, sauce	35.00		25.00	40.00		
Butter	400.00		225.00	325.00		
Creamer	125.00		100.00	150.00		
Cruet	700.00		325.00	645.00		
Novelty bowl	55.00		30.00	55.00		
Pitcher	650.00		325.00	475.00		
Tumbler	100.00		65.00	80.00		
Shakers, pair	175.00		125.00	165.00		

214

Pattern Name	Blue	Green	White	Vaseline/Canary	Cranberry	Other
Spooner	125.00		100.00	125.00		
Sugar	200.00		125.00	200.00		
JEWELED HEART						
Bowl, master	65.00	60.00	50.00			
Bowl, sauce	30.00	25.00	20.00			
Butter	325.00	300.00	225.00			
Condiment set (four pieces, complete)	1,000.00	1,000.00	750.00			
Compote	150.00	150.00	100.00			
Creamer	175.00	150.00	100.00			
Cruet	400.00	400.00	310.00			
Novelty bowl	50.00	40.00	30.00			
Pitcher	400.00	300.00	200.00			
Tumbler	100.00	65.00	40.00			
Plate, small	75.00	70.00	55.00			
Shakers, pair	350.00	350.00	275.00			
Spooner	175.00	150.00	100.00			
Sugar	200.00	195.00	125.00			
Sugar shaker	350.00	350.00	275.00			
Syrup	500.00	475.00	400.00			
Toothpick holder	250.00	250.00	200.00			
Tray	250.00	225.00	200.00			
JEWELS & DRAPERY & VARIANT						
Novelty bowl	75.00	65.00	35.00	125.00		70.00 Aqua
Vase	85.00	75.00	45.00			75.00 Aqua
JOLLY BEAR						
Bowl, very rare	425.00	375.00	275.00			
JUBILEE						
Bowl	100.00					
KEYHOLE						
Bowl	55.00	60.00	40.00			
Bowl, tricorner J.I.P. whimsey	70.00	75.00	60.00			
Rose bowl whimsey	150.00	150.00	125.00			
KING RICHARD						
Compote	200.00		150.00	225.00		
KING'S PANEL						
Novelty bowl in holder	85.00		95.00			
Creamer	35.00		50.00			
Sugar, open	30.00		40.00			
KING'S X						
Spill, rare	145.00					
KITTEN'S (FENTON)						
Cup, very rare						650.00 Amethyst
Saucer, very rare						550.00 Amethyst
LABELLE						
Toothpick				70.00		
LADY CAROLINE						
Basket	60.00			60.00		
Creamer	60.00			60.00		
Sugar, two shapes	55.00			55.00		
Whimsey, three handled	75.00			70.00		
Spill	65.00			65.00		
Spill vase whimsey						
Handleless	75.00			75.00		
LADY CHIPPENDALE						
Basket	80.00			115.00		80.00 Cobalt
Butter	165.00			195.00		125.00 Cobalt
Compote, tall	140.00			160.00		100.00 Cobalt
Creamer or spooner	60.00			65.00		50.00 Cobalt
Novelty bowls, various	40.00-70.00			50.00-80.00		35.00-55.00 Cobalt
Sugar	75.00			90.00		65.00 Cobalt
LADY FINGER (DAVIDSON)						
Spill vase	150.00			150.00		
LADY SLIPPER						
Novelty vase	185.00		125.00	250.00		
LATE COINSPOT						
Pitcher	150.00	150.00	110.00			
Tumbler	45.00	35.00	25.00			
LATTICE (ENGLISH)						
Vase				95.00		
LATTICE & DAISY						
Tumbler, very scarce	90.00		60.00	125.00		
LATTICE & POINTS						
Bowl, novelty			55.00			
Hat shape			60.00			
Vase			75.00			

Pattern Name	Blue	Green	White	Vaseline/ Canary	Cranberry	Other
LATTICE MEDALLIONS						
Bowl	55.00	50.00	40.00			
Nut bowl whimsey	75.00	65.00	50.00			
Rose bowl	75.00	65.00	50.00			
LAURA (SINGLE FLOWER FRAMED)						
Bowl, scarce	55.00	50.00	35.00			
Nappy, scarce	60.00	55.00	35.00			
Plate, ruffled, rare	150.00	150.00	125.00			
LAUREL SWAG & BOWS						
Shade, gas						125.00 Amethyst
LEAF & BEADS						
Bowl, footed or dome	60.00	55.00	35.00			
Bowl, whimsey, pulled points	75.00	65.00	45.00			
Rose bowl	85.00	75.00	55.00			
LEAF & DIAMONDS						
Bowl	50.00	65.00	30.00			
LEAF & LEAFLETS (LONG LEAF)						
Bowl	60.00		45.00			
LEAF CHALICE						
Novelty compote (found in several shapes from same mould)	80.00	85.00	65.00	110.00		175.00 Cobalt
Whimsey, four cornered	85.00	90.00	70.00	135.00		
LEAF GARLAND						
Bowl, small				75.00		
Compote	100.00					
LEAF GARLAND & RIBS						
Creamer, 3"				70.00		
LEAF ROSETTE & BEADS						
Bowl, low, very scarce	200.00	200.00	125.00			
LEAFY STRIPE						
Basket whimsey				250.00		
Bride's bowl, 9"						250.00 Honey amber
LILY PAD						
Epergne, with bowl and lily				250.00		
LILY POOL EPERGNE						
Epergne	275.00		225.00	300.00		
LINED HEART						
Vase	40.00	40.00	30.00			
LINKING RINGS						
Bowl	125.00			160.00		
Compote	185.00			250.00		
Juice glass	70.00			95.00		
Milk pitcher	145.00			225.00		
Pitcher	375.00			500.00		
Tray	110.00			130.00		
LITTLE NELL						
Vase	40.00	35.00	20.00			
LITTLE SWAN* (DUGAN OR NORTHWOOD)						
Novelty, two sizes	100.00	100.00	50.00	90.00		
LORDS & LADIES						
Butter	100.00			125.00		
Celery boat (in wire basket)	200.00			225.00		
Creamer	70.00			85.00		
Open sugar	75.00			90.00		
Plate, 7½"	100.00			125.00		
LORNA						
Vase (add 50% for whimsey vase shape)	40.00		30.00	45.00		
LOTUS						
Bowl with underplate	160.00		140.00	160.00		
LOVE FLOWER						
Loving cup, handled	200.00					
LUSTRE FLUTE						
Bowl, master	200.00	275.00	175.00			
Bowl, sauce	45.00	60.00	30.00			
Butter	475.00		275.00			
Creamer	150.00		90.00			
Custard cup	50.00		30.00			
Pitcher	400.00		325.00			
Tumbler	100.00		65.00			
Spooner	150.00		95.00			
Sugar	235.00		150.00			
Vase	85.00		65.00			
MANY DIAMONDS						
Bowl on metal stand						110.00 White w/blue crest
MANY LOOPS						
Bowl, ruffled	50.00	45.00	35.00			

216

Pattern Name	Blue	Green	White	Vaseline/Canary	Cranberry	Other
Bowl, deep round or tricorner	60.00	55.00	40.00			
Rose bowl, scarce	75.00	70.00	45.00			
MANY RIBS (MODEL FLINT)						
Vase	95.00		55.00	100.00		
MAPLE LEAF						
Jelly compote	100.00	100.00	70.00	200.00		
MAPLE LEAF CHALICE						
One shape	75.00	85.00	50.00	65.00		
MARKHAM SWIRL BAND WITH OPAL COBWEB						
Oil lamp	300.00		250.00	325.00	550.00	
MARY ANN						
Vase, rare	300.00		250.00			
*Reproduced in white opal						
MARY GREGORY						
Small pitcher with lid			325.00			
MAVIS SWIRL						
Barber bottle	100.00		85.00	145.00		
Pitcher	185.00		125.00	250.00		
Tumbler	65.00		50.00	75.00		
Rose bowl	70.00		60.00	85.00		
Shakers, pair	125.00		100.00	145.00		
Toothpick holder	90.00		75.00	90.00		
Trinket dish	40.00		30.00	45.00		
MAY BASKET						
Basket shape	80.00	75.00	60.00	100.00		
MEANDER						
Bowl	60.00	55.00	35.00			
Nut bowl whimsey	70.00	65.00	45.00			
MEDIEVAL ARCHES						
Bowl, square				70.00		
MELON OPTIC SWIRL						
Bowl, rare	80.00	90.00	60.00	85.00		
MELON SWIRL						
Pitcher	450.00					
Tumbler	75.00					
MERMAIDS & SHELLS						
Novelty bowl			200.00	425.00		400.00 Rose opalescent
MICA SPATTER						
Vase, J.I.P. Shape						250.00 Cranberry spatter
MINIATURE EPERGNE						
Epergne, one lily	150.00			150.00		
MIRROR FRAME						
Mirror, round				100.00		
MODEL FLINT REVERSE SWIRL						
See Reverse Swirl						
MONKEY (UNDER A TREE)						
Pitcher, rare			1,200.00			
Tumbler, rare			500.00			
Mug, very rare			600.00			
MURANO FLORAL						
Vase, decorated, speckled			390.00			
MYSTIC MAZE						
Vase, blown				200.00		
NATIONAL'S #17						
Bouquet vase, 8"	150.00	150.00		150.00		
Bouquet vase, 10½"				175.00		
NATIONAL SWIRL						
Pitcher	275.00	275.00				
Tumbler	50.00	50.00				
NESTING ROBINS						
Bowl			300.00			
NETTED CHERRIES						
Bowl			45.00			
Plate			65.00			
NETTED ROSES						
Bowl	70.00	90.00	50.00			
Plate	120.00	130.00	100.00			
NORTHERN STAR						
Banana bowl	75.00	70.00	50.00			
Bowl	65.00	60.00	40.00			
Plate	100.00	100.00	50.00			
NORTHWOOD'S MIKADO						
Nappy, with poppy interior, very rare				500.00		
NORTHWOOD'S POPPY						
Pickle dish, very rare	400.00					

Pattern Name	Blue	Green	White	Vaseline/ Canary	Cranberry	Other
NORTHWOOD SWIRL						
Tumbler	50.00			65.00		
OAK LEAF						
Novelty bowl	150.00			150.00		
OCEAN SHELL						
Novelty, footed, three variations	75.00	90.00	55.00			
OCEAN WAVE						
Advertising bowl, rare				275.00		
OHIO STATE SEAL						
Cup plate			75.00			
OKTOBERFEST						
Ale glass				250.00		
OLD MAN WINTER						
Basket, small	75.00	85.00	60.00			
Basket, large, footed	150.00	165.00	100.00	275.00		
ONYX ("FINDLEY")						
*All pieces, rare						
bowl						400.00-1,600.00
Butter, covered						1,300.00
Celery vase						900.00-1,800.00
Creamer						500.00-1,000.00
Cruet						700.00-1,500.00
Lamp						5,500.00
Pickle castor						700.00-1,200.00
Pitcher						1,200.00-1,500.00
Tumbler						500.00-1,800.00
Shakers						600.00-900.00
Sugar						550.00-1,100.00
Sugar shaker						600.00
Sauce						800.00
Spooner						600.00-1,300.00
Syrup						1,800.00
Toothpick holder						600.00

*All pieces are lustre ware with various accents; gold, silver, bronze, ruby, etc., and prices vary greatly pending such.

Pattern Name	Blue	Green	White	Vaseline/ Canary	Cranberry	Other
OPAL BLOSSOM						
Vase, 6"		275.00				
OPAL BULL'S EYE						
Mustard, with lid and spoon				140.00		
Opan salt in metal holder, 1½"				85.00		
OPAL DAISY						
Slanted box, two sizes				125.00-175.00		
OPAL DOT						
Water tray				125.00		
OPALESCENT SWIRL						
Shade, various shapes				100.00		
OPAL FLORAL						
Compote				85.00		
OPAL FLOWER						
Cylinder shade					165.00	
OPAL LOOPS						
Vase			110.00			
Decanter			160.00			
Flask			195.00			
Glass pipe			180.00			
OPAL OPEN* (BEADED PANELS)						
Bowl, novelty	50.00	55.00	30.00	50.00		
Compote	75.00	70.00	65.00	85.00		
Ring bowl, handled	100.00	90.00	55.00	85.00		
Rose bowl, novelty	50.00	60.00	30.00	50.00		
Vase, novelty	40.00	40.00	25.00	40.00		
OPAL SPIRAL						
Tumbler	325.00					
Sugar	90.00					
OPAL STRIPE						
Vase, with applied flowers				135.00		
OPAL URN						
Vase	80.00		50.00	80.00		
OPEN BLOSSOM						
Vase, 6"	150.00	150.00	125.00	200.00		
OPEN EDGE BASKET (FENTON)						
Bowl	40.00	35.00	25.00	40.00		
Console set, three pieces	250.00	275.00	200.00	250.00		
Nappy	50.00	40.00	35.00	40.00		
Plate	60.00	80.00	45.00	100.00		
OPEN O'S						
Bowl, novelty	55.00	50.00	25.00	45.00		

218

Pattern Name	Blue	Green	White	Vaseline/Canary	Cranberry	Other
Spittoon whimsey	125.00	100.00	75.00	100.00		
Rose bowl whimsey	100.00	90.00	55.00	85.00		
Vase, squat	85.00	75.00	65.00	95.00		
OPTIC BASKET						
One shape				150.00		
OPTIC PANEL						
Vase jip				100.00		
ORANGE TREE						
Mug, rare						250.00 Custard opal
OSCAR'S LEGACY						
Iris window insert				125.00		
OVAL WINDOWS						
Flower holder with metal frog/lid				150.00		
OVER-ALL HOB						
Bowl, master	75.00		40.00	70.00		
Bowl, sauce	30.00		20.00	25.00		
Butter	250.00		175.00	225.00		
Celery vase	75.00		50.00	75.00		
Creamer	100.00		50.00	90.00		
Finger bowl	60.00		30.00	60.00		
Mug	75.00		55.00	75.00		
Pitcher	225.00		165.00	200.00		
Tumbler	65.00		25.00	50.00		
Spooner	100.00		50.00	90.00		
Sugar	175.00		100.00	150.00		
Toothpick holder	200.00		135.00	200.00		
OVERLAPPING LEAVES (LEAF TIERS)						
Bowl, footed	175.00	175.00	150.00			
Plate, footed	250.00	275.00	195.00			
Rose bowl, footed	175.00	185.00	150.00			
PALISADES (LINED LATTICE)						
Bowl, novelty	45.00	50.00	35.00	55.00		
Rose bowl whimsey	45.00	50.00	40.00	50.00		
Vase, novelty	50.00	45.00	35.00	50.00		
PALM & SCROLL						
Bowl, footed	65.00	60.00	40.00	60.00		
Rose bowl, footed	75.00	70.00	50.00	70.00		
PALM BEACH						
Bowl, master	85.00			85.00		
Bowl, sauce, two sizes	40.00			50.00		
Butter	300.00			300.00		
Card tray whimsey, rare				500.00		
Creamer	150.00			140.00		
Jelly compote	175.00		150.00	200.00		
Nappy, handled, rare				425.00		
Pitcher	450.00			475.00		
Tumbler	100.00			100.00		
Plate, 8", rare	550.00			600.00		
Spooner	150.00			150.00		
Stemmed card tray, rare	500.00			500.00		
Sugar	225.00			225.00		
Wine, very rare				425.00		
PAN AMERICAN						
Vase, with embossed lettering	250.00			375.00		
PANELED ACORN						
Vase				150.00		
PANELED ACORN VASE						
Vase, rare				650.00		
PANELED CORNFLOWER						
Bowl, handled, pinched			75.00+			
Vase			135.00			
PANELED FLOWERS						
Nut cup, footed	85.00		50.00			
Rose bowl, footed	75.00		45.00			
PANELED FRONDS						
Basket	135.00					
PANELED HOLLY						
Bowl, master	200.00		150.00			
Bowl, sauce	75.00		35.00			
Butter	400.00		325.00			
Creamer	175.00		125.00			
Novelty bowl	90.00		65.00			
Pitcher	700.00		425.00			
Tumbler	110.00		85.00			
Shakers, pair	250.00		150.00			
Spooner	175.00		125.00			

Pattern Name	Blue	Green	White	Vaseline/Canary	Cranberry	Other
Sugar	250.00		175.00			
PANELED LATTICE BAND						
Tumbler, rare				150.00		
PANELED SPRIG						
Cruet			150.00			
Shakers, pair			125.00			
Toothpick holder			100.00			
PANELS WITH SPIRAL BAND						
Vase				95.00		
PEACOCK FEATHERS						
Bowl on metal stand						125.00 Rose pink
PEACOCKS (ON THE FENCE)						
Bowl, scarce	300.00		210.00			375.00 Cobalt
PEACOCK TAIL						
Tumbler, rare	100.00	95.00	75.00			
PEARL FLOWERS						
Novelty bowl, footed	60.00	50.00	30.00			
Nut bowl, footed	50.00	45.00	35.00			
Rose bowl, footed	70.00	80.00	40.00			
PEARLINE RIB						
Novelty bowl in holder	150.00			175.00		
PEARLS & SCALES						
Compote	65.00	60.00	40.00	75.00		80.00 Emerald
Rose bowl, rare	100.00	100.00	60.00	95.00		110.00 Emerald
PETALS WITH CUPPED PEARL						
Vase				100.00		
PHOENIX COINDOT						
Pitcher, rare				450.00		
PHOENIX DRAPE						
Butter	175.00				235.00	
Celery vase	80.00				100.00	
Juice glass	60.00				70.00	
Pitcher	225.00				325.00	
Punch cup	30.00				45.00	
Tumbler	65.00				80.00	
PHOENIX HONEYCOMB						
Pitcher, rare	375.00					
PIASA BIRD						
Bowl	55.00		45.00			
Plate, footed	125.00		100.00			
Rose bowl	90.00		75.00			
Spittoon whimsey	95.00		85.00			
Vase	75.00		65.00			
PICCADILLY						
Basket, small	100.00	90.00	70.00			
PICKET						
Planter, two sizes	75.00		60.00	75.00		
PILGRIM						
Candlestick, each			95.00			
PINEAPPLE						
Compote or open sugar	65.00					
PINEAPPLE & FAN (HEISEY)						
Creamer				600.00		
Sugar				650.00		
Vase, extremely rare				4,000.00		
PINWHEEL						
Cake plate, 12", stemmed	125.00			135.00		
PISTACHIO						
Pitcher				235.00		
Tumbler				70.00		
PLAID						
Bowl			225.00			
PLAIN JANE						
Nappy, footed	50.00	60.00	30.00	85.00		
PLAIN OPAL						
Creamer, footed				55.00		
PLAIN PANEL (NORTHWOOD)						
Vase	45.00	40.00	30.00			
PLUME PANELS						
Vase, rare	250.00	250.00	150.00			
PLUMES & SCROLLS						
Bowl	65.00					
POINSETTIA						
Bowl whimsey	150.00	125.00	100.00		200.00	
Fruit bowl, two sizes	125.00	110.00	85.00		175.00	
Pitcher, either shape	350.00-500.00	375.00-550.00	250.00-400.00		750.00-1,300.00	

Pattern Name	Blue	Green	White	Vaseline/Canary	Cranberry	Other
Tumbler	75.00		45.00		125.00	
Sugar shaker	300.00	300.00	200.00		450.00	
Syrup, various	300.00-700.00	350.00-750.00	200.00-450.00		450.00-900.00	
POINSETTIA LATTICE						
Bowl, scarce	300.00		125.00	475.00		
POLAR MEDALLIONS						
Milk pitcher				135.00		
POLKA DOT*						
Bowl, large	75.00		50.00		125.00	
Cruet	400.00		250.00		750.00	
Pitcher, rare	250.00		150.00		850.00	
Tumbler	70.00		30.00		125.00	
Shakers, pair	100.00		60.00		300.00	
Sugar shaker	200.00		150.00		300.00	
Syrup	250.00		125.00		725.00	
Toothpick holder	425.00		300.00		525.00	
POLKA DOT WITH THORN HANDLE						
One shape	75.00					
POMPEIAN (DUGAN)						
J.I.P. whimsey			75.00			
POPSICLE STICKS						
Bowl, footed	55.00	50.00	35.00			
Nut bowl whimsey	65.00	60.00	45.00			
Shade	60.00		35.00		200.00	
Toothpick holder					325.00	
POSEIDON						
Bowls, various			45.00-75.00	55.00-90.00		
Butter with lid				165.00		
Plate				80.00		
POSEIDON SHELL						
Footed bowl, 8½"x4¾"	85.00					
PRAM (AKA: CARRIAGE)						
Novelty bowl, 6½" x 3" wide	225.00					
PRAYER RUG (FENTON)						
Bon-bon, gilded, rare	150.00				225.00	
Vase, J.I.P. Shape, very scarce					165.00	
PREAKNESS						
Single lily epergne in metal holder			145.00			
PRESSED COINSPOT (#617)						
Card tray	75.00	100.00	50.00	100.00		
Compote	65.00	75.00	45.00	75.00		
Rose bowl whimsey			75.00			
PRESSED DIAMOND						
Bowl, boat shaped, 13"			125.00			
PRIMROSE (DAFFODILS VARIANT)						
Pitcher			900.00			
PRIMROSE SCROLL						
Bowl, 6"				100.00		
PRIMROSE SHADE						
Shade						250.00 Rubina verde
PRINCE CHARLES						
Bowl, 4"	65.00		50.00			75.00 Amber
PRINCESS DIANA						
Biscuit set (jar and plate, complete)	100.00			110.00		
Butter	125.00			110.00		
Compote, metal base	150.00			135.00		
Compote, large	90.00			110.00		
Creamer	55.00			50.00		
Novelty bowl	50.00			45.00		
Open sugar	70.00			65.00		
Pitcher	150.00			120.00		
Tumbler	50.00			40.00		
Plate, crimped	65.00			60.00		
Salad bowl	55.00			50.00		
Water tray	55.00			50.00		
PRINCE WILLIAM						
Basket, handled, 6½" long	300.00			300.00		
Creamer	65.00			60.00		
Open sugar	65.00			60.00		
Oval plate	65.00			70.00		
Pitcher	225.00			250.00		
Tumbler	45.00			35.00		
Toothpick holder	65.00					
PRISM HOBNAIL						
Creamer				80.00		

Pattern Name	Blue	Green	White	Vaseline/ Canary	Cranberry	Other
PULLED COINSPOT						
Mug					150.00	
PULLED LOOP						
Vase, two sizes, scarce	40.00-80.00	55.00-90.00	25.00-55.00			
PUMP & TROUGH*						
Pump	130.00		100.00	130.00		
Trough	75.00		50.00	75.00		
PUSSY WILLOW						
Vase, 4½"				85.00		
QUEEN'S CANDLESTICKS						
Candlesticks, pair				200.00		
QUEEN'S CROWN						
Bowl, small	40.00			45.00		
Compote, low	60.00			65.00		
QUEEN'S SPILL						
Spill vase, 4"	90.00			90.00		
Candlesticks	325.00			350.00		
QUEEN VICTORIA						
Plate	150.00			150.00		
QUESTION MARKS						
Card tray	75.00					
Compote	70.00	85.00	45.00	150.00		
QUILT						
Bowl, 5½"			140.00			
QUILTED DAISY						
Fairy lamp	500.00		375.00	450.00		
QUILTED PHLOX LATTICE						
Salt shaker			90.00		135.00	
Sugar shaker			125.00		200.00	
Syrup			165.00		240.00	
Toothpick			100.00		145.00	
QUILTED PILLOW SHAM						
Creamer	75.00			70.00		
Open sugar	75.00			65.00		
Oval butter	100.00			100.00		
QUILTED ROSE						
Pitcher			100.00			
Tumbler			25.00			
QUILTED WIDE STRIPE						
Finger bowl	55.00		40.00		70.00	
Pitcher	200.00		165.00		250.00	
Tumbler	65.00		45.00		80.00	
RAINBOW STRIPE						
Compote						250.00 Vaseline/cranberry
RAISED RIB (FENTON)						
Bowl, two shapes						125.00 Cameo opal
RASPBERRY PRUNTS						
Creamer				90.00		
RAY						
Vase	55.00	50.00	30.00			
RAYED HEART						
Compote	75.00	60.00	45.00			
RAYED JANE						
Nappy	50.00		25.00	65.00		
REEDS & BLOSSOMS						
Bowl		145.00				
REFLECTING DIAMONDS						
Bowl	60.00	65.00	40.00			
Bowl, ice cream shape	65.00	70.00	50.00			
Plate whimsey	85.00	80.00	65.00			
REFLECTIONS						
Footed Novelty bowls	30.00-50.00	30.00-50.00	20.00-40.00			
REGAL (NORTHWOOD'S)						
Bowl, master	125.00	150.00	100.00			
Bowl, sauce	35.00	45.00	20.00			
Butter	225.00	175.00	125.00			
Celery vase	150.00	175.00	100.00			
Creamer	100.00	65.00	50.00			
Cruet	750.00	750.00	600.00			
Plate, rare	165.00	150.00	100.00			
Pitcher	325.00	300.00	200.00			
Tumbler	100.00	85.00	45.00			
Shakers, pair	375.00	375.00	300.00			
Spooner	100.00	65.00	50.00			
Sugar	150.00	100.00	70.00			

Pattern Name	Blue	Green	White	Vaseline/ Canary	Cranberry	Other
REVERSE DRAPERY						
Bowl	45.00	45.00	25.00			
Plate	90.00	85.00	50.00			
Vase whimsey	100.00	100.00	75.00			145.00 Amethyst
REVERSE SWIRL						
Bowl, master	70.00		40.00	55.00	85.00	
Bowl, sauce	25.00		20.00	25.00	40.00	
Butter	200.00		165.00	175.00	250.00	
Celery vase	175.00		100.00	150.00	200.00	
Creamer	125.00		100.00	125.00	195.00	
Cruet	275.00		110.00	175.00	475.00	
Cruet set and holder, four pieces	300.00		200.00		375.00	
Custard cup	50.00		35.00		150.00	
Finger bowl	70.00		45.00		100.00	
Hanging lamp, rare					1,700.00	
Mini-lamp	375.00		200.00		325.00	
Mustard pot	80.00		45.00	75.00	125.00	
Oil lamp	350.00		300.00	345.00		
Pitcher	250.00		175.00	225.00	800.00	
Tumbler	60.00		35.00	60.00	100.00	
Rose bowl				75.00	95.00	
Shakers, pair	100.00		60.00	100.00	175.00	
Spooner	125.00		80.00	100.00	150.00	
Sugar	175.00		100.00	150.00	225.00	
Sugar shaker	175.00		125.00	150.00	275.00	
Syrup	175.00		100.00	150.00	425.00	
Toothpick holder	155.00		100.00	125.00	275.00	
Water bottle	150.00		100.00	150.00	200.00	
RIB & BIG THUMBPRINTS						
Vase	45.00	40.00	25.00			
RIBBED BEADED CABLE						
See Beaded Cable						
RIBBED COINSPOT						
Butter	325.00		295.00		425.00	
Celery vase	225.00		210.00		250.00	
Creamer	400.00		350.00		450.00	
Pitcher	1,000.00		800.00		1,300.00	
Tumbler	150.00		120.00		200.00	
Spooner	300.00		225.00		375.00	
Sugar	395.00		300.00		500.00	
Sugar shaker	465.00		385.00		550.00	
Syrup	950.00		725.00		1,150.00	
All pieces, very scarce to rare						
RIBBED EPERGNE						
Five-lily epergne in metal holder				350.00		
RIBBED (OPAL) LATTICE						
Bowl, master	70.00		45.00		150.00	
Bowl, sauce	30.00		20.00		40.00	
Butter	225.00		175.00		800.00	
Creamer	75.00		65.00		400.00	
Cruet	225.00		175.00		500.00	
Pitcher	275.00		225.00	850.00	1,000.00	
Tumbler	50.00		40.00		150.00	
Shakers, pair	145.00		100.00		300.00	
Spooner	75.00		65.00		400.00	
Sugar	125.00		100.00		650.00	
Sugar shaker, two sizes	140.00		100.00		425.00	
Syrup	175.00		150.00		600.00	
Toothpick holder	300.00		175.00		350.00	
RIBBED OPAL RINGS						
Pitcher, rare	675.00		525.00		825.00	
Sugar	185.00		155.00		225.00	
Tumbler	100.00		85.00		125.00	
RIBBED OPTIC						
Tumble-up	70.00	80.00	50.00	75.00	100.00	
RIBBED PILLAR						
Berry bowl, small					40.00	
Berry bowl, large					95.00	
Butter					200.00	
Celery vase					85.00	
Creamer or spooner					65.00	
Cruet					165.00	
Pitcher					300.00	
Tumbler					60.00	
Shakers, pair					135.00	
Sugar					65.00	

Pattern Name	Blue	Green	White	Vaseline/Canary	Cranberry	Other
Sugar shaker					125.00	
Syrup					155.00	
RIBBED SPIRAL						
Bowl, master	75.00		45.00	65.00		
Bowl, sauce	30.00		20.00	25.00		
Bowl, ruffled	55.00		40.00	50.00		
Bowl whimsey	100.00		85.00	115.00		
Butter	375.00		300.00	350.00		
Creamer	100.00		45.00	65.00		
Cup and saucer	110.00		60.00	100.00		
Jelly compote	70.00		50.00	65.00		
Pitcher	525.00		385.00	475.00		
Tumbler	115.00		60.00	100.00		
Plate	75.00		45.00	60.00		
Shakers, pair	225.00		125.00	225.00		
Spooner	110.00		50.00	75.00		
Sugar	200.00		150.00	175.00		
Toothpick holder	175.00		125.00	175.00		
Vase, squat, 4"-7"	60.00		35.00	75.00		
Vase, standard, 8"-14"	45.00		25.00	55.00		
Vase, funeral, 15"- 22"	145.00		90.00	200.00		
Whimsey, three handled				125.00		
RIBBED TRIANGLE & FANS						
Bowl, 9½" x 7½"	95.00					
RIBBON SWIRL						
Bowl	125.00	110.00	100.00			
Rose bowl	140.00	125.00	120.00			
Spittoon	200.00	175.00	165.00			
Vase	175.00	165.00	150.00			
RIBBON WAVE						
Salt dip, in metal holder						125.00 Rubina verde
RICHELIEU						
Basket, handled	100.00		60.00	80.00		
Bowl	70.00		50.00	65.00		
Cracker jar with lid	200.00		150.00	185.00		
Creamer	65.00		45.00	60.00		
Divided dish, rare	100.00		75.00	100.00		
Jelly compote	75.00		50.00	75.00		
Nappy, handled	90.00		70.00	95.00		
Open sugar	65.00		40.00	60.00		
Basket, open	100.00		70.00	100.00		
Pitcher	160.00		130.00	150.00		
Tumbler	30.00		20.00	30.00		
Tray	65.00		40.00	55.00		
Triple sweet dish	75.00		60.00	75.00		
RIC-RAC						
Vase				100.00		
RIGOREE						
Sauce						200.00 Rubina verde
RIGOREE SPILL						
Spill vase						150.00 Rubina verde
RINGED BARREL						
Toothpick holder	150.00			150.00		
RINGED FLUTE WITH BEADED MEDALLIONS						
Basket	90.00					
RING HANDLE						
Basket	145.00	150.00	120.00	160.00		
Ring tray	100.00	80.00	75.00	95.00		
Shakers, pair	100.00		75.00			
RINGS & ARCHES						
Bowl	70.00					
RINGS WITH WAVE BAND						
Vase				145.00		
RIPPLE						
Vase	250.00	175.00	150.00	300.00		
RIPPLED RIB						
Vase			40.00			
ROARING LION						
Cordial				100.00		
Goblet				165.00		
Glass, pilsner shape				150.00		
ROCOCO						
Bowl, bride's basket	300.00		250.00	300.00	400.00	
Plate, 6", rare			200.00			
Plate, 10", rare	400.00		350.00	400.00	600.00	

Pattern Name	Blue	Green	White	Vaseline/Canary	Cranberry	Other
ROLLED WIDE STRIPE (ENGLISH)						
Tumbler or spill vase	80.00		65.00	100.00		
ROSE ("ROSE & RUFFLES")						
Bowl, small	100.00			100.00		
Candlesticks, pair	250.00			250.00		
Cologne	250.00			250.00		
Vase, 6"	100.00			100.00		
Powder jar, two sizes	125.00			125.00		
Pomade	100.00			100.00		
Covered bowl, large	150.00			150.00		
Tray, dresser	100.00			100.00		
Pin tray or soap dish	75.00			75.00		
Tall compote	100.00			100.00		
Console bowl	80.00			80.00		
Tray, center handled	90.00			90.00		
ROSE BUSH						
Wall pocket, very scarce			150.00			
ROSE SHOW						
Bowl, rare	325.00		250.00			
ROSE SPATTER						
Pitcher, rare						400.00 Tortoise shell
Celery						190.00 Tortoise shell
ROSE SPRAY						
Compote, round	45.00	60.00	30.00			85.00 Amethyst
Compote, J.I.P.			75.00			
ROULETTE						
Bowls, various shapes	50.00	45.00	30.00			
Nut bowl whimsey	90.00	65.00	55.00			
Plate, square, scarce	100.00	100.00	60.00			
ROYAL DAISY						
Compote	225.00					
ROYAL FAN						
Posy vase				85.00		
ROYAL JUBILEE						
Basket, handled	110.00			110.00		125.00 Amber
ROYAL SCANDAL						
Wall vase	250.00		200.00	250.00		
ROYAL SUNBURST						
Bowl				85.00		
RUBINA DIAMONDS						
Jip vase						225.00 Rubina verde
RUBINA VERDE						
Jip vase						250.00 Rubina verde
RUFFLES & RINGS						
Novelty bowl	55.00	50.00	30.00			
Nut bowl	60.00	55.00	40.00			
Rose bowl	65.00	60.00	45.00			
RUFFLES & RINGS WITH DAISY BAND						
Bowl, footed	95.00	85.00	60.00			
SALMON						
Bowl, fish shape			325.00	450.00		
SCHEHEREZADE						
Novelty bowl	50.00	45.00	30.00			
SCOTTISH MOOR						
Celery vase	150.00		100.00			
Cracker jar	350.00		225.00			
Cruet	400.00		225.00			
Pitcher	350.00		275.00		475.00	1,500.00 Orange
Tumbler	80.00		65.00		90.00	275.00 Orange
Vase	90.00		60.00			
SCROLL						
Bowl				80.00		
SCROLL WITH ACANTHUS						
Bowl, master	55.00		40.00	50.00		
Bowl, sauce	25.00		20.00	25.00		
Butter	375.00		325.00	350.00		
Creamer	100.00		65.00	75.00		
Cruet	225.00		200.00	375.00		
Jelly compote	65.00		60.00	65.00		
Pitcher	400.00		325.00	350.00		
Tumbler	100.00		65.00	75.00		
Shakers, pair	225.00		195.00	200.00		
Spooner	85.00		70.00	75.00		
Sugar	175.00		150.00	165.00		
Toothpick holder	300.00		275.00	325.00		

Pattern Name	Blue	Green	White	Vaseline/Canary	Cranberry	Other
SCROLL WITH BUTTONS						
Creamer			95.00			
SCROLL WITH CANE BAND						
Bowl, rare		150.00				
SEA SCROLL						
Compote	125.00	135.00	95.00			
SEA SHORE						
Bowl	100.00					
SEA SPRAY						
Nappy, round or tricorner	55.00	55.00	40.00			
Whimsey	50.00	50.00	40.00			
SEAWEED						
Bowl, master	60.00		40.00		125.00	
Bowl, sauce	30.00		20.00		70.00	
Butter	475.00		225.00		650.00	
Celery vase	100.00		80.00		175.00	
Creamer	125.00		100.00		225.00	
Cruet, two shapes	425.00		200.00		725.00	
Finger bowl	250.00		200.00		500.00	
Pitcher	1,100.00		475.00		1,400.00	
Tumbler	70.00		45.00		125.00	
Pickle caster, complete					650.00	
Rose bowl			500.00			
Shakers, pair	150.00		125.00		350.00	
Spooner	125.00		100.00		175.00	
Sugar	175.00		145.00		225.00	
Sugar shaker	275.00		200.00		450.00	
Syrup	850.00		325.00		1,150.00	
Toothpick holder	325.00		225.00		500.00	
SEAWEED VARIANT						
Vase						135.00 White w/rubina top
SERPENT THREADS						
Epergne, 23"				425.00		
SHAMROCK						
Oil lamp				375.00		
SHARKS TOOTH						
Oil lamp, rare				800.00		
Spooner, rare				325.00		
Smoke shade, rare						500.00 Rubina
SHELDON SWIRL						
Lamp, either size	575.00		475.00	675.00	725.00	
SHELL						
Novelty shell, two sizes, rare	175.00		200.00			
SHELL & DOTS						
Novelty bowl	50.00		40.00	100.00		
Rose bowl	45.00		35.00			
Nut bowl	45.00	55.00	40.00			
SHELL & SEAWEED						
Rose bowl						450.00 Rubina verde
SHELL & WILD ROSE						
Novelty bowl, open edge	60.00	55.00	45.00	100.00		
Nut bowl whimsey	80.00	70.00	55.00	175.00		
SHELL BEADED						
Bowl, master	85.00	100.00	65.00			
Bowl, sauce	55.00	65.00	35.00			
Butter	500.00	675.00	400.00			
Condiment set, four pieces	800.00	900.00	700.00			
Creamer	150.00	180.00	145.00			
Cruet	500.00	700.00	400.00			
Pitcher	575.00	625.00	500.00			
Tumbler	100.00	115.00	75.00			
Shakers, pair	350.00	400.00	300.00			
Spooner	150.00	180.00	150.00			
Sugar	225.00	275.00	190.00			
Toothpick holder	475.00	675.00	500.00			
Jelly compote, very rare	900.00	900.00	700.00	900.00		
SHOE						
Novelty shoe	85.00					
SILVER OVERLAY						
Vase			75.00			
SIMPLE SIMON						
Compote	65.00	60.00	40.00			
SINGING BIRDS						
Mug, rare	600.00		450.00	800.00		
SINGLE POINSETTIA (FENTON)						
Bowl			275.00			350.00 Amethyst opal
SIR LANCELOT						
Bowl, footed	65.00	60.00	40.00			

Pattern Name	Blue	Green	White	Vaseline/ Canary	Cranberry	Other
SIX PETALS						
Bowl			75.00			
SKIRTED DOTS						
Salt, open sugar or marmalade				95.00		
SMOOTH RIB						
Bowl	25.00	20.00	15.00	50.00		
Bowl on metal stand			65.00			
SNAIL LOOP & BALL						
Creamer			65.00			
SNOWBALL ROYALE						
Christmas ornament, rare				500.00		
SNOWFLAKE						
Hand lamp	400.00		275.00		600.00	
Night lamp	1,300.00		800.00		1,800.00	
Oil lamp	325.00		225.00		550.00	
SNOWFLAKE SPATTER						
Vase	150.00	125.00	75.00			
SNOWSTORM						
Bowl					150.00	
Rose bowl					195.00	
SOLAR FLARE						
Plate				135.00		
SOMERSET						
Bowl, large	135.00			400.00		
Nappy, two shapes	50.00			90.00		
Oval dish, 5½"-9½"	40.00-95.00			60.00-125.00		
Pitcher, small	100.00			225.00		
Sugar bowl	90.00			175.00		
Tumbler, 3"	75.00			125.00		
Underplate for water set	80.00			110.00		
Waste bowl	65.00			90.00		
SOWERBY BASKET						
Basket, handled 3½" x 2"			125.00			
SOWERBY SALT						
Salt dish	65.00	70.00	55.00			
SPANISH LACE						
Bowl, master	100.00		65.00	80.00	150.00	
Bowl, sauce	30.00		25.00	30.00	40.00	
Bride's basket, two sizes	125.00		90.00	150.00	200.00	
Butter	425.00		225.00	400.00	500.00	
Celery vase	125.00		85.00	150.00	175.00	
Cracker jar	700.00				900.00	
Creamer	150.00		100.00	125.00	175.00	
Cruet	275.00		200.00	300.00	750.00	
Finger bowl	75.00		50.00	85.00	150.00	
Jam jar	300.00		200.00	325.00	500.00	
Liqueur jug					850.00	
Mini-lamp	200.00		125.00	225.00	350.00	
Pitcher	250.00-500.00	275.00-400.00	100.00-300.00	350.00-450.00	650.00-1,000.00	
Tumbler	60.00	50.00	40.00	55.00	125.00	
Perfume bottle	300.00		100.00	225.00	275.00	
Rose bowl, many shapes	75.00		50.00	75.00	150.00	
Shakers, pair	125.00		75.00	125.00	225.00	
Spooner	150.00		100.00	145.00	175.00	
Sugar	275.00		200.00	250.00	325.00	
Sugar shaker	150.00		100.00	150.00	225.00	
Syrup	250.00		175.00	350.00	650.00	
Vase, many sizes	100.00		50.00	125.00	225.00	
Water bottle	300.00		200.00	325.00	425.00	
SPATTER						
Vase, 9"	95.00	90.00	55.00	100.00		100.00 Orange
Bowl	55.00	50.00	30.00	55.00	125.00	
Pitcher	250.00	250.00	175.00	265.00	450.00	
Tumbler	35.00	35.00	20.00	30.00	95.00	
SPATTERED COINSPOT						
Pitcher					450.00	
Tumbler					100.00	
SPECKLED CELERY VASE						
Celery vase	140.00	140.00	100.00		185.00	
SPECKLED CHRYSANTHEMUM BASE						
Berry, small					65.00	
Berry, large					125.00	
Butter					385.00	
Celery vase					165.00	
Creamer or spooner					100.00	
Cruet					250.00	
Finger bowl					125.00	
Mustard					150.00	

Pattern Name	Blue	Green	White	Vaseline/Canary	Cranberry	Other
Pitcher					550.00	
Shaker					275.00	
Straw holder with lid					375.00	
Sugar					150.00	
Syrup					300.00	
Toothpick holder					225.00	
Tumbler					90.00	
SPECKLED STRIPE						
Barber bottle	290.00		265.00	290.00		
Covered jar	390.00		350.00	390.00		
Finger bowl and underplate	250.00		200.00	300.00		
Shakers, pair	240.00		190.00	240.00		
Sugar				50.00		
Vase, three sizes	110.00-200.00	100.00-190.00	75.00-150.00	100.00-185.00		
SPINEY CACTUS						
Vase, 3⅛" and 5"	50.00-75.00					
SPIRALEX						
Vase	55.00	60.00	40.00	90.00		
SPIRAL OPTIC						
Pitcher						250.00 Amethyst opal
Tumbler						50.00 Amethyst opal
SPIRAL WEB						
Marmalade in metal holder				465.00		
SPOKES & WHEELS & VARIANTS						
Bowl	55.00	50.00	35.00			
Plate, rare	85.00	80.00				75.00 Aqua
SPOOL						
Compote, either shape	50.00	50.00	35.00			65.00 Emerald
SPOOL OF THREADS						
Card tray whimsey	100.00					
Compote	60.00		40.00	55.00		
SQUARE						
Match holder or spill vase	80.00		60.00			
SQUIRREL & ACORN						
Bowl	185.00	175.00	170.00			
Compote	190.00	180.00	175.00	200.00		
Vase	190.00	180.00	175.00			
Whimsey	190.00	185.00	175.00			
S-REPEAT						
Bowl, master	85.00	100.00	65.00	200.00		
Pitcher	475.00		350.00			
Tumbler	65.00		45.00			
STAG & HOLLY						
Bowl, footed, rare			1,400.00			1,850.00 Amethyst
STAR BASE						
Square bowl	40.00					
STARFLOWER						
Vase				225.00		
STAR IN DIAMOND						
Bowl, oval, 5⅜" x 3½"	55.00					
STARRY NIGHT						
Bowl, various shapes			55.00			
STARS & BARS						
Pull knob, each			20.00			
STARS & STRIPES						
Barber bottle			100.00		300.00	
Compote (age ?)					375.00	
Lamp shade			65.00			
Pitcher			250.00		1,100.00	
Tumbler	100.00		75.00			
STIPPLED IVY						
Basket, very scarce	150.00					
STIPPLED SCROLL & PRISM						
Covered stemmed piece, two sizes	40.00-80.00	30.00-70.00	20.00-55.00			
Goblet, 5"	40.00	30.00	25.00			
Goblet, 7½"	55.00	35.00	30.00			
Goblet, 9"	75.00	40.00	35.00			
STORK & RUSHES						
Mug	150.00		175.00			
Tumbler			95.00			
STORK & SWAN						
Syrup			150.00			
STOURBRIDGE						
Creamer			85.00			
Sugar			70.00			
STRAWBERRY						
Bon-bon			125.00			

Pattern Name	Blue	Green	White	Vaseline/ Canary	Cranberry	Other
STRAWBERRY & DAHLIA TWIST						
Epergne with lily	450.00*	400.00*	325.00*			
STRIPE						
Barber bottle	160.00				300.00	
Bowl			60.00		100.00	
Condiment set	400.00				750.00	
Cruet					500.00-750.00	
Oil lamp					625.00	
Pitcher	275.00			350.00	575.00	
Tumbler	55.00			70.00	100.00	
Rose bowl	100.00				225.00	
Shakers, pair	100.00				250.00	
Spittoon	150.00				300.00	
Syrup	275.00				450.00	
Toothpick holder	250.00				400.00	
Vase			600.00		125.00	
STRIPE BRACKET LAMP						
Lamp in wall mounted holder	145.00		125.00	245.00	225.00	
STRIPE CONDIMENT SET						
Four piece set, complete with holder						450.00 mix of three colors
STRIPED LEMONESCENT						
Creamer				265.00		
Sugar				250.00		
Vase				225.00		
STRIPE WITH FAN						
Bowl shape, enameled decoration					125.00	
STRIPE WITH FLY						
Creamer in silverplated holder				250.00		
Creamer, polka dot pattern					225.00	
SUNBURST-ON-SHIELD (DIADEM)						
Bowl, master	150.00			200.00		
Bowl, sauce	40.00			40.00		
Breakfast set, two pieces	200.00			250.00		
Butter	375.00		275.00	400.00		
Creamer	100.00		80.00	135.00		
Cruet, rare	325.00		350.00	750.00		
Nappy, rare	225.00			350.00		
Pitcher	600.00			950.00		
Tumbler	125.00			200.00		
Spooner	125.00		90.00	145.00		
Sugar	225.00		175.00	250.00		
Novelty bowl, 7½"	100.00		75.00	100.00		
SUNDERLAND						
Basket	110.00					
Compote				150.00		
Tumbler	60.00					
SUNK HOLLYHOCK						
Bowl, scarce				125.00		
SUNK HONEYCOMB						
Bowl, very rare				225.00		
SUNSET						
Bowl, 9"	75.00					65.00 Pink
SURF SPRAY						
Pickle dish, very scarce	75.00	70.00	45.00			
SUSSEX						
Creamer	150.00			150.00		
Sugar, open	150.00			150.00		
SWAG WITH BRACKETS						
Bowl	50.00	45.00	30.00	45.00		
Bowl, master	78	65.00	45.00	65.00		
Bowl, sauce	35.00	35.00	25.00	30.00		
Butter	275.00	250.00	200.00	250.00		
Creamer	100.00	85.00	55.00	80.00		
Cruet	500.00	325.00	175.00	250.00		
Jelly compote	60.00	55.00	30.00	50.00		
Pitcher	300.00	300.00	200.00	290.00		
Tumbler	85.00	75.00	40.00	75.00		
Shakers, pair	200.00	175.00	125.00	200.00		
Spooner	100.00	110.00	55.00	100.00		
Sugar	150.00	140.00	75.00	125.00		
Toothpick holder	350.00	300.00	250.00	300.00		
Whimsey sugar	100.00	125.00		175.00		
SWASTIKA						
Pitcher	1,800.00	3,000.00	1,100.00		3,300.00	
Tumbler	175.00	225.00	100.00		425.00	
Syrup	1,550.00	2,000.00	900.00		3,800.00	
SWIRL						
Bowl, master	50.00	55.00	40.00		75.00	

Pattern Name	Blue	Green	White	Vaseline/Canary	Cranberry	Other
Bowl, sauce	20.00	25.00	15.00		35.00	
Butter	125.00	125.00	65.00		175.00	
Cheese dish			250.00		400.00	
Celery vase	75.00	85.00	50.00		150.00	
Creamer	75.00	85.00	40.00		100.00	
Cruet, two sizes	175.00	200.00	100.00		300.00	
Cruet set, complete					475.00	
Custard cup	40.00	50.00	30.00		75.00	
Finger bowl	65.00	60.00	35.00		100.00	
Fingerlamp			350.00		600.00	
Handled novelty whimsey			75.00			
Lampshade	100.00	100.00	40.00		175.00	
Mustard jar	100.00	110.00	60.00		150.00	
Pitcher, various shapes and tops	175.00-275.00	175.00-275.00	90.00-150.00	300.00-500.00	350.00-600.00	2,000.00 Amethyst
Tankard pitcher		800.00*				
Tumbler	30.00	25.00	15.00	45.00	95.00	
Rose bowl	60.00	70.00	40.00		90.00	
Shakers, pair	175.00	150.00	100.00		250.00	
Shot glass	80.00		65.00			
Spittoon	90.00	85.00	70.00		150.00	
Spooner	75.00	80.00	40.00		125.00	
Strawholder, rare	800.00		575.00		1,200.00	
Sugar	100.00	110.00	50.00		175.00	
Sugar shaker	150.00	100.00	75.00		175.00	
Syrup	125.00	115.00	75.00		160.00	
Toothpick holder	125.00	140.00	70.00		150.00	
Vase	60.00	65.00	35.00		150.00	
Water, bitters, and bar bottles, each	100.00-250.00	90.00-200.00	65.00-100.00		350.00-450.00	
SWIRLED INTERIOR FLUTE						
Vase	70.00					
SWIRLING MAZE						
Bowl, salad	100.00	90.00	60.00	90.00	150.00	
Pitcher, any (average)	500.00	450.00	300.00		800.00	
Tumbler	65.00	55.00	25.00		100.00	
TARGET						
Vase	75.00	70.00	45.00			
TARGET SWIRL						
Bottle whimsey	125.00		100.00		275.00	
Salt in metal holder, rare				175.00		
Tumbler	80.00		65.00		95.00	
Vase, two sizes	300.00		225.00		500.00	
Vase, squat, various shapes	300.00		200.00		500.00	400.00 Amethyst
TAZZA						
Compote				200.00		
THIN & WIDE RIB						
Vase	60.00	60.00	45.00	75.00		
THISTLE & WREATH						
Cup plate, 3½"			125.00			
THISTLE LILY						
Vase						250.00 Rubina verde
THISTLE PATCH (INTAGLIO POPPY)						
Novelty, footed	90.00		40.00	75.00		
Add 10% for goofus						
THISTLES						
Shade						200.00 Rubina verde
THOMAS WEBB CROCODILE						
Novely piece				425.00		
THORN LILY						
Epergne, three lily with base				375.00		
Epergne, one lily, various metal holers				150.00		
THORN VASE (THOMAS WEBB)						
Vase			325.00	400.00		
THOUSAND EYE						
Bottles, various			25.00-55.00			
Bowls, various			25.00-50.00			
Butter			125.00			
Celery vase			100.00			
Compotes, various			45.00-85.00			
Creamer			75.00			
Cruet			150.00			
Pitcher			110.00			
Tumbler			30.00			
Shakers, pair			75.00			
Spooner			75.00			
Sugar			100.00			
Toothpick holder			125.00			
THREAD & RIB						
Epergne	800.00	900.00	600.00	800.00		

Pattern Name	Blue	Green	White	Vaseline/ Canary	Cranberry	Other
THREADED GRAPE						
Banana boat	225.00					
Compote, 8", large	200.00	175.00	100.00			
Tri-corner whimsey			185.00			
THREADED MELON						
Basket	250.00					
THREADED OPTIC						
See Band & Rib						
THREADED STRIPE						
Bowl						100.00 Amber
THREE FINGERS & PANEL						
Bowl, master, rare	100.00		75.00	100.00		
Bowl, sauce, rare	40.00		25.00	40.00		
THREE FRUITS						
Bowl, scarce	225.00		145.00			
THREE FRUITS WITH MEANDER						
Bowl, footed	165.00		110.00			
THREE LILY WATERFALL						
Epergne	275.00		250.00	375.00		
TINES						
Vase		75.00				
TINY RIB						
Bowl, footed, 6"	100.00					
TINY TEARS						
Vase	50.00	45.00	35.00			
TOKYO*						
Bowl, master	45.00	40.00	25.00			
Bowl, sauce	30.00	30.00	15.00			
Butter	200.00	175.00	100.00			
Creamer	100.00	80.00	40.00			
Cruet	200.00	200.00	100.00			
Jelly compote	55.00	55.00	30.00			
Pitcher	350.00	300.00	175.00			
Tumbler	75.00	70.00	45.00			
Plate	70.00	70.00	35.00			
Shakers, pair	100.00	85.00	45.00			
Spooner	100.00	85.00	45.00			
Sugar	150.00	135.00	60.00			
Syrup	150.00	145.00	70.00			
Toothpick holder	250.00	200.00	125.00			
Vase	55.00	50.00	35.00			
TRAFALGER FOUNTAIN						
Epergne	325.00		275.00	350.00		350.00 Amber
TRAILING VINES						
Novelty bowl	120.00		85.00	135.00		
TREE FORM						
Posy vase	250.00		375.00			
TREE OF LIFE						
Handled whimsey	125.00					
Shakers, each	100.00		50.00			
Vase	100.00		60.00			
Vase whimsey, two shapes	125.00		75.00			
TREE OF LOVE						
Basket				250.00		
Butter, covered, rare			350.00			
Compote			55.00			
Handled whimsey, center handled			255.00			
Novelty bowl			45.00			
Plate, rare, two sizes			135.00			
TREE STUMP						
Mug	85.00	95.00	60.00			
TREE TRUNK						
Vase	45.00	50.00	35.00			
TRELLIS						
Tumbler				65.00		
TRIANGLE						
Match-holder	75.00		55.00			
TRIDENT						
Pitcher						425.00 Amber opal
Tumbler						75.00 Amber opal
TROUT						
Bowl			150.00			
TULIP						
Cylinder shade						145.00 Rubina verde
TULIP COMPOTE						
Compote whimsey						300.00 White/amethyst
TULIP VASE (RICHARDSON GLASS)						
Vase, 6"				375.00		

Pattern Name	Blue	Green	White	Vaseline/Canary	Cranberry	Other
TUT						
Whimsey vase	125.00	125.00	100.00	165.00		
TWIGS						
Vase, small, 5½"	65.00	75.00	50.00	75.00		
Vase, panelled, 7"	85.00	100.00	65.00	85.00		
Vase whimsey, various top shapes	100.00	110.00	80.00	75.00		
TWIGS AND LEAVES						
Basket, twig handle	250.00			300.00		
TWIST (MINIATURES)						
Butter	275.00		175.00	275.00		
Creamer	85.00		45.00	85.00		
Spooner	85.00		50.00	85.00		
Sugar	150.00		80.00	150.00		
TWISTED RIBS						
Vase	45.00	40.00	25.00			
TWISTED ROPE						
Vase, very rare	275.00	325.00	200.00	325.00		
TWISTED TRUMPET						
Epergne		195.00				
TWISTER						
Bowl	50.00	45.00	35.00			
Plate	100.00					
Vase whimsey	75.00	75.00	45.00			
UNIVERSAL EPERGNE						
Epergne, various patterns and bases	125.00	135.00	95.00	165.00		
UNIVERSAL NORTHWOOD TUMBLER						
Tumbler	80.00		65.00	85.00		
VENETIAN BEAUTY						
Lamp (mini night lamp)	125.00		100.00		300.00	
VENETIAN (SPIDER WEB)						
Vase	85.00					
VENETIAN DRAPE						
Bowl with underplate, decorated			175.00			
VENICE						
Oil lamp	400.00		350.00			
VICTORIA & ALBERT						
Biscuit jar	165.00		110.00	150.00		
Covered butter	155.00		110.00	150.00		
Creamer	80.00		50.00	75.00		
Sugar	90.00		60.00	85.00		
VICTORIAN						
Vase, applied flowers and vine	165.00	175.00	110.00	165.00		175.00 Amber opal
VICTORIAN HAMPER						
Handled basket	75.00			75.00		
VICTORIAN STRIPE WITH FLOWERS						
Vase				300.00		
VICTORIAN SWIRL WITH FLOWERS						
Vase, decorated			200.00	275.00		
VIKING						
Bowl, boat shaped, 8½"	200.00					250.00 Amber opal
VINTAGE (FENTON)						
Bowl, rare	100.00		75.00			150.00 Amethyst opal
VINTAGE (JEFFERSON/NORTHWOOD)						
Bowl, dome base	55.00	55.00	30.00			
WAFFLE						
Epergne						700.00 Olive opal
WAR OF THE ROSES						
Bowl	75.00			70.00		
Boat shape, large	125.00			125.00		
Boat shape, small	100.00			100.00		
Compote, metal stand	150.00			150.00		
WATERLILY & CATTAILS (FENTON)						
Bon-bon	75.00	65.00	45.00			85.00 Amethyst
Bowl, master	75.00	70.00	50.00			85.00 Amethyst
Bowl, sauce	35.00	30.00	25.00			40.00 Amethyst
Bowl whimsey	85.00	75.00	65.00			100.00 Amethyst
Breakfast set, two pieces	150.00	135.00	100.00			175.00 Amethyst
Butter	400.00	350.00	250.00			425.00 Amethyst
Creamer	100.00	75.00	60.00			125.00 Amethyst
Gravy boat, handled	60.00	55.00	45.00			80.00 Amethyst
Novelty bowl	45.00	40.00	30.00			55.00 Amethyst
Pitcher	425.00	400.00	250.00			425.00 Amethyst
Tumbler	75.00	65.00	30.00			85.00 Amethyst
Plate	100.00	85.00	55.00			125.00 Amethyst
Relish, handled	100.00	90.00	70.00			125.00 Amethyst
Rose bowl	85.00		50.00			135.00 Amethyst
Spooner	100.00	75.00	60.00			150.00 Amethyst
Sugar	200.00	150.00	100.00			225.00 Amethyst

Pattern Name	Blue	Green	White	Vaseline/Canary	Cranberry	Other
Vase whimsey			150.00			
WATERLILY & CATTAILS (NORTHWOOD)						
Pitcher, rare	375.00					
Tumbler, rare	85.00					
WAVES						
Decanter	165.00			195.00		
Guest set	200.00			265.00		
Light shade	80.00			125.00		
Pitcher	450.00			575.00	525.00	
Tumbler	70.00			85.00		
WEBB CENTERPIECE						
Fancy centerpiece epergne, very rare			850.00			
WEST VIRGINIA STRIPE						
Pitcher	225.00		165.00		400.00	
Tumbler	65.00		45.00		90.00	
WHEAT						
Oil lamp				475.00		
WHEEL & BLOCK						
Novelty bowl	45.00	40.00	30.00			
Novelty plate	135.00	100.00	65.00			
Vase whimsey	55.00	45.00	35.00			
WIDE PANEL						
Epergne, four lily, scarce	800.00	850.00	600.00	925.00		
WIDE RIB						
Vase	125.00		100.00	145.00		
WIDE STRIPE						
Cruet	200.00	500.00	175.00		550.00	
Pitcher	250.00		175.00		450.00	
Tumbler	60.00		40.00		100.00	
Shakers, pair			150.00		250.00	
Sugar shaker	175.00		150.00		275.00	
Syrup	225.00		200.00		325.00	
Toothpick holder	275.00	400.00	225.00		350.00	
WILD BOUQUET						
Bowl, master	200.00	175.00	100.00			
Bowl, sauce	65.00	50.00	40.00			
Butter	500.00	450.00	325.00			
Creamer	200.00	150.00	100.00			
Cruet	400.00	425.00	250.00			
Cruet set with tray	475.00	425.00	300.00			
Jelly compote	175.00	135.00	100.00			
Pitcher	275.00	250.00	200.00			
Tumbler	120.00	100.00	50.00			
Shakers, pair	200.00	175.00	125.00			
Spooner	200.00	150.00	100.00			
Sugar	300.00	275.00	195.00			
Toothpick holder	425.00	375.00	225.00			
WILD DAFFODILS						
Mug	85.00		65.00			100.00 Amethyst
WILD GRAPE						
Bowl			40.00			
Compote			40.00			
WILD ROSE						
Banana bowl	70.00		50.00			80.00 Amethyst
Bowl	60.00		40.00			75.00 Amethyst
Shade			75.00			
WILLIAM & MARY						
Bowl	95.00			165.00		
Butter, covered	175.00			250.00		
Cake plate, stemmed	140.00			160.00		
Celery vase	90.00			110.00		
Compote	100.00			90.00		
Creamer	65.00			60.00		
Master salt	50.00					
Open sugar, stemmed	70.00			65.00		
Plate	100.00			95.00		
WILLOW REED						
Basket	175.00					
WILTED FLOWERS						
Bowl	50.00	60.00	40.00			
Handled basket	100.00	110.00	65.00			
Rose bowl, very scarce			85.00			
WINDFLOWER						
Bowl, rare	175.00		125.00			
Nappy, rare			285.00			
WINDOWS (PLAIN)*						
Barber bottle					325.00	
Fingerbowl	50.00		45.00		75.00	

Pattern Name	Blue	Green	White	Vaseline/Canary	Cranberry	Other
Mini lamp	175.00				1,850.00	
Oil lamp					625.00	
Pitcher, various	150.00-200.00		90.00-150.00		350.00-550.00	
Tumbler	55.00		35.00		125.00	
Shade	60.00		35.00		200.00	
Toothpick holder					325.00	
WINDOWS (SWIRLED)						
Barber bottle	225.00		175.00		375.00	
Bowl, master	55.00		40.00		100.00	
Bowl, sauce	40.00		30.00		55.00	
Butter	400.00		300.00		550.00	
Celery vase	100.00		50.00		175.00	
Creamer	100.00		75.00		225.00	
Cruet	325.00		225.00		475.00	
Cruet set, complete	275.00		200.00		625.00	
Mustard jar	75.00		55.00		150.00	
Pitcher, various	300.00-425.00		200.00-300.00		600.00-800.00	
Tumbler	85.00		65.00		125.00	
Plate, two sizes	125.00		65.00		250.00	
Shakers, pair	175.00		125.00		300.00	
Spooner	10.00		75.00		225.00	
Sugar	250.00		175.00		350.00	
Sugar shaker	150.00		125.00		325.00	
Syrup, two shapes	300.00		200.00		500.00	
Toothpick holder	300.00		175.00		375.00	
WINDOWS ON STRIPES						
Oil lamp				450.00		
WINDSOR STRIPE						
Vase					125.00	
WINGED SCROLL						
Nappy, rare				425.00		
Sauce, rare				700.00		
WINTER CABBAGE						
Bowl, footed	50.00	45.00	35.00			
WINTERLILY						
Vase, scarce	225.00	250.00	175.00			
WISHBONE & DRAPERY						
Bowl	50.00	45.00	35.00			
Plate	60.00	60.00	50.00			
WOOD VINE LAMP (GAIETY BASE)						
Oil lamp			450.00			
WOVEN WONDER						
Novelty bowl	55.00		40.00			
Rose bowl	60.00		45.00			
WREATH & SCROLL						
Oil lamp				525.00		
WREATH & SHELL						
Bank whimsey, rare					235.00	
Bowl, master	100.00		70.00		125.00	
Bowl, sauce	40.00		25.00		35.00	
Butter	250.00		150.00		225.00	
Celery vase	200.00		100.00		175.00	
Cracker jar	600.00		475.00		550.00	
Creamer	175.00		85.00		150.00	
Ivy ball, rare	175.00		125.00		165.00	
Ladies spittoon	100.00		65.00		125.00	
Novelty bowl	75.00	150.00	55.00		65.00	500.00 Pink
Pitcher	600.00		200.00		375.00	
Tumbler, flat or footed	125.00		50.00		75.00	
Rose bowl	100.00		65.00		85.00	
Salt dip	140.00		85.00		100.00	
Spooner	175.00		80.00		125.00	
Sugar	200.00		100.00		150.00	
Toothpick holder	300.00		200.00		275.00	

Note: add 10% for decorated items.

Pattern Name	Blue	Green	White	Vaseline/Canary	Cranberry	Other
WREATHED GRAPE & CABLE						
Centerpiece whimsey			300.00			
Orange bowl, footed, very rare			350.00			
X-HATCH						
Bowl, ruffled						175.00 Rubina verde
ZINFANDEL						
Pitcher, decorated						350.00 Rose opal
Tumbler, decorated						75.00 Rose opal
ZIPPER & LOOPS						
Vase, footed	65.00	70.00	45.00			
ZIPPERED FLUTE						
Vase		125.00				

After much deliberation, I've decided to add a price guide for items made after 1930 that are shown in the book. To have taken on the pricing of all items made in the last 73 years would have been a massive task and since this book is geared to only old glass (I only include these after 1930 patterns to illustrate what to be aware of in buying old glass), it was something I wouldn't consider, now or in the future.

Here then are prices for the items I show in this book in the colors shown. I hope it will give readers some idea of what newer glass is selling for and is meant to be only a ballpark reference and not a price setter.

Pattern Name	*Blue*	*Green*	*White*	*Vaseline/ Canary*	*Cranberry*	*Other*
ADAM'S RIB						
Candlesticks, pair	80.00					
APPLE TREE WHIMSEY VASE						
Vase, from pitcher, rare				225.00*		
BUTTERFLY						
Atomizer, complete	75.00					
CACTUS						
Vase, 9"	60.00		50.00	70.00		
CANTERBURY						
Baskets, various	40.00-80.00		25.00-60.00			30.00-70.00 Pink opal
Bowls, various	25.00-55.00		20.00-45.00			25.00-50.00 Pink opal
Vases, various	30.00-65.00		25.00-55.00			30.00-50.00 Pink opal
CHECKERBOARD						
Celery tray				45.00		
COIN DOT (FENTON)						
Barber bottle					75.00	
Vase					55.00	
CORN VASE REPRODUCTION						
Vase	55.00			70.00		60.00 Amber
COSMOS FLOWERS ATOMIZER						
Atomizer	70.00	70.00	55.00			
CUBIST ROSE						
Bowl			225.00			
DAISY & BUTTON						
Compote, covered	45.00			60.00		
Fan vase	25.00			30.00		
Rose bowl on stand	65.00					
DAISY & BUTTON WITH THUMBPRINT						
Goblet	45.00			65.00		
DANCING LADIES						
Vase, footed			285.00			
DECO DAISY						
Plate			55.00			
DEVILBISS WIDE SWIRL						
Atomizer			135.00*			
DIAMOND OPTIC WATER CARAFE						
Water bottle					75.00	
DOGWOOD						
Bowl			225.00			
DUNCAN & MILLER						
Ashtray				30.00		
Vase	30.00					
EASTER CHICK						
Plate, 7½"	25.00					
ELLEN						
Vase, 5"		30.00	20.00			25.00 Pink
EYE DOT						
Oil lamp			90.00			
FENTON COIN DOT						
Basket with handle	40.00				50.00	
Pitcher	80.00				95.00	
FENTON HAND VASE						
Vase, 3½"	25.00		15.00			
FENTON HOBNAIL						
Atomizer	60.00	60.00	45.00	75.00	90.00	
Compote, covered	35.00	35.00		60.00	75.00	
Fan vase	60.00	50.00	40.00	70.00	85.00	80.00 Plum
Hat shapes, various sizes	35.00-80.00	35.00-80.00	30.00-60.00	45.00-90.00	65.00-135.00	
Lamp, two sizes and shapes	125.00		85.00		165.00	
Pitcher	75.00					
Tumbler	15.00					

Pattern Name	Blue	Green	White	Vaseline/Canary	Cranberry	Other
Vase, made from pitcher mold	90.00					
*Condensed list. Many shapes and colors too numerous to list.						
FENTON RIB						
Ashtray	25.00					
FENTON'S #37 MINIATURES						
Creamer	20.00		15.00	25.00		
Vase	15.00		10.00	20.00		
FENTON'S BEATTY HONEYCOMB						
Vase	30.00	35.00				
FENTON SPANISH LACE						
Pitcher	70.00				95.00	
FENTON SWIRL						
Bowl, with separate base standard	70.00					
Hat shape	65.00	70.00	50.00	80.00	90.00	
Vase, various shapes and sizes	55.00	60.00	40.00	80.00	85.00	
*Condensed list. Many shapes and colors too numerous to list.						
FISHBONE SCROLL (SCROLL FLUTED)						
Celery tray	25.00	25.00	20.00	30.00		
Creamer	25.00	25.00	20.00	30.00		
Rose bowl	30.00	30.00	25.00	35.00		
Sugar	25.00	25.00	20.00	30.00		
FOSTORIA HEIRLOOM						
Bowl	30.00		20.00	40.00		
Plate	35.00		25.00	45.00		
Novelty bowl	40.00		30.00	50.00		
Vase, various sizes	15.00-40.00	15.00-40.00	15.00-45.00	15.00-50.00		
FRISCO						
Rose bowl		25.00				
GIBSON SPITTOON						
Spittoon whimsey		25.00				
GRAPE & VINE						
Vase, J.I.P. Shape	45.00					
HOBNAIL (CZECHOSLOVAKIAN)						
Puff box	35.00	40.00		50.00	60.00	
Tumbler	15.00	15.00		25.00	25.00	
HOBNAIL (WESTMORELAND)						
Creamer	45.00					
Goblet	35.00					
Sugar	40.00					
HOBNAIL VARIANT						
Vase	25.00		15.00			
HONEYCOMB WITH FLOWER RIM						
Vase	25.00					
JERSEY SWIRL						
Compote, low covered				45.00		
Compote, high covered				65.00		
Goblet				35.00		
Plate, 6"				25.00		
Plate, 10"				35.00		
Salt dip				20.00		
Master salt				25.00		
Footed sauce				20.00		
Wine				25.00		
LACE-EDGED BASKETWEAVE						
Vase, footed	30.00	35.00	25.00			
LACE-EDGED BUTTONS						
Bowl	25.00	25.00	20.00			
LACE-EDGED DIAMONDS						
One shape, with handles	25.00	25.00	20.00			
MOON & STARS						
Goblet	20.00			30.00		
NAUTILUS						
Compote, very rare				400.00		
NEEDLEPOINT						
Tumbler, three sizes	15.00-25.00	15.00-25.00				20.00-30.00 Orange
OPALBERRY						
Plate			225.00			
OPEN-EDGE BASKETWEAVE						
Bowl, various shapes	25.00	25.00	20.00	30.00		
PANACHE						
Atomizer	80.00					
PEACOCK GARDEN VASE						
Vase, 4", 6", 8" 10"			300.00-600.00			
PETTICOATS ATOMIZER						
Atomizer	60.00		40.00	75.00		

236

Pattern Name	Blue	Green	White	Vaseline/ Canary	Cranberry	Other
PINECONE & LEAVES						
Bowl			65.00			
PINECONE SPRAY						
Plate			55.00			
PLUME TWIST ATOMIZER						
Atomizer, 4"			75.00	115.00		
PLYMOUTH						
Pilsner			35.00			
QUEEN'S PETTICOAT						
See "Fostoria's Heirloom"						
QUILTED PINECONE						
Atomizer	70.00					
RING						
Pitcher			70.00			
SEAWEED & SHELL						
Bowl, 5¾"	75.00					
SPIRAL OPTIC (FENTON, 1930s – 1950s)						
Candy with lid					80.00	
Hat	60.00	65.00	55.00	80.00	90.00	
Vase	50.00			45.00	70.00	
Vase, #894, 10½", either top	70.00	75.00	65.00	100.00	125.00	
Condensed list. Many shapes and colors known.						
SPIRAL WAVES						
Plate, 15"			65.00			
STAMM HOUSE DEWDROP						
Bowl, large				65.00		
Bowl, small				25.00		
STARS & STRIPES						
Basket with handle	45.00				60.00	
Bottle	50.00				75.00	
Creamer	25.00				40.00	
Cruet	55.00				60.00	
Finger bowl	25.00				25.00	
Tumbler	20.00				25.00	
Syrup	60.00				60.00	
SWAN BOWL						
Bowl, with swan neck handles	135.00	140.00				160.00 Rose opalescent
SWIRL						
Pitcher	90.00					
SWIRLED FEATHER						
Candy dish	30.00	30.00	25.00		35.00	
Cruet	45.00	45.00	35.00		55.00	
Fairy lamp	30.00	30.00	25.00		40.00	
Hurricane lamp	60.00	60.00	50.00		65.00	
Tumbler	20.00	20.00	15.00		25.00	
Vanity set	95.00	95.00	75.00		115.00	
Vase	25.00	25.00	20.00		35.00	
SYLVAN						
Bowls, various	35.00-90.00		25.00-60.00			35.00-80.00 Pink opalescent
Relish trays, various	25.00-80.00		20.00-65.00			30.00-90.00 Pink opalescent
Vases, various	45.00-100.00		35.00-70.00			50.00-110.00 Pink opalescent
TOKYO REPRODUCTION						
Compote	25.00					
TROUT (FENTON)						
Bowl			75.00			
TWIGS REPRODUCTION						
Vase	30.00	30.00	25.00	35.00		
WATER BALLET						
Plate, or low bowl			100.00			
WILDFLOWER						
Goblet	25.00			30.00		
WINDOWS (L.G. WRIGHT)						
Creamer	20.00				35.00	
Cruet	45.00				60.00	
Epergne	75.00				100.00	
Fairy lamp	30.00				40.00	
Finger bowl	20.00				25.00	
Lamps, various	50.00-95.00				65.00-125.00	
Tumbler	15.00				25.00	
Syrup	40.00				50.00	
Vase	30.00				40.00	
WREATHED CHERRY						
Creamer	20.00			30.00		
WRIGHT'S THREAD & RIB EPERGNE						
Epergne	175.00			195.00		

Other Titles by Mike Carwile

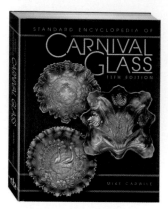

Standard Encyclopedia of Carnival Glass, 11th Edition

Mike Carwile

This edition covers over 2,000 color patterns. New sections on base/feet identification and Inca bottle variations are also included. The bound-in price guide includes virtually every piece of carnival glass ever made with prices given for various colors. Both American and foreign companies are represented, including Dugan, Fenton, Imperial, Northwood, Westmoreland, Fostoria, Heisey, McKee, Jeannette, and the U.S. Glass Company. 2008 values.

Item #7623 · ISBN: 978-1-57432-576-8 · 8½ x 11 · 400 Pgs. · HB · $29.95

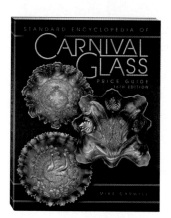

Standard Ency. of Carnival Glass Price Guide, 16th Edition

Mike Carwile

This price guide is bound into the *Standard Encyclopedia of Carnival Glass, Eleventh Edition,* but is also offered separately. The more than 25,000 alphabetical pattern name listings feature updated values, company names, sizes, and prices given for 10 different colors. 2008 values.

Item #7624 · ISBN: 978-1-57432-577-5 · 8½ x 11 · 96 Pgs. · HB · $9.95

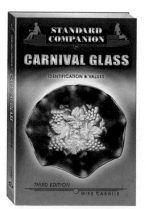

Standard Companion to Carnival Glass, 3rd Edition

Mike Carwile

This easy-to-use, small format book highlights the approximately 250 carnival glass patterns available. Each pattern shines with all necessary facts and a detailed photograph to illustrate the pattern. Data about each piece includes name of pattern, manufacturer, year of production, colors and shapes available, and information on reproductions. 2007 values.

Item #7347 · ISBN: 978-1-57432-531-7 · 5½ x 8½ · 288 Pgs. · PB · $17.95

Standard Encyclopedia of Pressed Glass, 5th Edition

Bill Edwards & Mike Carwile

American pressed glass, which was at its zenith in the 1870s, entails hundreds of patterns and dozens of shapes with elaborate geometric, animal, fruit, and floral designs. Available in crystal and sparkling colors, this collectible glassware flourished until the end of the 1920s. This all-new encyclopedia features approximately 230 new photographs, most of them for new patterns, bringing the total to more than 1,600 photos showcasing the exquisite patterns and beautiful colors of the quality pressed glass produced for 60 years in America. 2007 values.

Item #7364 · ISBN: 978-1-57432-548-5 · 8½ x 11 · 464 Pgs. · HB · $29.95

Standard Companion to Non-American Carnival Glass

Bill Edwards & Mike Carwile

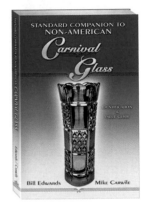

Focusing on non-American carnival glass, this handy pocket guide showcases over 350 of the best collectible patterns from Australia, England, Germany, Czechoslovakia, Finland, Sweden, and India. A brief section on foreign marks adds interest. Data given for each pattern includes maker, date of manufacture, shapes, colors, and values. 2006 values.

Item #6927 · ISBN: 978-1-57432-488-4 · 5½ x 8½ · 336 Pgs. · PB · $16.95

Standard Encyclopedia of Millersburg Crystal

Bill Edwards & Mike Carwile

This book is filled with almost 200 photos, including opalescent, frosted, gilded, ruby and lime stained, and maiden blush stained glass. An extensive history of the factory, old advertisements, and factory and employee photos are highlights. Also featured are Butler Brothers catalogs and Jefferson's Canadian Glass Factory catalogs from Ontario. 2001 values.

Item #5832 · ISBN: 978-1-57432-225-5 · 8½ x 11 · 144 Pgs. · HB · $24.95

For these and other great titles from **COLLECTOR BOOKS**

visit www.collectorbooks.com

or call 1.800.626.5420

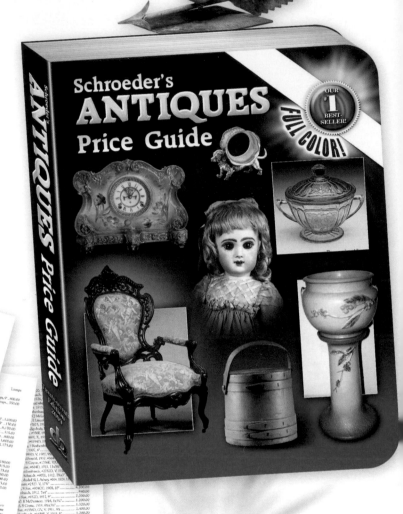